Invest
Like the
Best

Invest Like the Best

Using Your Computer to Unlock the Secrets of the Top Money Managers

James P. O'Shaughnessy

McGraw-Hill

New York   San Francisco   Washington, D.C.   Auckland   Bogotá
Caracas   Lisbon   London   Madrid   Mexico City   Milan
Montreal   New Delhi   San Juan   Singapore
Sydney   Tokyo   Toronto

Library of Congress Cataloging-in-Publication Data

O'Shaughnessy, James P.
     Invest like the best : using your computer to unlock the secrets
of the top money managers / by James P. O'Shaughnessy.
          p.   cm.
     ISBN 0-07-047984-4 (HC)   ISBN 0-07-913754-7 (PBK)
     1. Investment analysis—Date processing.   2. Finance, Personal—
Data processing.   3. Portfolio management—Data procesing.
I. Title.
HG4521.083   1994
332.6'0285'536—dc20   93-41389
                                                                 CIP

McGraw-Hill

A Division of The McGraw·Hill Companies

     4 5 6 7 8 9 0   DOC/DOC   9 9 8 7 6 5   (HC)
   3 4 5 6 7 8 9 0   DOC/DOC   9 0 2 1 0 9 8   (PBK)

ISBN 0-07-047984-4 (HC)
P/N 048247-0
Part of ISBN 0-07-913754-7 (PBK)

*The sponsoring editor for this book was Caroline Carney, the editing
supervisor was Fred Dahl, and the production supervisor was Donald F.
Schmidt. It was set in Palatino by McGraw-Hill's Professional Book Group
composition unit.*

Printed and bound by R. R. Donnelley & Sons Company.

 This book is printed on recycled, acid-free paper containing a
minimum of 50% recycled, de-inked fiber.

To my wife, Melissa,
and my children Patrick and Kathryn.
I love you all very much.

Contents

Preface

Imagine yourself in a room with the quarterly reports for 1600 companies. Assuming each of the 6400 reports is about an eighth of an inch thick, stacking them up would build a 66-foot-high tower of information! The reports would include myriad data on the companies, such as earnings, dividends, stock prices, and price-to-earnings ratios. If each report covered just 59 individual pieces of information for each of the 1600 stocks, you'd have more than 377,600 different pieces of data, *just for one year.*

Now imagine your response if your boss walks into the room and tells you to sift through each of these reports and isolate all the stocks that meet just four criteria, telling you to make sure that *only* the stocks that meet *each* of the four criteria are included. You'd probably quit on the spot! Isolating a handful of stocks from 1600 is overwhelming for most people.

A New Age on Wall Street and Main Street

But it is not overwhelming for a computer. Scanning the 377,600 bits of information on the 1600 stocks and picking only the stocks that meet all your criteria is simple for a computer. The task is completed before you can take a sip of water. What used to take armies of stock analysts weeks of research to accomplish can now be executed in minutes by an individual using a computer. The leverage a computer gives an individual is astounding. In the comfort of your home, you can create powerful stock-picking models that are every bit as good as those used by Wall Street's most highly paid and respected professionals.

Top stock pickers do much better than the market because they've discovered a superior stock selection method: Their portfolios beat the market because they are filled with stocks that are *very different* from the market. These stocks are different not necessarily in terms of the types of businesses the issuing companies are engaged in, but very distinct in terms of the factors, or underlying characteristics, like earnings, dividends, and growth rates, that define the stocks in the portfolio.

Let's say your boss walks into the room stacked with quarterly reports, pulls out the reports for 30 companies held by a top-performing mutual fund, and tells you it's your job to demonstrate exactly how those 30 companies differ from the market as a whole.

Without a computer, you couldn't do it. A computer gives you the power to quickly and precisely discover how these 30 stocks differ. By entering the 30 stocks into a database like Value Line's Value/Screen III, you can see exactly how they differ from the market and what rules, or model, guided the person putting the portfolio together.

What works for these 30 stocks works with portfolios built by anyone, including the masters of the trade. *By putting the portfolios of great managers on a computer, you can quickly analyze their stocks to see which factors, or underlying characteristics, they most value. With this information, you can develop a stock-picking model that scans the vast amounts of information in the computer database, selecting only the stocks that consistently meet the master's standards.* Indeed, you can simply use their standards as a *starting point,* moving a step beyond to design models that have a greater clarity, simplicity, and precision than the master's own portfolio.

Do as They Do, Not as They Say

If you've read other books on the stock market, you know how confusing and conflicting the advice can be. Reading some of the thousands of books on the market could leave you completely disoriented, thinking the stock market is hopelessly complicated and mysterious. *Invest Like the Best* lets you avoid this confusion by giving you the tools to see exactly how top managers put together portfolios and then showing you how to mirror them by using their favorite factors.

By designing your models around what the pros actually *do*, rather than what they *say* they do, you filter out all extraneous information and superstitions, leaving only relevant data for the purpose at hand: designing a winning portfolio. This is important, since often there's an enormous difference between what someone *says* they do and what they *actually* do. According to studies done by Paul Slovic, a respected researcher of human cognition, the emphasis that brokers and other market professionals initially *said* they put on various inputs varied significantly from what they *actually* used when buying stocks. Moreover, while they said they used a huge number of variables when picking stocks, they actually used only a few. Indeed, if you study the techniques used by the greatest investors throughout time, you'll find that most of them used simple, elegant, and direct strategies *consistently*.

Great Managers Act Consistently

Yet only a handful of investors beat the market over the long term because few have the discipline to consistently implement a superior investment strategy. If you learn only one thing from this book, it should be that all managers with long-term success in the stock market made it to the top by consistently using a superior investment strategy. John Neff built the Windsor fund, one of the most successful value funds, by sticking with his strategy of buying undervalued companies with low price-to-earnings ratios. He never once deviated from what mutual fund rating service Morningstar calls "his extremely disciplined and patient approach ... [even] when huge weightings in financial and cyclical issues led to disastrous results in 1990, he held on."

Neff is a great investor because he has the intelligence to understand that, no matter how superior his investment ideas are, they won't do him any good if he second-guesses them.

The Four Horsemen

Refusing to act emotionally and second-guess your methods is one of the toughest assignments investors face. Most fail. The four horsemen of the investment apocalypse are Ignorance, Greed, Fear, and Hope. These four are responsible for larger losses than any single economic depression ever caused. Only Ignorance is easily corrected. It's also the only one of the four that isn't an emotion. By understanding exactly how the masters make their stock selections, you'll be well on your way to slaying Ignorance. Removing Ignorance lets you tame the other three and move on to outstanding investment performance.

After reading *Invest Like the Best*, you'll:

- Know how to uncover the strategy of *any* money manager and take what you've learned to create a computerized stock-picking program that consistently beats the market and the portfolios of the nation's top stock-picking gurus.

- Know which factors all top-performing managers of any given style share and how to use them to develop outstanding portfolios.

- Be able to systematically review any investment strategy, be it from a book or a broker. You'll see how it performed in the past and how it's likely to perform in the future. Moreover, you'll understand how risky it is, and whether or not the risk is at a level you can tolerate.

- Know how to use factor profiles to avoid mutual funds or money managers that are headed for disaster.

- Never again make a random, unplanned purchase of a stock or a mutual fund based on a hunch, tip, or untested recommendation. You'll understand immediately if a stock fits your criteria and if it would make a good addition to your portfolio.

- Know how to unite the best of two styles of investing to create a high-yielding portfolio that also has tremendous capital appreciation potential, while keeping risk in line with the market as a whole.

- Have the power of knowledge and the ability to act with conviction. You'll see how it works for the pros, and you'll know it can work for you.

Acknowledgments

I'm deeply indebted to my wife, Melissa, for all her help on this book. Her summa cum laude degree in journalism came in especially handy when it was time to edit and rewrite the manuscript. Without her expert and thorough hand, this book could never have been finished.

Thanks also go to Caroline Carney, my editor at McGraw-Hill, for seeing the promise of this book and championing it at every turn. Thanks also to my office staff, especially Cheryl Clifford and Jennifer O'Doherty, for putting up with me during the many hours I bothered them while combating writer's block.

James P. O'Shaughnessy

Value/Screen III:*
A Quick Start
Guide for IBM
and Compatibles

This is a quick start "crib sheet" so that you can start using the companion disk right away. This requires a high-density disk drive, a hard disk, and at least 640K of memory.

To use this disk, type VS at the A: > prompt.

Main Functions

A. Stock Selection (Data Base Screening)

B. Stock Report

C. Statistical Analysis

D. Portfolio Management

*Value/Screen II was used to prepare this manuscript, but the latest version is Value/Screen III. The methods and system described in the book, however, remain the same.

Function Keys

Esc (ESCAPE) Returns you to the previous screen

F1 Help.

F2 Executes a command.

F3 Save/Recall/Delete Criteria

F4 Save/Recall/Delete Lists

F5 View Screening Results

F6 Produces the User Define Variables from the Screening mode. Merges two selected ticker lists in Create-Edit Ticker List mode.

F7 Generates a Single Ticker Report

F8 Produces a histogram showing frequency distribution for selected variable in the Screening mode.

F9 Allows you to insert a line of data when screening, preparing reports, or editing portfolios.

F10 Deletes a line of data when screening, preparing reports, or editing portfolios.

Special Keys

+ and −   The plus and minus keys toggle through alternative responses while screening the database.

Home, then Ctrl and F10 simultaneously   Clears all data entered on your screen.

Alt C Changes the background color on your screen.

News About Value/Screen III

Pressing **N** from the Main Menu provides you with information on Value/Screen. This information comes from the README file, which provides a Business Summary on Turner Broadcasting Systems and pricing information on the demonstration disk.

A Sample Screening

From the Main Menu, press **S** to select Screen Database and type the following:

1. **M1**   Recent Price **Enter**   The cursor moves to the right.
2. Use the + or − key to select >, and press **Enter**. The cursor moves to the right.
3. Type **20** and press **Enter.**
4. Using the same method enter:

    M4   Current P-E ratio < (less than) 20.
    M9   Market Cap. < (less than) 500 ($mill).
    G5   Projected EPS Growth > (greater than) 20.

5. Press **F2** to see the number of stocks passing this test. Press **F5** to view the names of the companies. After viewing the list, press **Esc** twice to return to the Main Menu.

Producing Reports in Value/Screen III

Selecting **R** from the Main Menu allows you to select different reports. Tabular, Portfolio, Statistical Summary, and Comparison reports are all available from the Reports Submenu.

Reporting on a Screened List Using a Tabular Report R

The Tabular Reports feature allows you to easily construct reports containing columns of stock data.

1. Once in the Tabular Report screen, press the + or − key to toggle through the various report formats. For demonstration purposes select SCREEN as the method for the report generation and press **Enter**. The cursor moves to the right.
2. Type the variables for your report as follows:

    11   Company Name **Enter**
    12   Ticker Symbol **Enter**
    M1   Recent Price **Enter**
    M4   Current P-E Ratio **Enter**
    H9   5-year Dividend Growth **Enter**

Once all the variables are selected, choose a "Ticker list" or a "Screened list" to report on. If the top of your screen reads "Tabular Report on: Last Screening," the program will produce the Tabular Report based on the results of the last ticker list used for screening.

You may select a previously saved ticker list by pressing **F4** and recalling a list.

Press **F2** to generate and view this report. After viewing, press **Esc** twice to return to the Main Menu.

Obtaining Single-Stock Reports

Pressing **F7** from the Screen Database function produces a Single Ticker Report. Type the ticker symbol AAPL and press **Enter**. The cursor moves up. Toggle to the desired format SCREEN or PRINT and press **F2**. You may use your arrow keys to view the entire report. After viewing all of the information for Apple Computers, Inc., press **Esc** twice.

Exporting Reports as WKS and Text Files

Creating a report in any of these formats will allow you to export information for use in other programs, such as spread-sheet, database, or text editing programs. Use the + or − key to toggle to FILE: WKS and press **Enter**. WKS files are commonly used in spreadsheet programs. Press **F2**, name the file, and press **Enter**. After the report has been calculated, the program returns to the Tabular Report screen. A new file has been created, and can be found in the program's directory.

1

The Underlying Secret of Portfolio Performance

We beat the market by over 20 percent last year!
Our long-term performance is 100 percent better
than the market!
Our secret strategy gives us high returns at low
levels of risk!

You see ads like these all the time. They're in *The Wall Street Journal, Investor's Business Daily, Forbes, Fortune, Business Week,* and anywhere you look for advice on the market.

How did these funds do it? How did the funds at the top of the long-term rankings outperform the market for so long? Are the people running these market-beating funds geniuses? (They think so!) Do they have access to some secret known only by the rich? Are they in the know, always one step ahead of the many hapless investors who never make their decisions consistently or consciously?

The answers are some *are* geniuses. Others *do* possess superior methods. And, yes, the best performers *do* take advantage of investors who refuse to act consistently and consciously in the market. But these responses don't get at the core of the matter. Essentially, these portfolios did so much better than the market by being very *different* from the market. Managers regularly do

1

much better or worse than the market by keeping their portfolio's characteristics different from the market as a whole.

For example, great sports teams do much better than pick-up teams playing a weekend game because they are composed of people with very different attributes than those of the average weekend warrior. Compare the underlying characteristics, or factors, that define the Dream Team players who won the gold medal for basketball in the 1992 Summer Olympics to a profile of randomly selected people. Are they similar? No way. Nor are they very similar to people who play basketball every weekend, although they have slightly more in common with this second group. Yet the factors that make them so unbeatable—their height, their speed, their ability to make gravity-defying shots—all these things substantially differentiate them from all others.

The same is true on Wall Street. Portfolios with the best returns generate them by being *very* different from the S&P 500. The difference is not necessarily in terms of the types of businesses that the issuing company is involved in or the location of their headquarters, but rather in terms of the factors defining the company's stock. The factors favored by market participants in any given year determine how the top performing portfolios will differ from the market. When growth is in fashion, the best performers often have much higher earnings per share growth rates than the S&P 500. When value is in vogue, they often have much lower price-to-earnings ratios. The *more* a portfolio's factors differ from the market, the *more* its performance will differ from the market.

At times, the actual names of the funds give clues about the factors in vogue that year. At the end of 1991, many funds with *aggressive growth* or *growth* in their names were at the top of the list. A few years earlier, many at the top had the word *value* in their names. In short, many fund names reflect the underlying *style* that determines the stocks the fund's manager will buy and sell. All investors have a style, a perspective on the market that determines how their portfolios differ from the market. Investment styles determine the factors that an investor values and the stocks that the investor buys. Apart from the names given funds, managers also give clues to their investment style by what they say:

- You can beat the market by investing in stocks with low price-to-earnings ratios.

- Our goal is to beat the market by 5 percent per year. To do this, we will buy stocks with two characteristics. First, they must have five-year earnings-per-share percentage gains above 20 percent. Second, forecasted earnings gains must be greater than the market.

- We believe stocks with high yields do better than the market.

- The only way to beat the market over the long term is to own stocks with rapidly growing earnings and small market capitalizations.

These are examples of managers explaining their styles in terms of the factors they use to select stocks. They also reflect the influences of the two main schools of investing, growth and value.

The School of Investing Determines Which Factors You Value

Growth investors buy stocks that have higher-than-average growth in sales and earnings per share. A classic growth company's earnings just keep getting better and better. Growth investors believe in a company's future prospects, thinking that a stock's price will follow its earnings higher. If growth stock investing were a song, its name would probably be "The Future's So Bright, I Gotta Wear Shades."

Value investors buy stocks with current market values substantially below true or liquidating value. Value managers use factors like price-to-earnings ratios and price-to-sales ratios to identify when a stock is selling below its intrinsic value. They bargain hunt, looking for stocks where they can buy a dollar's worth of assets for 70 cents. Value investors believe in a company's current balance sheet, thinking that a stock's price will eventually reflect its intrinsic value. If value stock investing were a song, its title would most likely be "Been Down So Darn Long That It Looks Like Up to Me."

Each style also has highly defined subgroups. In the growth category you find:

- *Aggressive growth* investors who buy emerging companies whose earnings are growing at rates far in excess of the market. This type of stock has much greater volatility than established growth stocks.

- *Established growth* investors who buy companies that have, and that are expected to have, earnings and sales gains above the market as a whole. Established growth companies have longer track records than aggressive growth companies, and their share prices are less volatile.

- *Momentum growth* investors who buy stocks that are currently experiencing a rapid growth in earnings and price appreciation, and who quickly sell any stock that falters, however briefly.

- And *other investors* whose styles combine those listed.

In the value category you find:

- *Low price-to-earnings ratio* investors who buy only stocks with the lowest price-to-earnings ratios.

- *Low price-to-book ratio* investors who buy only stocks with very low price-to-book ratios, usually with current prices below book value.

- *High-yield* investors who buy stocks either when their yields rise sharply relative to past yields or when their absolute yield goes above a certain level.

- *Defensive,* or *quality* investors who buy stocks with very high financial ratings, price stability, and balance sheet quality.

- And *other investors* who combine the styles listed.

Both styles are also segmented into managers who invest in companies with large market capitalization (*large cap*) and managers who invest in companies with small market capitalization (*small cap*). When looking at actual investors, you'll usually find that they value ideas from many of the various schools. Commonly, a manager who is essentially either a growth or a value manager uses factors popular with the other style. For example, a growth manager might buy stocks with high five-year earnings per share growth rates *and* low price-to-earnings ratios in an attempt to weed out high flying growth stocks that might crash.

The style used to build a portfolio determines the sort of stock the portfolio manager chooses to buy or sell. This, in turn, determines the factor profile of the overall portfolio. Generally, growth investors like *high* while value investors like *low*. Growth investors want high earnings and sales growth, and usually don't care if the stock has a high price-to-book ratio. High price-to-book ratios terrify value investors. A high price-to-book ratio means investors have high hopes for the stock. High hopes, the value investor reasons, are usually dashed, along with the price of the stock. That's why they usually insist on a low price-to-book ratio.

It's Not the Stock, It's the Style and Factors

When buying stocks, many investors still make decisions based on personifications of the stock and fail to focus on the underlying factors. To illustrate the importance of consistently looking at a stock's factors, let's create a portfolio containing just one stock: IBM. International Business Machines is one of the best known companies in the world. Mention the name IBM and you immediately think about computers. IBM became a legend for its ability to continually expand earnings growth and brilliantly outperform its rivals. IBM was a stock that managers were praised for buying and holding. IBM had the largest market capitalization and best visibility of all the stocks on the New York Stock Exchange, and its name was shorthand for a high-quality blue chip growth stock. It even had a nickname that everyone knew: Big Blue.

Had you bought this one stock on December 31, 1980, when IBM's underlying factors were those of a growth stock, and held until December 31, 1985, you would have made over 182 percent, or 23.1 percent on an annual compounded basis. Compared to the S&P 500's return of 98.5 percent, or 14.7 percent annual compounded return, this was extraordinary. Not only was IBM doing much better than the S&P 500 on an absolute basis, it was doing a lot better when you took risk into account. IBM was one of the safest stocks on the exchange, with the largest market capitalization and an A++ rating from all the financial rating services.

At the end of 1985, had you been thinking of IBM as a well-managed company and the world's biggest computer maker, you would miss part of the picture that people who pay attention to factors would not miss: At the end of 1985, IBM no longer had the factors of a growth stock. Not only did IBM see its annual earnings per share percentage change decline, but the forecast for the next year was more of the same. Value Line estimated that IBM's earnings would decrease by a little over 1 percent in 1986. Despite its grand reputation, IBM had nothing to recommend it to a growth investor at the end of 1985. It was no longer a growth stock and it surely wasn't a value stock. It had a mediocre yield and its price-to-book and price-to-sales ratios were high. As Fig. 1-1 shows, its factor profile simply wasn't good for a growth *or* a value portfolio. Only people who considered more than IBM's reputation as the world's best known computer maker and looked further at its underlying factors could make a good investing call.

Between December 31, 1985 and December 31, 1989, IBM appealed to neither a growth nor a value investor, since its underlying factors continued to show earnings growth rates below the market, while price-to-earnings ratios and the like were above the market. Over those four years, IBM lost over 30

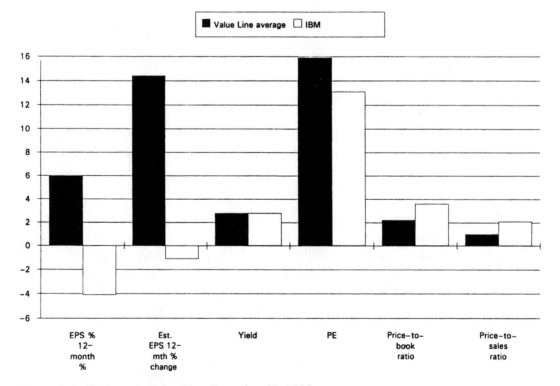

Figure 1-1. IBM versus Value Line, December 31, 1985.

percent of its value, an annual compounded return of −8.6 percent. The S&P 500, on the other hand, gained 89.9 percent, or 17.4 percent on a compounded annual basis.

Then, as at the end of 1985, something happened. Thinking conventionally, you'd have seen a troubled growth stock that had disappointed investors for more than four years. Had you looked at IBM in terms of its underlying factors, however, you would have seen the profile presented in Fig. 1-2. During 1989, IBM became a superb value stock. Most of its underlying factors were now similar to those that value managers find attractive. A yield twice that of the average stock in the Value Line 1600 with price-to-book, price-to-sales, and price-to-earnings ratios well below the market average. With all of this, IBM was still ranked as one of the safest companies on the exchange, with an A++ financial ranking. At the end of 1989, any value manager using factor analysis would have found IBM a great stock and incluein his or her portfolio. Beginning in 1991, however, IBM's strong

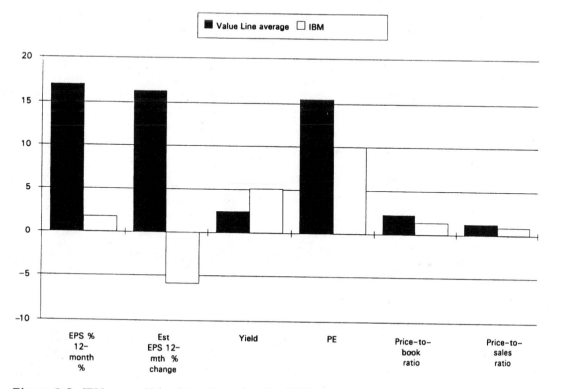

Figure 1-2. IBM versus Value Line, December 31, 1989.

return of 19.8 percent over the previous year knocked it out of the value category again. Thus, as 1991 began, IBM was once again appealing to neither a growth nor a value manager.

IBM might spend the coming few years moving into and out of the value category, but the point remains: You could perceive and act on these dramatic changes in IBM's investment appeal only by looking at its underlying factors.

A Manager's Style Determines His Performance

What's true for individual stocks is true for portfolios. In a multi-year review of how various portfolios performed versus the market as a whole, I found that a manager's inherent style foretells the portfolio's performance, with as much as 80 percent of a portfolio's return attributable to the manager's underlying style. For instance, a value manager's portfolio will have a tough time beating a market hot on growth stocks, while a growth manager's portfolio will pop in that same market. A portfolio's factors have an overwhelming impact on its performance.

Consider 1991, for example, a year the average mutual fund in the Morningstar database went up around 30 percent. That year, growth stocks were in favor on Wall Street. Funds that invested in stocks with factors valued by growth investors did well, with the average aggressive growth fund going up 46 percent, 16 percent better than the average mutual fund.

Consider the power that factors have on a portfolio's performance. What if we took two factors highly associated with growth investing—the five-year earnings per share growth rate and the percentage gain or loss in earnings per share over the last 12 months—and used them to create a portfolio. Starting on December 31, 1990, we will buy the 50 stocks that in the previous year had the highest annual earnings per share percentage change and five-year earnings per share growth rates greater than 20 percent. That's all we do to create our portfolio: simply use two factors that are highly desirable to growth stock investors.

Figure 1-3 is the factor profile of our 50-stock portfolio compared to the market. (In this instance, the Value Line 1600 stocks are used to represent the market, as I'll continue to do throughout the book, unless otherwise stated.) See how different our

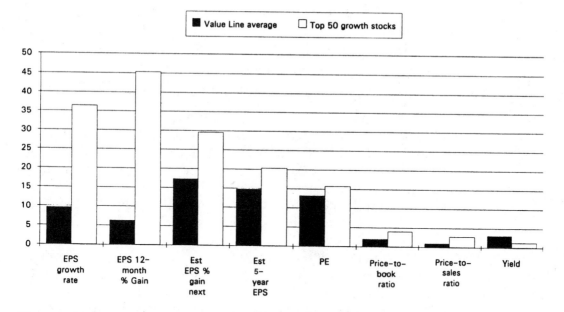

Figure 1-3. Factor profiles of Value Line and top 50 growth stocks.

two-factor growth portfolio is from the market? The 50 stocks, held for a year, were up 60.1 percent. No trades were made in the portfolio. Nor were stocks bought or sold because of their names or industries. We simply used two factors associated with growth stocks and equally weighted all the stocks that made the list.

Do you see the power that a portfolio's factors have on its performance? While growth managers who did well will trumpet their "brilliance" in advertisements announcing 1991 performance, the fact is that *anyone* who had a portfolio even *mildly* based on the growth stock philosophy would have done well in 1991.

A Mutual Fund's Style and Factors Determine Its Performance

What's true for a single portfolio is also true for a group of mutual funds. Again in 1991, take the growth funds in the Morningstar database and isolate three factors:

1. A cash position below 5 percent, signifying an aggressive position

2. Earnings per share growth rates above 20 percent

3. Return on assets below 12 percent

You'll end up with just five funds. These funds have similar factors, but invest in different stocks. If you looked at the names of the stocks in each of their portfolios, you would see very different names, ranging from Coca Cola to Tetra Technologies. Remember, it's not the stocks so much as the portfolio's underlying factors that determine performance. Because their factors are so similar, the returns on our five mutual funds ranged from a low of 67.04 percent to a high of 72.72 percent, a spread of only 5.68 percent.

Investment styles and a portfolio's factors are also responsible for poor performance. The first half of 1992 was rough for growth managers, with the average aggressive growth manager losing over 5.8 percent. Our two-factor growth portfolio was down over 12 percent in the first half of 1992. The five mutual funds we just discussed posted an average loss of over 13 percent for the same six-month period. Our growth portfolio and mutual funds were down in 1992 for the same reason they had been up in 1991—because of their underlying factors, not because some of the stocks in their portfolios were named Biomet, Merck, or Home Depot.

Styles come into and out of favor. The best long-term managers do well by finding a great style and sticking with it throughout the various market cycles.

Portfolios with Similar Factors Have Similar Performance

Now we'll see how portfolios with similar factor profiles have similar returns. If you saw a portfolio that was identical to the S&P 500 in terms of its underlying attributes, or factors, how do you think it would perform? The portfolio featured in Fig. 1-4 has factors that are identical to the S&P 500. It has the same price-to-earnings ratio, price-to-book ratio, five-year earnings per share growth rate, yield, and debt level. It should come as no surprise that this portfolio and the S&P 500 performed the

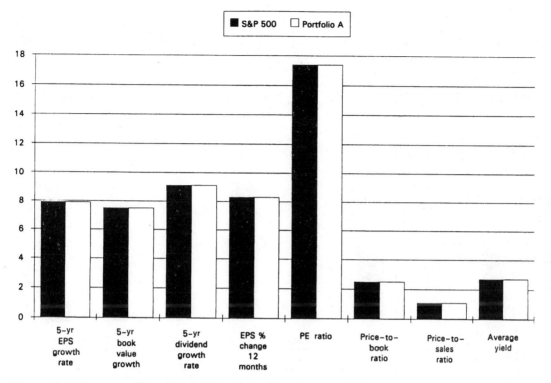

Figure 1-4. Factor profiles of S&P 500 and portfolio A.

same. Portfolio A is an "index" fund's factor profile. Index funds contain the same stocks as the S&P 500 in order to duplicate its performance.

Index funds don't even have to replicate the S&P 500 by purchasing all 500 stocks in the index. They can buy just a representative sample and virtually duplicate the S&P 500's performance. I've confirmed this by selecting stocks with attributes that are identical to those in the S&P 500. As long as the portfolio's factors remained similar to the S&P 500, so did its performance. The same is true of any portfolio. As long as the factors defining the portfolios are the same, their performance will be nearly the same.

What happens to a portfolio that's very different from the S&P 500? The portfolio depicted in Fig. 1-5 differs dramatically from the S&P 500 in price-to-earnings ratio, price-to-book ratio, earnings per share growth rates, yields, and debt levels. We can

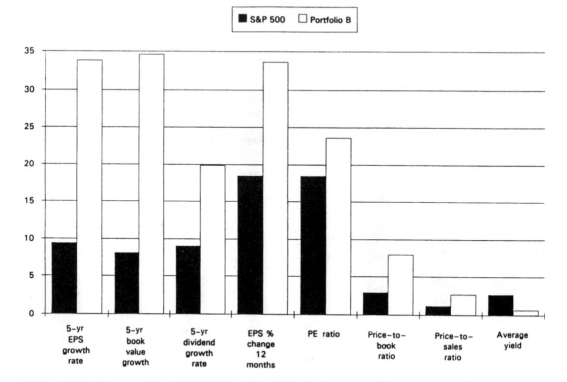

Figure 1-5. Factor profiles of S&P 500 and portfolio B.

predict from these differences that its performance will not mimic the S&P 500 and may differ substantially. In fact, the portfolio's return did differ substantially. Table 1-1 lists the stocks in portfolio B, along with their performance for the one-year period following this factor analysis. As you can see, their performance differed markedly from the S&P 500.

If, however, you compared this portfolio to another growth portfolio with highly similar factors, you'd find that in any given year the two would also have highly similar performance. Figure 1-6 depicts a portfolio with factors that are remarkably similar to portfolio B, yet it contains none of the same stocks. Table 1-2 shows that its performance was very close to portfolio A, not because it contained the same stocks or invested in the same industries, but because it had similar underlying factors. If the goal is simply to match a portfolio's performance, the first step is to match its underlying factors.

As a consultant to a large pension fund, I created "shadow

Table 1-1. The Stocks in Portfolio B and
Their Subsequent One-Year Return

Ticker	Stock	1992 return (%)
CC	Circuit City Stores	12.2
CTB	Cooper Tire & Rubber	37.3
HDI	Harley Davidson, Inc.	72.1
HD	Home Depot	51.1
MIKE	Michael's Stores	86.4
MSFT	Microsoft	16.6
PEP	Pepsico	24.4
RBK	Reebok International	5.3
USHC	U.S. Healthcare	59.9
VAL	Valspar	14
Portfolio total		48.5
S&P 500		6.8

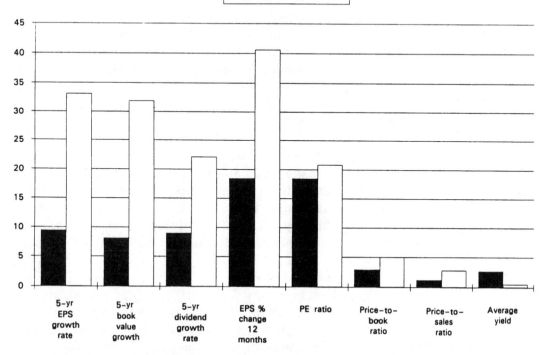

Figure 1-6. Factor profiles of S&P 500 and portfolio C.

Table 1-2. The Stocks in Portfolio C and
Their Subsequent One-Year Return

Ticker	Stock	1992 return (%)
AIG	American International Group	20.6
CCN	Chris Craft Ind.	32
DDS	Dillard Department Stores	21.2
DIS	Walt Disney	54.2
ERTS	Electronic Arts	119.6
GLK	Great Lakes Chemical	18.5
NKE	Nike Inc.	15.9
PGR	Progressive Corp.	59.7
SHX	Shaw Ind.	90
SUP	Superior Industries	74.1
Portfolio total		50.58
S&P 500		6.8

portfolios" for the plan's money managers using factor analysis
and multifactor modeling. That's a fancy way of saying that I
studied their portfolios to see which factors they valued, used
those factors to screen the database for stocks, and then created
another portfolio with highly similar underlying factors. To see
a real time example of how portfolios with similar factors have
similar returns, we'll look at one of the plan's managers as an
example. This manager was followed in real time starting in
1990, with the pension committee reviewing both the manager
and the shadow each quarter.

This manager is a classic growth manager, investing over $10
billion for a variety of clients. When analyzing the portfolio, I
found that the manager used an established growth style. Figure
1-7 shows the portfolio's factors compared to the market (only
those factors that were substantially different from the market
are listed). Looking at factors is a minicourse in how various
schools of investing ply their trade. You see instantly that the
portfolio is made up of stocks with very high five-year growth
rates for dividends, book value, and earnings per share. Recent
earnings growth has been good, with earnings per share percentage gains for the last quarter and 12-month period substantially higher than the average stock in the Value Line database.
The portfolio also ranks high on ancillary factors associated
with growth stock investing. Figure 1-8 shows these factors.

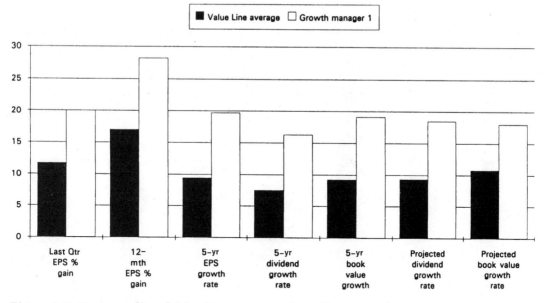

Figure 1-7. Factor profiles of Value Line average and growth manager 1.

Imitating the Style of a Selected Portfolio

Once we see how this manager builds his portfolio, it is easy for us to use the factors he most values to create a portfolio just like his in terms of underlying factors. First, we rank the factors by *how much* they differ from the market. We find that it deviates most from the market in terms of historical growth rates for dividends, earnings per share, and book value. We also see that recent earnings percentage changes are considerably higher than the market. Profit margins, price-to-sales ratios, and price-to-cash-flow ratios are also high. Finally, we notice that the projected five-year growth rates for dividends and book values are considerably higher than the market. These are the factors we will use later when constructing our multifactor screening model.

We can replicate the important deviations from the market by using the following model as a screen on the Value Line 1600:

1. Five-year earnings per share growth rates must be higher than 10.5 percent or the Value Line average, whichever is greater.

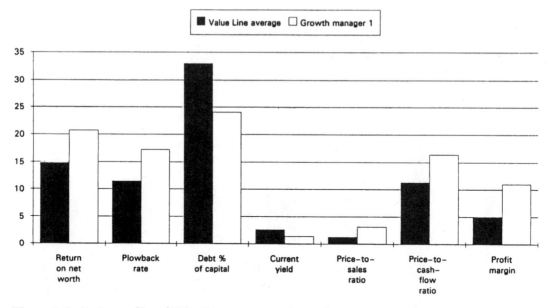

Figure 1-8. Factor profiles of Value Line average and growth manager 1.

2. Five-year dividend growth rates must be higher than the Value Line average.

3. Five-year book value growth rates must be higher than the Value Line average or 10 percent, whichever is greater.

4. Twelve-month earnings per share percentage gains must be higher than the Value Line average.

5. Projected three- to five-year earnings per share and book value growth rates must be higher than the Value Line average.

6. Projected three- to five-year dividend growth rates must be higher than zero.

7. Market capitalization must be lower than $8 billion.

That's it. Those are the only factors we need to create a portfolio with factors that are like our growth manager's. Figures 1-9 and 1-10 show that there is almost no difference between the two portfolio's factors. Both have similar five-year growth rates for earnings per share, dividends, and book values. Both have similar recent earnings-per-share percentage gains. They both have similar projections for three- to five-year growth rates in terms

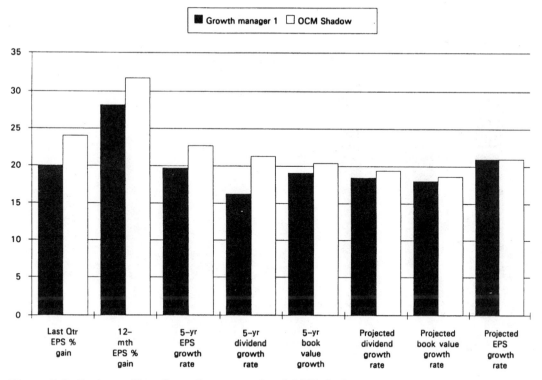

Figure 1-9. Factor profiles of growth manager 1 and OCM shadow.

of earnings per share, book value, and dividends. Looking at secondary factors, both have similar return on net worth, plowback ratios, debt levels, profit margins, and yields. At the factor level, these two portfolios are virtually the same, even though someone just looking at the names of the stocks in each portfolio wouldn't find much similarity at all, in that they held only about 30 percent in common.

Now compare their annual returns, featured in Fig. 1-11. From 1989 on, we see virtually identical performance. The individual managing the account was changed at the end of 1988. Since we were using a factor model based on the new manager's factor preferences, this explains the big performance difference in 1988. (My client wished that the managers had switched sooner!) In each of the next three years, the performance of the portfolio designed by our multifactor model was virtually identical to the conventional manager. It came that close *without any optimization* (i.e., using factors that have tested better than the ones

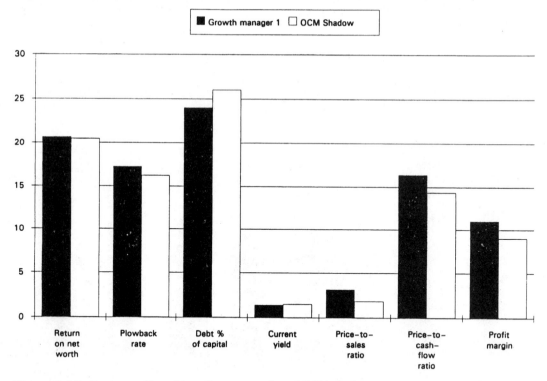

Figure 1-10. Factor profiles of growth manager 1 and OCM shadow.

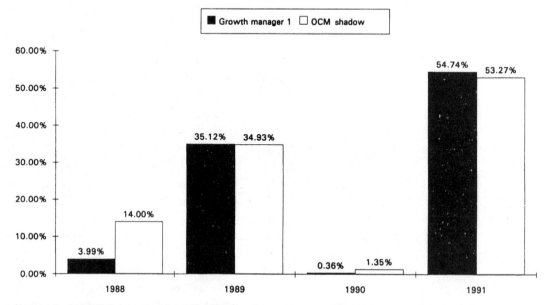

Figure 1-11. Factor profiles of growth manager 1 and OCM shadow.

used) or use of factor *combinations* that I know would work better for an established growth model. The shadow portfolio also
had very high commissions attributed to it; so trading costs
didn't dampen the return of the manager's portfolio versus his
shadow portfolio. I compared only the return on stocks, without
taking cash positions into account. Had you invested $10,000
with the manager on December 31, 1987, it would have grown
to $21,821 at the end of 1991. The same $10,000 invested in the
multifactor generated portfolio designed to shadow the manager would have been worth $23,895 at the end of 1991. This man-
ager was of interest because he religiously sold stocks that no
longer met his criteria and replaced them with ones that did. By
doing so, he kept the factor profile of his portfolio consistent in
each year of the study.

When managers don't have the discipline to replace stocks
that no longer fit their profile, their portfolios suffer in performance, even if the managers have great ideas. Another manager
shadowed for this client is a good example. His return was 38
percent below his shadow simply because he failed to continually and rigorously sell stocks that no longer met his criteria. The
manager had good ideas, but he didn't consistently act on them.
He cost himself 30 percent over four years by letting his portfolio drift, so that each year saw his factor profile become slightly
less sharp than before. Managers who fail to keep a portfolio
tilted to precisely the factors they value tend to underperform
the market, and they might even take more risk while doing so.

*Consistently applying a profitable style is the one thing that all
great money managers share.* By using a nonoptimized model
based on factors identical to those in the manager's underlying
portfolios, we were able to generate performance substantially
better than the manager simply because our models made buy
and sell decisions rigorously and consistently.

Emulating the Best Managers

Now that we've seen that portfolios with similar factors have
similar performance, we know how to learn from the best managers. We can look at the essence of great managers' styles by
looking not at the names of the stocks they buy, but at their
underlying characteristics. With this information, we can devel-

op a model that consistently picks stocks to meet the masters'
standards. We can also use their standards as our starting point,
moving beyond them to design models that have a greater clarity, simplicity, and precision than the masters' own portfolios.
We can stand on the shoulders of the great managers and look
farther, using the insights learned to design models that give us
even better performance.

2

Factors That Determine Investment Performance

In this chapter, you will become acquainted with the factors we'll be using throughout the book. I recommend using Value Line's Value/Screen database for factor analysis and model building for the following reasons:

- *Price.* It's relatively cheap. Value Line offers a lot of data for a price that most individual investors can afford.

- *Liquid stocks.* The stocks Value Line covers account for 95 percent of the trading volume on the exchanges. If a stock is in the Value Line, the chances are high that it has good trading liquidity. It wouldn't do you any good to find a stock that looks like it will double in a month only to discover that it never trades. Value Line's stocks are highly liquid, ensuring a low spread between the stock's bid and asked price.

- *Widely followed.* Stocks in the Value Line database are widely followed on Wall Street. This causes an "information saturation" that forces all estimates for a stock's future earnings to move closer and closer to one another, because researchers use what the competition is forecasting as feedback when making their own forecasts. This effectively moves statistical forecasts, like those available from Value Line, very close to the mean consensus estimates available from all of Wall Street's expensive forecasters.

■ *Easy to use.*   The home version of the Value Line database is easy to use. It is fairly intuitive and will not cause you to rip out your hair in despair.

Therefore, we'll define the factors in the same order you would find them listed in Value/Screen's database. Value Line groups factors according to section names. The names we'll look at are:

1. The Ratings & Estimates Section.

2. The Market Data Section.

3. The Historical Measures Section.

4. The Fiscal Year Data Section.

5. The Growth Projections Section.

6. The Identification Section.

7. The User Defined Section.

The Ratings & Estimates Section

In Value Line's first group of factors, under the Ratings & Estimates Section, you'll find the following nine factors:

1. Beta

2. Current earnings per share (EPS)

3. Current dividend

4. Financial strength rank

5. Industry rank

6. Price stability rank

7. Safety rank

8. Technical rank

9. Timeliness rank

Beta.   This is a mathematical formula measuring the sensitivity of rates of return on individual stocks compared to the market as a whole. A high beta suggests the stock's price will be more volatile than the market, whereas a low-beta stock should be less volatile than the market. You would expect a stock with a beta of 1.25 to go up or down 25 percent more than the market over any given period. If the market is up 20 percent for the year, the stock with a beta of 1.25 should be up around 25 percent.

Beta has recently moved from an article of faith among academics to one of questionable validity. New academic studies are proving what market practitioners have always known: Beta doesn't work very well as a predictive factor.

Current Earnings per Share. Covering a 12-month period, this rank stands for Value Line's estimated earnings per share for the coming six-month period added to the actual earnings per share for the two most recent quarters.

Current Dividend. This consists of dividends per common share to be declared within the next 12 months.

Financial Strength Rating. Value Line rates each stock's financial strength relative to all the others in the database. The ratings range from A++ to C in nine steps. Value Line awards companies with the best financial strength an A++ rank, indicating an ability to weather hard times better than almost all the other companies in the database. The ratings continue down on a relative basis, moving from A++ to A+, all the way down to C, the lowest of the nine ratings. Value Line gives its lowest rating of C to companies with very serious financial problems.

Industry Rank. This numerical rating is based on the average Value Line Timeliness ranks for the stocks within particular industries. The rank indicates how Value Line estimates the industry as a whole is likely to perform relative to all the other industries in the coming 12 months.

Price Stability Index. An index based on the weekly percentage changes in the price of a stock over the last five years: the lower the standard deviation of the price changes, the more stable the stock. Stocks ranking in the top 5 percent (lowest standard deviation) carry a rank of 100; the next 5 percent, a rank of 95; and so on, down to a rank of 5, which has the highest standard deviation of price changes. One standard deviation is the range around the average weekly percentage price change that encompasses about two-thirds of all the weekly percentage change figures over the last five years. When the range is wide, the standard deviation is high and the stock's price stability is low. As an example, the average stock in the Dow Jones Industrial Average has a price stability index rank of 76, whereas the average stock in a small capitalization growth fund has a rank of 30.

Safety Rank. Value Line developed this measure to quantify the potential risk associated with specific, individual common stocks, rather than large, diversified portfolios. Value Line bases a stock's Safety rank on the stability of its price. The Safety rank reflects a stock's sensitivity to the overall market as well as its inherent volatility (adjusted for trend) and other factors, including company size, the penetration of its markets, product market volatility, the degree of financial leverage, earnings quality, and the overall condition of the balance sheet. Safety ranges from 1 (highest) to 5 (lowest). Thus, a rank of 1 or 2 would mean the stock was highly stable and wouldn't be too risky for conservative investors, whereas ranks of 4 or 5 signify speculative, highly volatile issues.

Technical Rank. This is Value Line's prediction of a stock's expected price movement over the next three to six months. A stock's Technical rank is a function of its price action relative to all stocks followed by Value Line. Value Line expects stocks ranked 1 (highest) or 2 (above average) to outpace the market. Those ranked 4 (below average) or 5 (lowest) are not expected to outperform most stocks over the next six months. Stocks ranked 3 (average) are expected to advance or decline in line with the market as a whole.

Timeliness Rank. Value Line ranks a stock's probable performance relative to the market in the year ahead. Stocks ranked 1 (highest) or 2 (above average) are likely to outpace the market. Stocks ranked 4 (below average) and 5 (lowest) are not expected to outperform the market over the next 12 months. Value Line expects stocks ranked 3 (average) to perform about the same as the market.

Timeliness is Value Line's most important rank. Value Line derives it using a cross-sectional analysis that compares each stock with every other stock in the database. Therefore, the rank is comparative, not predicative. The analysis has five elements, all based on earnings and price behavior over the last ten years. Value Line gives higher ranks to stocks with higher earnings per share and price in relation to their ten-year average, whereas stocks with lower earnings and price compared to their ten-year rank get lower rankings. Additional points go to stocks with lower price-to-earnings ratios, and with recent relative strength in earnings-per-share percentage gains and price performance. Finally, Value Line gives special consideration to stocks whose earnings were a "surprise" (i.e., exceeding Value Line's estimates). When all of this historical information is tabulated and each stock in the database is compared to every other stock, Value Line's Timeliness ratings are the result.

Some Factors Coincide

These nine factors define different attributes of any given stock, but as you start doing factor analysis, you'll see how certain factors usually clump together. Of the nine factors just defined, six of them are unique to the Value Line database. The Timeliness, Technical, Safety, and Industry Ranks are all available only from Value Line and are in themselves multifactor models. The Financial Strength and Price Stability ratings are also Value Line innovations. These "multifactor factors" can be useful shortcuts in creating databases that reflect a manager's style.

For example, you'll very often see a growth manager holding stocks with Timeliness ranks of 1 or 2, Technical ranks of 1 or 2, and Industry ranks well below the mean. If the manager you were looking at specialized in emerging growth stocks, the stocks in his portfolio might also have low Price Stability indexes and Safety ranks. If the manager concentrated on established growth stocks, the stocks might score *high* on these ranks. Conversely, a conservative manager's preferred database of stocks might show Safety ranks of 1 or 2, Price Stability ranks above 70, and Financial Strength ratings above the grade of A.

The key thing to remember is that the various management styles tend to value similar profiles when it comes to their portfolio's underlying factors. Table 2-1 lists some of the factors that you would normally find in a traditional growth manager's portfolio.

Table 2-1. Factors Found in a Traditional Growth Manager's Portfolio

Factor	Reading relative to the average stock in the database
Timeliness	Low, usually between 1 and 3
Industry rank	Low, usually below the mean for the database
Technical rank	Low, usually below 3
13- and 26-week percentage gain	High, usually well above the average for the database
Return on net worth	High
Retained to common equity	High
Debt as percentage of capital	Low
Last quarter EPS % change	High, usually substantially above the database average
12-month EPS % change	High, usually substantially above the database average
5-year EPS growth rate	High
5-year book value growth rate	High
Estimated change EPS fiscal year	Fairly high
Projected EPS growth	High
Shares outstanding	High
Price-to-cash-flow	High
Profit margins	High
Payout ratio	Low
Yield	Low

The Market Data Section

The nine factors found in the Market Data Section of the Value Line database are:

1. Current price-to-book value ratio (P/B).

2. Current price-to-earnings ratio (PE).

3. Current yield.

4. 52-week high.

5. 52-week low.

6. Market value in millions of dollars.

7. Recent price.

8. 13-week percentage price change.

9. 26-week percentage price change.

Let's define these nine factors.

Current Price-to-Book Value Ratio (P/B). The current price per share is divided by the current book value per share (current price ÷ current book value). Stocks with a very high price-to-book ratio are generally rapidly growing firms, expected to experience great growth in underlying book value in the coming years. Stocks with very low price-to-book ratios are generally in older, more established industries. Investors use P/B as a yardstick to measure a company's cheapness relative to other stocks in the market.

Current Price-to-Earnings Ratio (PE). A stock's recent market price is divided by current earnings per share (current price ÷ current earnings per share). The higher the price-to-earnings ratio, the more investors are paying for earnings, and the larger the expectations for future earnings growth. Stocks with high PEs are typically rapidly growing companies. Stocks with low price-to-earnings ratios usually are low-growth stocks in mature industries. A stock's PE is the most common measurement for how cheap or expensive it is relative to other stocks.

Current Yield. Dividends per share to be paid within the next 12 months are divided by current price (current dividend ÷ current price). Like price-to-earnings ratios and price-to-book ratios, current yield serves as the basis for entire market philosophies. The dividend often accounts for more than half the total return you get from a stock.

52-Week High. This is the highest price for the stock during the 52 weeks ending prior to the most recent database update.

52-Week Low. This is the lowest price for the stock during the 52 weeks ending prior to the most recent database update.

Market Value in Millions of Dollars (Market Cap). This, the total value in dollars of the company, is calculated by multiplying the number of shares outstanding by the current price (total shares outstanding × current price). You can identify some schools of investing by the market cap of their stocks. Small-cap investors concentrate on stocks with small market values, and large-cap investors buy stocks with larger market values.

Recent Price.   The most recent price for a stock is taken immediately prior to updating the Value Line database.

13-Week Percentage Price Change.   This is the amount by which the recent price of a stock differs from the market price of 13 weeks earlier. Negative numbers indicate price declines. You can use this factor to test the relative performance of each stock versus the database as a whole. Stocks with percentage changes greater than the market as a whole have *positive relative strength*, whereas stocks with percentage changes less than the market have *negative relative strength*.

26-Week Percentage Price Change.   This is the amount by which the recent price of a stock differs from the market price of 26 weeks earlier. Negative numbers represent price declines. Again, this factor is another gauge of relative strength, but here it's for six-month performance.

Several of these factors are the "bread and butter" factors of stock market analysis. Entire market schools revolve around buying stocks with low PE ratios and high yields, whereas others swear by buying stocks that have extremely good relative strength in price performance. These factors are also among the most widely studied and reported. Any good newspaper will usually carry a stock's price, 52-week high and low, PE, and dividend yield.

Value managers are usually most interested in stocks that have low PE ratios, low P/B ratios, and high yields, whereas growth managers aren't as concerned with these ratios, provided the stock has excellent earnings growth rates with expectations for continued rapid growth. Table 2-2 lists some of the factors that you would normally find in a traditional value manager's portfolio.

The Historical Measures Section

The ten factors found in the Historical Measures Section of the Value Line database are:

1. Book value per share.

Table 2-2. Factors Usually Found in a Traditional Value Manager's Portfolio

Factor	Reading relative to the average stock in the database
Safety rank	Low, usually 3 or below
Timeliness	Usually no 1 or 2 ranks
Current price-to-earnings ratio	Low, usually below the database average
Yield	High, usually above the database average
Price-to-sales ratio	Low, usually below the database average
Earnings yield	High
Price-to-cash-flow ratio	Low
Price-to-book value ratio	Low
Earnings per share percentage gains	Low
Forecasted earnings gains	Low

2. Debt as percentage of capital.

3. Five-year book value growth rate (5-Yr Bk Val Growth).

4. Five-year dividend growth rate (5-Yr Divd Growth).

5. Five-year earnings per share growth rate (5-Yr EPS Growth).

6. Last quarter earnings per share percentage change (Last Qtr EPS % Chg).

7. Percentage retained net worth (% Ret Net Worth).

8. Percentage retained to common (% Retained to Common).

9. Sales in millions of dollars [Sales ($ mill)].

10. 12-month earnings per share percentage change (12-Month EPS % Chg).

Book Value per Share. The common shareholders' equity at the end of the most recent fiscal year is divided by the number of shares outstanding (shareholders' equity ÷ shares outstanding).

Debt as Percentage of Capital. Long-term debt is expressed as part of total capital.

Five-Year Book Value Growth Rate (5-Yr Bk Val Growth). This is the compound annual growth rate of book value per share. You calculate it by comparing the average book value of the latest three years with the average book value of the three-year period a half-decade earlier.

Five-Year Dividend Growth Rate (5-Yr Divd Growth). The compound annual growth rate of dividends per share is calculated by comparing the average dividends of the latest three-year period with the average dividends of the three-year period a half-decade earlier.

Five-Year Earnings per Share Growth Rate (5-Yr EPS Growth). The compound annual growth rate of earnings per share. You calculate it by comparing the average earnings of the latest three-year period with the average earnings of the three-year period a half-decade earlier.

Last Quarter Earnings per Share Percentage Change (Last Qtr EPS % Chg). The percentage increase or decrease of earnings per share for the latest reported quarter, compared with same quarter the year before.

Percentage Retained Net Worth (% Ret Net Worth). Net income is divided by net worth, expressed as a percentage (net income ÷ net worth). This is the same as return on equity, and is a very important measure of a company's profitability.

Percentage Retained to Common (% Retained to Common). Net income, less all dividends (common and preferred), is divided by common stockholders' equity (i.e., net worth less the liquidating or redemption value of preferred stock outstanding) and expressed as a percentage. Many investors also call this ratio the *plowback ratio* because it shows the percentage of earnings the company retains (or "plows back" into the company), relative to common equity. It is an excellent measure of the extent to which a company is reinvesting itself.

Sales in Millions of Dollars [Sales ($ mill)]. This is the amount of sales generated by a company in the prior year.

12-Month Earnings per Share Percentage Change (12-Month EPS % Chg). The percentage increase or decrease of earnings per share for the latest reported 12-month period is compared with the preceding 12-month period.

Most of these factors measure how a company has done historically. Have earnings been growing rapidly or not at all? Has the company loaded up on debt? Has it been reinvesting its earnings in itself or paying them out in dividends? Investors who use a so-called "quality" investment strategy would use some of these factors to determine whether the stock was of a high enough caliber to make it into their portfolio. Such investors might buy only stocks with excellent five-year growth rates for book value, dividends, and earnings, with generous returns on net worth and high retained to common percentages that nevertheless had low debt relative to capital. Table 2-3 lists some of the other factors that core, or "quality," managers like in stocks.

The Fiscal Year Data Section

The eight factors found in the Fiscal Year Data Section of the Value Line database are:

Table 2-3. Factors Usually Found in a Traditional Core High-Quality Manager's Portfolio

Factor	Reading relative to the average stock in the database
Timeliness rank	Usually below 4
Safety rank	Usually 3 or below
Financial strength rating	High, usually B++ or better
Price stability rank	High, usually above the database average
Return on net worth	Usually equal to or above database average
Debt as percentage of total capital	Close to or lower than the database average
Current price-to-earnings ratio	Close to the market's
Current yield	Usually higher than the database average
Market value ($ mill)	High, usually above one billion
Five-year EPS growth rate	Usually equal to or above database average
Five-year dividend growth rate	Usually equal to or above database average
Five-year book value growth rate	Usually equal to or above database average
Cash flow per share	High
% institutional	High
Shares outstanding	High

1. Cash.
2. Cash flow per share.
3. Current assets.
4. Current liabilities.
5. Long-term debt.
6. Net profit.
7. Net worth.
8. Total assets.

Cash.   This consists of all cash on hand plus any short-term securities that can be quickly converted to cash.

Cash Flow per Share.   The sum of net profit and depreciation, less any preferred dividends, is divided by shares outstanding {[(Net profit + depreciation) − preferred dividends] ÷ shares outstanding}.

Current Assets.   This can be cash or any asset the company expects to convert into cash within one year. Current assets include all marketable securities such as stocks, bonds, commercial paper, and the like, as well as accounts receivable, inventories, prepaid expenses, and any other assets that could be expected to be sold, consumed, or otherwise converted to cash within 12 months.

Current Liabilities.   All debts due within a year are included in this category. Current liabilities include all accounts payable, short-term loans, any long-term debt maturing within a year, declared dividends not yet paid, and all expenses incurred but not yet paid.

Long-Term Debt.   All debts that are coming due more than 12 months after year end, including capitalized leases, make up this category.

Net Profit.   This category consists of income for the year after all income taxes are deducted but before extraordinary charges or credits are taken.

Net Worth. Total assets minus current liabilities, long-term debt, and all other noncurrent liabilities at year end constitute net worth.

Total Assets. This is the sum of all current and long-term assets at year end.

These eight factors are most useful when you combine them with other factors and create new ratios. For example, when you divide a stock's price by its cash flow per share, you have an excellent ratio for measuring how cheap or dear the stock's price is relative to other stocks. When you divide net income by net sales, you get the net profit margin, which allows you to see how profitable the stock is relative to others in the database.

We'll cover these and other ratios in the "User Defined Section" later in this chapter.

Growth Projections

The eight factors in the Growth Projections Section of the Value Line database are:

1. Estimated percentage change in earnings per share for quarter one (Est. % Chg EPS Qt. 1).

2. Estimated percentage change in earnings per share for quarter two (Est. % Chg EPS Qt. 2).

3. Estimated percentage change in earnings per share for fiscal year (Est. % Chg EPS Fis Yr).

4. Projected book value growth rate (Prj Book Val Growth).

5. Projected dividend growth rate (Prj Divd Growth).

6. Projected earnings per share growth rate (Prj EPS Growth).

7. Projected three- to five-year price percentage appreciation (Prj 3-5 Yr Apprec %).

8. Projected three- to five-year average annual return (Prj 3-5 Yr Av Return).

Estimated Percentage Change in Earnings per Share for Quarter One (Est. % Chg EPS Qt. 1). This is Value Line's estimate of the percentage increase or decrease of earnings per share from the preceding year's quarter.

Estimated Percentage Change in Earnings per Share for Quarter Two (Est. % Chg EPS Qt. 2). Value Line estimates the percentage increase or decrease for the quarter immediately following the current one. If you were doing a factor analysis of a portfolio on January 1, this estimate would be for the percentage increase or decrease in earnings for the second quarter of the year.

Estimated Percentage Change in Earnings per Share for Fiscal Year (Est. % Chg EPS Fis Yr). Value Line estimates the percentage increase or decrease from the prior year's earnings.

Projected Book Value Growth Rate (Prj Book Val Growth). The compound annual rate of growth of book value per share is projected by Value Line for the next three to five years. You calculate it by dividing the average annual result for the latest three years into the average projected result for the period three to five years hence.

Projected Dividend Growth Rate (Prj Divd Growth). The compound annual rate of growth of dividends is projected by Value Line for the next three to five years. You calculate it by dividing the average annual result for the latest three years into the average projected result for the period three to five years hence.

You can also use this projection to find the expected return for the stock market based on discounted cash flow analysis. In that model, you arrive at the expected return for the market by adding the yield for the market or for the index you're working with, such as the S&P 500, to the projected growth rate for dividends. People wishing to judge whether the market is fairly priced compute this figure and then compare it to the returns available in the bond market.

Projected Earnings per Share Growth Rate (Prj EPS Growth). The compound annual rate of growth of EPS is projected by Value Line for the next three to five years. You calculate it by dividing the average annual result for the latest three years into the average projected result for the period three to five years hence.

Projected Three- to Five-Year Price Percentage Appreciation (Prj 3-5 Yr Apprec %). This is the expected percentage price gain for a stock if Value Line's profit and price-earnings projections for the period three to five years hence are on target.

Projected Three- to Five-Year Average Annual Return (Prj 3-5 Yr Av Return). This is similar to the projected three- to five-year appreciation, but it includes the sum of all dividend disbursements expected over the next three to five years along with capital appreciation. You divide it all by the recent price of the stock, and express it as a compound annual growth rate.

Earnings projections are the lifeblood of Wall Street. Wall Street financial institutions spend more money trying to get their estimates for future earnings closer to what the company eventually reports than on any other underlying factor. They pay some analysts more than $1 million a year to predict future corporate earnings. Shares react swiftly to actual earnings that are surprisingly higher or lower than the consensus estimates. Therefore, it's important for you to understand that you can use Value Line's estimates with confidence.

Several companies collect the estimates of Wall Street's analysts and publish them. The Institutional Brokers Estimate Service (IBES) publishes one that is available over Compuserve, a dial-up computer information service. Having done several studies comparing Value Line's estimates for EPS percentage change for the coming fiscal year with the IBES numbers, I find statistically little difference between the two. Value Line's estimates for the coming year are virtually identical to the IBES numbers, with a correlation factor above 95 percent. What's more, the *Value Line estimates were many times better at projecting true earnings than the consensus of the highly paid Wall Street analysts!*

As an example, in mid-1992, I programmed my computer to randomly select five stocks from the Value Line Database of 1600 stocks. Noting Value Line's estimate for EPS change for the coming fiscal year, I got the IBES consensus numbers from Compuserve. Here are the results:

Stock	Value Line estimate (%)	IBES consensus (%)	Difference (%)
American General	9.4	10	0.6
Norwest Bank	15.8	15	− 0.8
Yellow Fright Sys	60.0	53.0	− 7
Beverly Enterprises	48.6	49.0	0.4
Lawson Products	5.7	6.0	0.3

Thus, you can be confident that Value Line's estimates are usually very similar to the consensus on Wall Street for annual or quarterly estimates.

The Identification Section

The three factors here are:

1. Exchange code.
2. Shares outstanding.
3. Percentage institutional holdings (% Institutional).

Exchange Code. The code is for the exchange on which the stock trades.

Shares Outstanding. This is the number of common shares outstanding at the end of the most recently reported fiscal year.

Percentage Institutional Holdings (% Institutional). This, the number of shares of a company's stock reported held by large investment institutions such as pension plans and mutual funds, is expressed as a percentage of shares outstanding at the end of the most recent fiscal year.

Many "emerging growth" stock investors like to buy companies with a limited number of shares outstanding and *some* institutional sponsorship. One study found that 95 percent of the greatest stock market winners over a 35-year period had fewer

Table 2-4. Factors Usually Associated with an Emerging Growth Manager's Portfolio

Factor	Reading relative to the average stock in the database
Timeliness rank	Very low, usually 1 or 2
Price stability rank	Low, usually well below the database average
Beta	High
Technical rank	Very low, usually 1 or 2
Market value ($ mill)	Low
Return on net worth	High
Percent retained to common	High
13- and 26-week percentage gain	Very high, usually in the upper third of the database
Debt as percentage of capital	Low
Last quarter EPS percentage change	Very high, usually in the upper quarter of the database
12-month EPS percentage change	Very high, usually in the upper quarter of the database
Estimated change EPS quarter 1	Very high
Estimated change EPS fiscal year	Very high
Projected EPS growth rate	High
Yield	Low
Shares outstanding	Low

than 25 million shares outstanding when they had their greatest earnings improvement and stock market performance.

Table 2-4 lists some of the other factor characteristics found in emerging growth investor's portfolios.

The User Defined Section

The last section we'll look at is the User Defined Section of the database. Unlike the other sections, this one lets you define your own factors using the other factors in the database. This feature is handy when you need to look at a factor that's not in the database but that is nevertheless popular, like price-to-sales ratios or price-to-cash-flow ratios. You can also use the User Defined Section to build "multifactor factors."

We'll first look at 12 popular factors that aren't in the Value Line database but that you can create in the User Defined Section. Then we'll see how you can build handy combinations of factors using this section.

1. Cash per share
2. Common equity

3. Current ratio

4. Earnings yield

5. Net profit margin

6. Price-to-cash-flow ratio

7. Price-to-sales ratio (PSR)

8. Payout ratio

9. Recent price as percentage of 12-month high

10. Recent price as percentage of 12-month low

11. Return on total assets

12. Sales per share

Cash per Share.   Cash is divided by shares outstanding (cash divided by shares outstanding). The cash per share figure lets you see how much of a stock's price is supported by cash holdings. For example, a company that has $5 of cash per share with a price of $6 might be very attractive to a value investor.

Common Equity.   A company's book value per share is multiplied by the number of shares outstanding (book value per share × shares outstanding). This factor shows the total equity in a corporation shared by all common stockholders.

Current Ratio.   A company's current assets is divided by its current liabilities (current assets ÷ current liabilities). This factor is a measure of a company's ability to meet its short-term obligations: generally, the higher a company's current ratio, the higher its short-term liquidity. This is often a sign of a conservative management. Very high current ratios may reduce profitability.

Earnings Yield.   A company's earnings per share is divided by the current price of the stock (EPS divided by current price). You can also get the earning's yield by dividing 1 by the price-to-earnings ratio (1 divided by PE). The earning's yield is also called a company's capitalization rate. It helps show the total theoretical return to the shareholder (i.e., dividend growth plus the growth in the net assets of the company).

Net Profit Margin.   The net profit margin is a company's net income divided by net sales (net income divided by net sales).

The net profit margin is a measure of management's overall efficiency in managing operations, investing idle cash successfully, and borrowing at good rates.

Price-to-Cash-Flow Ratio.   The current price of a stock is divided by the cash flow per share (current price divided by cash flow per share). The price-to-cash-flow ratio can help you get a fix on how popular a stock is on Wall Street. Investors have high hopes for stocks with very high price-to-cash-flow ratios. Stocks with very low price-to-cash-flow ratios reflect modest expectations.

Price-to-Sales Ratio (PSR).   The PSR is a measurement of the relative value of an individual stock or a portfolio of stocks. You find it by dividing a stock's recent price by its sales per share (recent price divided by sales per share). PSRs are like price-to-earnings ratios because they measure a stock's current popularity with investors. In this case, we're looking at how much investors will pay for sales. The higher the PSR, the more popular the stock.

Payout Ratio.   This is the percentage of common share earnings that the company pays out in dividends. You find the ratio by dividing dividends per share by earnings per share (dividends divided by earnings per share). Generally, younger, rapidly growing companies retain their earnings to reinvest them in their business and thus have a low payout ratio. Older, more mature companies are more apt to have a higher dividend payout ratio.

Recent Price as a Percentage of 12-Month High.   The current price of a stock is divided by its 12-month high. This gives you a quick look at where a stock is trading relative to its own highs and lows, and it is useful to track in conjunction with its relative strength versus the market as a whole.

Recent Price as a Percentage of 12-Month Low.   The current price of a stock divided by its 12-month low. Like the preceding factor, it is a good way of seeing where a stock is relative to its low price over the last 12 months.

Return on Total Assets.   A stock's net profit is divided by its total assets (net profit divided by total assets). This factor is a measurement of the operating efficiency of a company.

Sales per Share. A company's sales are divided by total number of shares outstanding (sales divided by shares outstanding). This factor is an important indicator of a company's health and a component of the price-to-sales ratio.

Additional Uses

These 12 user defined factors are not all the ones that you might want to look at when doing factor analysis and modeling, but they are among the most popular of those not included within the fixed variable menus of the Value Line database. You could also use this section to define relative factors such as relative PE (a stock's PE divided by the S&P's or Value Line's), relative yield (a stock's yield divided by the S&P's or Value Line's), and so on.

You can use this section of the database to create "multifactor factors." For example, some managers rely on a *value score* made up of three individual factors to rank stocks. The three factors that make up the "value score" are percentage retained to common, current yield, and earnings yield. They add the three together and then rank the stocks on their total score, with some managers believing the higher the score, the better the stock.

To create this value score in the User Defined Section, you would first create a factor called "value1" and define it as the percentage retained to common equity plus the current yield (% retained to common + current yield). Next, create a factor called "value score" and define it as "value1" (the previously defined factor, plus the earnings yield). All told, you need to define three separate factors to get the one factor called value score. But, once it's defined, you can use it to screen the database on that multifactor model.

Factor Profiles Overlap

Not all factors are created equal. Of the 59 factors just defined, you'll find that the same few factors keep showing up as the dominant ones in a manager's portfolio. Which factors they are is contingent on the style of the manager. In general, you find that the most important factors for one growth manager will also show up when you do a factor analysis of another growth manager. You'd be hard pressed to find a growth manager with a portfolio of stocks that had negative 12-month earnings gains and negative projected earnings. If that were the case, you could hardly consider them growth managers. The same holds true for value managers. They may hold a portfolio of stocks with very high PEs and expected earnings growth rates, and they may be successful. But they're not value managers.

As you do factor profiles of successful managers, composite profiles begin to emerge. You'll see that one successful manager after another concentrates on the same factors. You'll also be able to identify which factors they are, and how you can build a model based only on the factors that the best managers all use. The same holds true for managers of any style. In all instances you'll be able to see the factors that all the top performing managers like to focus on and then configure them in a multifactor model for maximum impact.

The same is true for mediocre managers. If you did a factor profile of several managers' portfolios that were selected for their mediocre to bad performance, you would find that the mediocre performers had very few highly defined factor differences from the market as a whole. When you looked at the poor performers, you'd find portfolios that had taken a lot of uncompensated risk and had strange factor combinations. For example, you might see a portfolio that had a very high price-to-sales ratio and a very high price-to-cash-flow ratio, and yet also had poor 12-month earnings and low projected earnings. High price-to-sales ratios and price-to-cash-flow ratios are not desirable; they are usually only a consequence of a stock that is very popular due to a fantastic rise in earnings or other outstanding prospects. Doing analysis on poor performers will let you see what not to do when designing a multifactor model.

In the next chapter, we'll see how doing a factor analysis on 1991's most successful mutual fund will show us exactly what factors were responsible for that fund's almost triple-digit return.

3

The Secrets
of a Master

Now let's go step-by-step through a factor analysis. You'll learn how to find the information you need, put it into your computer, and analyze it. I recommend reading this chapter in front of your computer. Even though the data used will differ from what you have on your disk, if you actually look at the Value/Screen program while reading this, you'll understand a lot faster. Without a computer, it's like trying to teach you how to swing a baseball bat without the bat. You'd understand what I'm talking about, but never really get it until you do it.

This chapter lays out a blueprint for you to follow. The underlying stocks of all the managers we analyze here will have changed by the time you read this. Yet the basic factor analysis and stock-picking method are always the same, regardless of the stocks comprising the portfolio.

A Simple, Easy-to-Use Method

This book's method of factor analysis doesn't even need a spreadsheet. All you'll need is Value/Screen, the Value Line database recommended in Chapter 2. This will let you start right away, without worrying about how to set up and manipulate data in a spreadsheet program.

Though simple, this method is more than adequate for most readers. In addition to a computer and Value Line's software, you'll need a pen, paper, and calculator.

Using Morningstar Mutual Funds to Find the Stocks

You can do a factor analysis of any stock portfolio. Just remember that, while it's easy to emulate the majority of managers, *the majority of them aren't worth emulating!* You want to learn from the masters of money management, who are very rare. A study published in July of 1991, in the trade magazine *Pensions & Investments,* showed that when you throw out the top 10 percent of managers from any given style, *the remaining 90 percent failed to beat the S&P 500!* The top 10 percent of money managers accounted for all of any style's ability to do better than the S&P 500. That's why you'll want to concentrate on only the best managers.

You can discover the stocks in the portfolio of any manager (with any style) by looking in *Morningstar Mutual Funds.* Morningstar's service covers more than 2300 open-ended mutual funds. Each page has a wealth of information, but all you'll need is the list of the top 30 equity holdings in the fund.

Who Should You Analyze?

The manager you select to analyze should reflect your goals. If you are very aggressive, you'll emulate a much different manager than if you are very conservative or need high income with little risk. One simple thing to do is to look at a manager's long-term record, and then look at how he or she has done relative to the S&P 500 in any single year. You might love doing 30 percent better than the S&P 500, but can you stomach doing 30 percent worse? Look at the volatility of a style over several years; then level with yourself. Decide how much risk you can live with, and incorporate it into your goals for your stock market investments. Be conservative. If at first you think you can take doing 30 percent worse than the S&P 500, think about the anguish you would feel if the market was up 10 percent and you were down 20 percent. Then reduce your estimate. If you don't set your risk tolerance level correctly, you'll buckle when you approach its limit—at exactly the time when you should be *most* committed to your investment program. Understand your goals, and then look up the best performing manager using that style.

The Best Performing Mutual Fund

The first example is 1991's best performing nonspecialty fund. (Specialty funds invest in one industry or sector, such as health care or natural resources.) As it turned out, the fund also ranks as the best performer for the last three and ten years. Its name is CGM Capital Development. CGM finished 1991 up 99.08 percent, some 68 percent better than the S&P 500. A $10,000 investment in CGM made in June of 1982 would be worth $85,831.64 in June of 1992. That's a total return of 758.38 percent, more than double the 339.2-percent return of the average growth fund, and 324.69 percent better than the S&P 500's return of 433.69 percent.

(Before you decide to forget this do-it-yourself approach and give your money to CGM, you should know that the fund is closed to new investors. The manager, Ken Heebner, has other funds still open to new money, but their performance is nowhere near CGM Capital Development's, since they have different objectives.)

Sizing Up CGM

First, locate CGM's page in Morningstar and look at the stocks in its portfolio. For this example, use CGM's portfolio as of December 31, 1991. The portfolio, listed here in Table 3-1, is worth over $300 million. Looking at the list, you see right away that the manager is willing to make aggressive bets, since it holds just 23 stocks, with a heavy concentration of money in the top five stocks. These five positions account for over 34 percent of the portfolio's net assets. Therefore, these five stocks will have a much greater impact on the portfolio than the five stocks with the lowest percentage of net assets.

We're interested in the underlying characteristics of the typical stock in CGM's portfolio. We'll be creating models based on the factors the manager values most overall, not on the weight he gives to each stock. If we paid attention to the weight, our emulation of CGM would require about five different multifactor models, which is an unnecessary complication of our task.

I recommend making equal investments in each stock in our portfolio to smooth out our bets. For example, what if the manager was betting wrong? Generally, a manager's love for a stock

Table 3-1. The Stocks in CGM's Portfolio as of
December 31, 1991

Stock	Value ($ 000)	% net assets
Philip Morris	30,020.0	9.21
Countrywide Credit	23,777.6	7.29
Telefonos De Mexico	20,390.6	6.29
Sci-Med Life Systems	20,160.0	6.18
Standard Federal Bank	18,543.6	5.69
Pfizer	17,818.9	5.47
Collective Bancorp	17,640.0	5.41
Merck	16,650.0	5.11
SLMA	16,280.0	4.99
American Home Products	16,078.8	4.93
Syntex	15,343.5	4.71
Onbancorp	14,932.5	4.58
Charter One Financial	14,602.5	4.48
Bankers Trust New York	14,343.8	4.40
Tyco Toys	13,770.0	4.22
International Game Technology	13,340.0	4.09
Tech Data	9604.0	2.95
Medtronic	9400.0	2.88
Green Tree Acceptance	5798.6	1.78
Hasbro	5605.2	1.72
Royal Appliance Manufacturing	4441.2	1.36
Metropolitan Financial	2379.8	0.73
Washington Savings Bank	2362.5	0.72

is reflected by the weight he gives it. There's very little doubt
that Heebner loves Philip Morris and Countrywide Credit, since
they account for over 16 percent of the total portfolio. But does
that mean he doesn't love Washington Savings Bank and
Metropolitan Financial since they amount to just 1.45 percent of
the total portfolio? Actually, what matters is that he found factors in all these stocks that made them worth buying, and they
all met his criteria. Therefore, you'll give the underlying factors
of Philip Morris and Washington Savings Bank equal weight.

Moving to Value/Screen

Once you have a list of the stocks in CGM's portfolio, go to
Value/Screen to find the stock's ticker symbols. Open the

Value/Screen program, and screen on the variable *Recent price* > 0.

This gives you all the stocks currently in Value/Screen. Select *View List*. You'll see a list of all the stocks, along with their ticker symbols. Looking for the first stock, Philip Morris, you see that its ticker symbol is MO. Make a note of this next to its name and go on to the next stock, Countrywide Credit. You'll find that its ticker symbol is CCR.

When you get to Standard Federal Bank (MI), you'll find that the stock is not in Value/Screen. Simply note that it was not available by writing N/A next to the stock's name. This should not concern you. All you need is a representative list of the stocks CGM likes. You don't have to have all the stocks to identify which factors CGM likes in stocks. The only time to be wary is when most of the stocks in a manager's portfolio are not in Value/Screen. This indicates the manager specializes in stocks outside the mainstream. If that's the case, don't try to emulate the manager with Value Line data.

When you finish the CGM portfolio, you'll find that Value/Screen didn't cover eight of CGM's stocks in its database. Yet our list of 15 stocks is more than adequate, accounting for over 74 percent of the total assets of the portfolio, reflecting very well the factors CGM admires.

Creating the Portfolio

Now that you have the ticker symbols, you can create the portfolio for analysis in Value/Screen. Do this by entering the ticker symbols from CGM's portfolio into a ticker list in Value/Screen. Select *Edit Ticker List*. Enter the symbols one at a time, pushing the Enter key after each symbol. After you've entered the symbols from CGM's portfolio, save the list, calling it *CGM*.

Opening the Ticker List

Now replace what Value/Screen calls the *Starting List* with the CGM ticker list. To do this, open the CGM ticker list, select *Price* > 0, and press Enter. You'll now have replaced the entire Value Line database with the stocks in CGM's portfolio, and you can begin doing the factor analysis.

Doing a Factor Analysis on CGM's Portfolio

Now you'll need your pen, paper, and calculator. Using the *Analysis of Screened List* section of the Value/Screen database, begin in the *Ratings & Estimates* section. Table 3-2 shows the factors, which Value/Screen calls variables, listed in the *Ratings & Estimates* section.

As you move through the list, factor by factor, you will write down your findings as you go. Then take these steps:

Step 1.   Start with *Timeliness* as your first *Selected Variable*, and make a note of its ranking. Recall that a Timeliness rank of 1 is the best rating, and a 5 is the worst. You see that the sample (i.e., the 15 stocks in the CGM sample) has a high Timeliness rank of 3, a low of 1, a mean of 2, and a median of 2.

Step 2.   Write down the mean, but not the median, unless it is significantly different from the mean. (This usually occurs when one or two stocks have very high or low numbers that are bringing the mean way up or down.)

Step 3.   Review the sample size. In this case it's 15, which means that all 15 stocks from the CGM portfolio have a rank for Timeliness. This isn't always the case, because many of the stocks will not have a figure available for the factor being analyzed. When the number of stocks in the sample falls well below

Table 3-2. Factors
Covered in Value/Screen's
Ratings & Estimates Section

Timeliness rank

Industry rank

Current EPS

Safety rank

Price stability rank

Current dividend

Financial strength rank

Beta

Technical rank

---

the original sample size, make a note of it with an asterisk (*). This reminds you that the number is based on a significantly reduced sample size.

Step 4. Note the average for this variable for the Value Line Database as a whole, so that you can compare the CGM and Value Line averages.

The first line on your pad should look like this:

Variable	High	Low	Mean	Value Line average	Difference (%)
Timeliness	3	1	2	3	−33

The difference column is the percentage difference between the sample (i.e., CGM in this instance) and the database. The average CGM stock has a better Timeliness rank than the average stock in the database.

Use the same four steps for each variable in the *Ratings & Estimates* section of the Value/Screen list, doing exactly the same thing for each variable, or factor, you analyze.

As an example, *Safety Rank* follows *Timeliness,* and here you find that the high was 4, the low 1, the average 3, and the median 3. Since the median is very similar to the mean, don't note it. The second line on the pad should look like this:

Variable	High	Low	Mean	Value Line mean	Difference (%)
Safety Rank	4	1	3	3	0

Do the same four-step review for every factor in the *Ratings & Estimates Section* until you've covered them all. At this point, your paper should look like Table 3-3.

Step 5. Now look at the dispersion of the various Value Line ranks using the *Tabular Reports* section of Value/Screen. Here list Timeliness, Safety, Industry Rank, and Technical ranks, and send the tabular report to the screen. Table 3-4 shows you the results of the Tabular Report. Only one stock, Bankers Trust, has a Timeliness rank of 3. All the others rank 1 or 2. Make a note of this under the Timeliness section of your notepad. The Safety

Table 3-3. 9 Factors from Ratings & Estimates Section

Variable	High	Low	Mean	Value Line mean	Difference (%)
Timeliness rank	3	1	2	3	−33
Safety rank	4	1	3	3	0
Financial Strength rank	C++	A++	B++/A	B+	Higher
Industry rank	35	1	11	49	−77
Price Stability rank	95	5	49	52	−5
Beta	1.40	0.95	1.16	1.06	9.75
Current EPS	7.89	1.19	3.65	1.73	40
Current dividend	2.80	0	1.80	0.74	40
Technical rank	3	1	2	3	−33

Table 3-4. Tabular Report on Value Line Ranks for CGM Portfolio

Company	Timeliness rank	Safety rank	Industry rank	Technical rank
American Home Products	1	1	1	2
Bankers Trust	3	3	25	2
Countrywide Credit	1	4	14	1
Green Tree	1	4	14	1
Hasbro	2	3	12	1
International Game Tech	1	3	35	1
Medtronic	1	2	10	2
Merck	1	1	1	2
Pfizer	2	1	1	2
Philip Morris	2	1	3	2
Scimed Life	2	4	10	2
Student Loan	2	4	14	3
Syntex	2	2	1	3
Telefonos De Mexico	1	3	9	1
Tyco Toys	2	4	12	1

rank and Technical rank are widely dispersed, but the Industry rank is also of interest. Here, only two stocks, Bankers Trust and International Game Technology, have Industry ranks above 15. Make a note of this under the Industry Rank section of your notepad. You do this to get a better understanding of the factors in the sample you are studying. All but one or two of the stocks in the CGM portfolio have Timeliness ranks of 1 or 2 and Industry ranks below 15, giving the sample a more focused profile than before.

Step 6. Now review the factors you've analyzed under the *Ratings & Estimates* section. Tables 3-3 and 3-4 show what you are looking at. Here's what you would see:

- The average stock favored by CGM has excellent Timeliness, Technical, and Industry ranks as assigned by Value Line.
- Safety and Financial Strength ratings are good.
- The median rank of A is better than the mean of B++. Both are above the database mean, indicating seasoned, strong companies.
- Average Price Stability is almost the same as that of the average stock in the Value Line database, showing us that this group of stocks is not more volatile than the database average.

From this section alone, you see timely stocks in timely industries that have good financial strength and overall price stability close to the market. Note all of these in longhand so that you can refer to them when building your model to emulate this style.

The Market Data Section

Move to the *Market Data* section. Do the same four-step review of each of the factors found in this section that you did in the first section. After you've reviewed each factor in this section, your notepad should have the additions shown in Table 3-5.

The *Market Data* section gives a lot more information about the factors CGM likes. A review shows:

- The prices of CGM's stocks are higher than the average stock in the database. Generally, the recent price of the average CGM stock is very close to its 52-week high. The average stock in the database is closer to its high than its low, but not by as much as the CGM sample.

- The average price-to-earnings ratio of the CGM stocks is 20.4, just 15 percent higher than the database average. This is quite unusual for a growth manager, where you normally find price-to-earnings ratios much higher than the market (i.e., it's standard to see an aggressive growth manager's portfolio have a PE 50 percent higher than the market). Thus, on your

Table 3-5. 9 Factors from the Market Data Section

Variable	High	Low	Mean	Value Line mean	Difference (%)
Recent price	166.5	34	68.42	29.82	129
52-week high	165.7	33	69.51	33.63	107
52-week low	82	7.38	30.83	19.95	55
Current PE	38.70	8.1	20.4	17.6	15.8
Current yield	4.4	0	1.4	2.4	−42
Price-to-book	16.8	2.04	7.98	2.83	182
13-week % price change	73.6	−10.90	27.8	5.2	435
26-week % price change	108.3	21.4	52.6	9.6	448
Market value ($ mill)	74,329	226.4	16,839/5596	2661	533

list, make a note of the price-to-earnings ratio being similar to the database average.

- The price-to-book value ratio for CGM is considerably higher than the database. That is normal for growth stocks.

- The 13- and 26-week price percentage change for the average CGM stock is dramatically higher than the average stock in the database. This means that the CGM portfolio has excellent *Relative Strength* when you compare its three- and six-month returns to those of the average stock in the database.

- The mean market value of CGM's stocks is $16.8 billion. (This time, also note the median of $5.6 billion since it varies significantly from the mean.) The low figure of $226 million in market value shows that the manager is willing to buy stocks with market values below $1 billion, meaning he doesn't appear to use a big-cap strategy or cutoff.

The Historical Measures Section

Move to the *Historical Measures* section. Do the same four-step review of the factors found in this section that you did in the first two sections. After you've reviewed each of these factors, your notepad should have the additions shown in Table 3-6.

In this section, you would see that:

- CGM likes stocks with a return on net worth and percentage of earnings retained to common equity almost double the

Table 3-6. 10 Factors from the Historical Measures Section

Variable	High	Low	Mean	Value Line mean	Difference (%)
Sales ($ mill)	51,169	111.8	6259	3303	89.49
% ret net worth	46.5	3.5	24.33	13.6	79
% retained to common	41.4	3.5	19.5	9.9	96.97
Book value per share	31.19	3.29	10.92	15.58	−29.89
Debt as % of capital	96	0	33.53/23	33	1.23
Last qtr EPS % chg	117.6	−8.60	41.2/19.6	10.7	285
12-month EPS % chg	117.6	0.10	34.4/20.5	3.1	1011
*5-yr EPS growth	27.5	−23	13.2/17.3	9	46.3
*5-yr divd growth	52.5	8	20.9	9.6	117.2
5-yr bk val growth	42	−14	12.6	9.1	38.6

average stock in the database. This means that, while these companies are earning more on their net worth, they are also retaining those earnings and reinvesting them in their businesses, not paying them out in dividends.

- In one of the most significant deviations, the percentage change of last quarter earnings per share is 285 percent higher than the database, and the percentage change of the 12-month earnings per share is 1011 percent higher than the database average!

- You see an asterisk (*) by five-year EPS percentage change and five-year dividend percentage change, because several of the 15 stocks didn't have this information available. The numbers you're looking at are for a smaller sample than our original 15 stocks. You'll want to remember that when you start experimenting with which factors you'll use to build an emulation of CGM.

The Fiscal Year Data Section

Move to the *Fiscal Year Data* section. Do the same four-step review of the factors here that you did in the first three sections. After you've reviewed each factor in this section, your notepad should have the additions shown in Table 3-7.

These factors aren't as important as the others in and of themselves. They're useful when used to model other ratios that help

Table 3-7. 8 Factors from the Fiscal Year Data Section

Variable	High	Low	Mean	Value Line mean	Difference (%)
Cash	11,251.3	6.6	1468	342.9	328
Current assets	12,367	78.8	2386.5	1597.8	49.4
Total assets	63,596	101.6	12,728	5952.7	113.8
Long-term debt	24,242.9	0	3155.5	931.5	238.8
Current liabilities	11,360	13.8	1633.9	1267.4	28.9
Net worth	11,947	87.4	2408.8	1323.2	82
Net profit	3540	3.4	662.6	155.2	327
Cash flow per share	5.3	1.04	2.97	3.44	−13.7

define the underlying characteristics of a style. The only one to note now is the cash flow per share. You use it to derive the price-to-cash-flow ratio, a measure that's used to value how cheap or expensive a company's stock is relative to others.

The Growth Projections and Identification Sections

Finally, move to the last of the preprogrammed Value/Screen sections, *Growth Projections and Identification.* Do the same four-step review of the factors that you did in the first four sections. After you've reviewed the factors in these sections, your notepad should have the additions shown in Table 3-8.

Here you see that:

- The average stock in CGM's portfolio has forecasted earnings gains for the coming fiscal year 266 percent greater than the database average.

- The stocks in CGM's portfolio also have high forecasts for projected growth in earnings per share, book value, and dividends over the coming five years.

- In several projections, CGM's stocks do worse than the average Value Line stock. The projected three- to five-year appreciation percentage figure for CGM's stocks shows that Value Line estimates that the average stock in CGM's portfolio will appreciate just 47.8 percent over the next three to five years compared to a 91 percent gain for the database. But Value

Table 3-8. 8 Factors from the Growth Projections Section

Variable	High	Low	Mean	Value Line mean	Difference (%)
Est. % chg EPS qt. 1	96.9	15.4	30	26	15.4
Est. % chg EPS qt. 2	86.1	2.6	23.0	34.8	−34
Est. % chg EPS fis yr	330	2.6	50.47	13.8	266
Prj 3-5 yr apprec %	92	−29	47.8	91	−47.5
Prj EPS growth	44.5	11.5	22.8	14.5	57
Prj div growth	N/A	N/A	N/A	N/A	N/A
Prj book val growth	40	9	20.7	9.7	113.8
Prj 3-5 yr av return	19	−8	11	18	−38.9

Line uses a value bias when making these long-term projections. Consequently, they expect stocks that have done tremendously well recently to "regress to the mean" and do worse over the next period, whereas they expect stocks that have lagged the market to do better over the next period. I don't pay attention to this factor because I've done studies that prove it to be unreliable.

- CGM's stocks have more shares outstanding and a larger institutional ownership than the average stock in the Value Line. A large number of shares outstanding is usually a good thing, since it increases a stock's liquidity and makes trading large blocks easy. But large institutional ownership can be *bad* for growth stocks. If the stock fails to meet investor's expectations for earnings growth and has a large institutional ownership, they can cut its price in half when they run en masse for the door. Large institutional ownership in popular growth stocks is fairly unavoidable, though. Put this in the "grin and bear it" category of growth stock investing.

The User Variables Section

You've finished the sections with preprogrammed histogram screens. These Value Line histograms cover more than 90 percent of the factors you'll use to design models for emulating any manager. However, you can analyze many more factors within

Table 3-9. Definitions of Additional User Defined Factors

Variable	Definition
Price-to-cash-flow	Current price ÷ Cash flow per share
Earnings yield	1 ÷ P/E expressed as percent
Margins	Net profit ÷ Sales expressed as percent
Price-to-sales ratio	Market value ÷ Sales
Payout ratio cent	Current dividend ÷ Current EPS expressed as per-

Value/Screen using the *User Variable* section. In this section, you'll look at some additional factors by first defining them in the *Define User Variable* section, and then getting the results in the *Tabular Reports* section. A list of factor definitions is provided elsewhere in the book. Refer to this list when defining your own variables.

Table 3-9 defines the additional factors you'll look at in the *Define User Variable* section. Look at Table 3-9, and see how we define each of these additional factors by dividing one variable by another. You then express this result as either a decimal or a percentage. For example:

$$\text{Price-to-cash-flow} = \frac{\text{Stock price}}{\text{Cash flow per share, expressed as a decimal}}$$

If a stock's current price is 10 and its cash flow per share is 5, its price to cash flow would be 2.

Conversely, a stock's payout ratio is:

$$\text{Payout ratio} = \frac{\text{Current dividend per share}}{\text{Current earnings per share}}$$

expressed as a percentage. If the dividend is 50 cents per share and earnings are $1, the payout ratio would be 50 percent.

Step 1.   Go to the *Define User Variables* section and enter the definitions provided in Table 3-9.

Step 2.   Go to the *Tabular Reports* section and get a report on each of the new variables just defined. Note the results. Then

Table 3-10. CGM's 5 User Defined Factors

Variable	Mean	Value Line mean	Difference (%)
Price-to-cash flow	24.43	10.7	128
Earnings yield	5.83	4.16	40
Margins	14.94	5.43	175
Price-to-sales ratio	4.7	1.32	256
Payout	24.48	27.91	−12

clear the current ticker list so that you're back to the entire Value Line database.

Step 3. Go back to the *Tabular Reports* section and press Go again. This time, you'll get a report for all the stocks in the database. Scroll down to the end and note the averages next to the numbers for CGM's stocks. Your pad should have the additions listed in Table 3-10. Value Screen doesn't list the highs and lows in the *Tabular Reports* section, just the means. You'd have to sort by each variable to get its high and low, a very time-consuming process. If there is something significant that you notice and want the high and the low, select the variable and sort by it in the *Tabular Reports* section. For now, the mean will suffice.

The two largest deviations for CGM are margins and price-to-sales ratios. CGM's stocks have much better profit margins than the database average. They also have high price-to-sales ratios. Remember, a stock's price-to-sales ratio is another measurement of value along with price-to-book and price-to-earnings. CGM's high ratio is typical for a growth manager.

Reviewing the Most Important Factors

Now let's review all the factors and see where CGM's portfolio deviates most from the average Value Line stock. These are the factors we'll use when emulating CGM's style.

Identifying the Key Factors

Take a new sheet of paper and scan the factors. As a headline, write "KEY FACTORS" at the top of the page. Some of the key factors that are common to most growth and aggressive growth managers are listed in Tables 2.1 and 2.4 in Chap. 2. In this instance, we'll move down your list, looking for the largest deviations CGM has from the database. Where are these deviations? As you go down the list, notice that the largest deviation from the Value Line database is the 12-month earnings per share percentage change, with the average CGM stock 1010 percent higher than the database. On your paper, write:

1. *12-Month EPS % Change 1010 percent higher.*

Next, you see that the average market value of the CGM portfolio is 532 percent higher than the database. Yet you also note that there is no apparent segregation by market capitalization, since the low in the CGM profile is just $226 million. Therefore, *don't list market value since there is no apparent buy or sell decisions made on this factor.* This is an ancillary factor, not an essential one.

Note that the 13- and 26-week percentage change in price is between 424 and 448 percent higher than the average stock in the database. Also note that the low for the 26-week price changes in the CGM sample is 21.40 percent, a very high number and an excellent gauge to screen on. On your list, write:

2. *Strong relative strength. 26-week percentage change is an average of 448 percent higher than the database, with a low of 21.4, more than double the database average.*

Now you see that last quarter earnings per share percentage change is 285 percent higher for the CGM stocks. So you write:

3. *Last quarter EPS % Change 285 percent higher than the database.*

Finally, note that the estimated percentage change for earnings per share for the coming fiscal year is 265.8 percent higher than the database. You write:

4. *Est % Change EPS Fiscal Year 265.8 percent higher than database.*

Note also that, except for one stock:

- All stocks in the CGM sample had Value Line Timeliness ranks of 1 or 2.
- All the CGM stocks except two had Industry ranks below 15

Table 3-11. List of Key Factors

Key Factors
1. 12-month EPS % Change 1010% higher
2. Strong relative strength. 26-week percentage change is an average of 448% higher than the database, and the low for sample is 21.4, more than double the database average.
3. Last quarter EPS % change 285% higher than the database
4. Est % change EPS fiscal year 265.8% higher than database
5. Timeliness less than 2, Industry ranks less than 15

by writing the number 5, followed by *Timeliness less then 2, Industry Ranks less than 15.*

Table 3-11 shows how this sheet of paper should look when you complete the key factors section.

Secondary Factors

Write another headline, calling it "SECONDARY FACTORS." Note all the other important factors of the portfolio. Is the price-to-sales ratio important? Yes, so list it here. How about the cash position? No, that is not as important for this type of analysis; so you'll skip it. Margins? These are important; so list them, along with return on net worth and retained to common, all important factors with significant deviations from the database. Table 3-12 shows the secondary factors I feel are important. These are the factors you'll utilize when using a trial-and-error method of model design.

Mysterious No Longer

That's all there is to it. See how your thinking has changed about CGM Capital? Instead of being awed by how well it did last year, by what stocks it owns, or by the industries they're in, you see things in a completely different light. You see an outstanding historical performance record, and you see the underlying factors that are responsible for it. You no longer think,

Table 3-12. List of Secondary Factors

Secondary Factors
6. Price-to-book average 182% higher, with low of 2.04
7. Current PE ratio average just 16% higher than database, with high of 39
8. Return on net worth and percentage retained to common both high
9. Projected 3- to 5-year growth in EPS and book value both high, with projected book value average more than double the database mean
10. Price-to-cash-flow high, with low of 11.93
11. Price-to-sales high, average 256% higher than the database
12. Margins are high, 175% higher than the database

"They own a lot of Philip Morris, so maybe I should buy that stock." Now you think of factors that are easy to identify and emulate. CGM concentrates on stocks with outstanding 12-month and last-quarter earnings-per-share gains. They show excellent relative performance. They have very high estimates for earnings gains in the coming fiscal year, and they sport Timeliness and Industry ranks that are in the upper tier of the Value Line ratings. They exhibit many ancillary factors that are common to growth stocks, and share many of the same risks.

Now you have the information you need to design a multifactor model using the same factors that CGM so highly values. You've identified the underlying factors that define how CGM differs from the market, and you know the actual factors that made CGM the best performing mutual fund in the Morningstar database.

In the following chapter, you'll use this knowledge to design a portfolio that has an even more clearly defined factor profile than CGM's. This will result in a portfolio that is easy for both individuals and professionals to buy and monitor.

4

Making the Best Better

In this chapter, we develop a model that emulates CGM's investment style. Our goal isn't to copy CGM. If that's what we wanted to do, it would be easier just to buy the stocks in CGM's portfolio. We want to develop a model based on the same factors that have worked so well for CGM, and then apply them in a rigorous, consistent manner to create our own portfolio. This lets us short-circuit the emotional, hit-or-miss methods that hurt investment performance. *Remember that the one characteristic shared by all successful money managers is a consistent implementation of their preferred styles.* Insisting on a consistent application of our model will improve our chances of beating the market enormously.

Reviewing CGM's Factor Profile

We want to stand on CGM's shoulders and develop a consistent strategy for picking stocks that performs *better* than CGM's portfolio. Our first step is to see how *all* of CGM's factor preferences interact by using *all* the significant deviations we find in the CGM portfolio as our factor bets in a first model. We'll then see how the resultant portfolio would have done in 1991. Next, we'll narrow down the factors to those that best reflect CGM's profile.

Entering the Factors

CGM's key and secondary factors are listed in Tables 3-11 and 3-12 in Chap. 3. We will test all these factors as screens and look at the performance results for 1991.

Step 1. Enter the key factors. With Value/Screen ready, start by noting that CGM's portfolio had 12-month EPS percentage changes that were 1010 percent higher than the databases. In Value/Screen, list 12-month EPS percentage change as your first variable, and set the minimum value acceptable as greater than the database mean. (We're using data from January 1, 1991, and the screen would read 12-month EPS % Chg $\geq$ 6.3.)

Do this for all the key factors. For example, the next one on the CGM list is strong relative strength. Using the 26-week percentage price change as a proxy for relative strength, enter it as your second variable and require that all stocks have 26-week price percentage changes greater than the database mean. We've picked the mean instead of some higher number because we're using 15 factors, and each one will narrow the list of acceptable stocks.

Table 4-1 shows you what the Value/Screen list will look like after you've finished entering all the key factors from the CGM list. Notice that, while we set most of the factors above the database mean, we set a few, such as Timeliness rank and Industry rank, to reflect what we found in the CGM factor profile.

Step 2. Enter the secondary factors. Now we'll enter all the factors from CGM's list of secondary factors. You can find them in Table 3-12 in Chap. 3. You'll enter these just as you did the key factors, except for a few entries where we will not use the database average. For example, when doing the factor analysis on CGM, we found that its portfolio had a high price-to-sales ratio. We capture that by requiring that price-to-sales ratios are

Table 4-1. Key Factors for CGM Entered into Value/Screen as of January 1, 1991

12-Month EPS % Chg $\geq$ 6.3 (the database mean)

26-Wk % Price Chg $\geq$ $-$ 16.1 (the database mean)

Last Qtr EPS % Chg $\geq$ 13 (the database mean)

Est % Chg EPS Fis Yr $\geq$ 17.3 (the database mean)

Timeliness rank $\leq$ 2 (from the CGM information)

Industry rank $\leq$ 15 (from the CGM information)

Table 4-2. Complete Factor Screen for CGM Entered into Value/Screen as of January 1, 1991

12-Month EPS % Chg ≥ 6.3 (the database mean)

26-Wk % Price Chg ≥ −16.1 (the database mean)

Last Qtr EPS % Chg ≥ 13 (the database mean)

Est % Chg EPS Fis Yr ≥ 17.3 (the database mean)

Timeliness rank ≤ 2 (from the CGM information)

Industry rank ≤ 15 (from the CGM information)

Price-to-book value ≥ 2.12 (the database mean)

Current PE ratio ≤ 39 (the high found in the CGM portfolio)

% Return Net Worth ≥ 14.5 (the database mean)

% Retained to Com Eq ≥ 10.8 (the database mean)

Prj EPS Growth ≥ 14.8 (the database mean)

Prj Book Val Growth ≥ 10.1 (the database mean)

Price-to-cash-flow ratio ≥ 11.93 (the low found doing the CGM factor analysis)

Margins ≥ 6 (from the CGM factor analysis)

Price-to-sales ratio ≥ 1 (used in place of mean to establish high-PSR stocks)

greater than 1. The same will hold true for margins and price-to-cash-flow ratios.

Table 4-2 shows what the complete Value/Screen screen should look like after you've entered the secondary factors from the CGM list.

That's all we do on this round: just enter all the factors where the CGM portfolio deviated significantly from the market, and set the minimums and maximums in the Value/Screen database to reflect those deviations.

Looking at Our First Clone Portfolio

Now, with all the factors entered, press Go to instruct the Value/Screen program to retrieve all the stocks in the database that meet all 15 of our CGM-inspired criteria. As of January 1, 1991, 17 stocks out of the 1600 in the Value Line database met

Table 4-3. 17 Stocks Meeting all 15 CGM-Inspired Criteria as of January 1, 1991

Ticker	Stock	Industry
RTG	Racal Telecom	Foreign telecom
MRK	Merck & Co.	Drug
SGP	Schering-Plough	Drug
LLY	Lilly, Eli	Drug
MYL	Mylan Labs	Drug
WLA	Warner-Lambert	Drug
CORD	Cordis Corp.	Medical supply
SMLS	Scimed Life Systems	Medical supply
STJM	St. Jude Medical	Medical supply
USS	U.S. Surgical	Medical supply
BMET	Biomet	Medical supply
STRY	Stryker Corp.	Medical supply
SODA	A&W Brands	Beverages
KO	Coca-Cola	Beverages
PG	Procter & Gamble	Household products
CHW	Chemical Waste	Environmental
WMX	Waste Management	Environmental

all 15 of our criteria. Those stocks and their industries are listed in Table 4-3.

Notice how just a few factors have a big impact on the number of stocks making the final cut. Just by setting Industry rank to 15 or below, we effectively wiped out all but 226 stocks from the 1600 in the database. Due to the nature of the Industry rank, we would see that these 226 stocks shared many factor similarities with the CGM portfolio, such as big EPS gains over the last year. The 226 stocks in the top 15 industries, as ranked by Value Line, had earnings gains of 25.2 percent compared to the database average of 6.3. If you add in the effect of requiring Timeliness ranks of 2 or better, the number of stocks making the cut drops to 124, and the earnings gains for those 124 stocks moves up to 32.8.

Our portfolio of 17 stocks is concentrated in just six industries, with two of them, drug and medical supply companies, accounting for over 64 percent of the portfolio. Quite a difference from the database!

Looking at the Portfolio's Underlying Factors

Let's see how much the portfolio deviates from the database by looking at the histograms provided under the *Analysis of Screened List* section. Figures 4-1 and 4-2 show some of the portfolio's most significant deviations.

Not surprisingly, we find the same deviations in this portfolio that we found when doing the factor analysis of the CGM portfolio. Relative Strength is quite strong, with a positive 26-week price percentage gain of 4.36 percent compared to a *loss* of over 16 percent for the average stock in the database. Like the CGM portfolio, earnings gains are quite strong, with 12-month earning per share gains almost 500 percent higher than the database. We find that this portfolio contains all the factors with significant deviations we listed under "Key Factors" when doing our factor analysis of CGM in this portfolio.

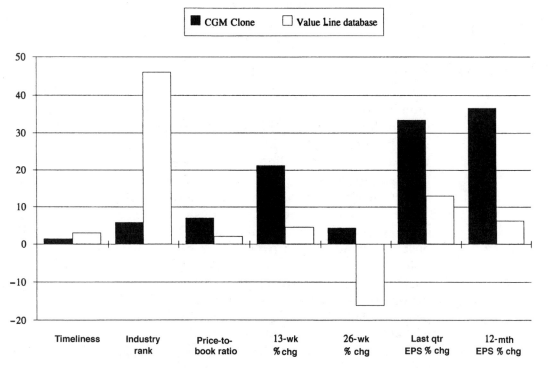

Figure 4-1. Factor profiles of CGM clone and Value Line database.

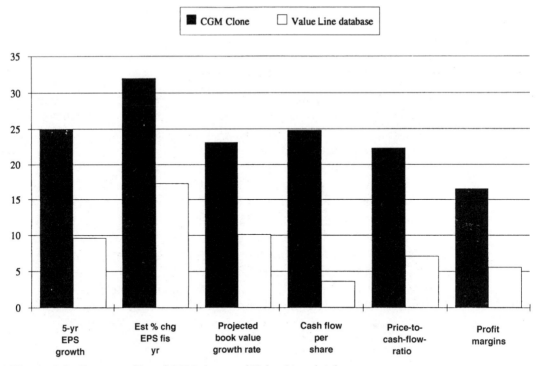

Figure 4-2. Factor profiles of CGM clone and Value Line database.

Examining Performance

Next, we'll review how the portfolio performed over the first six months of 1991. Since CGM is an aggressive growth manager, it's prudent to review the portfolio at least twice a year. Thus, we'll hold these 17 stocks for six months, or until June 30, 1991. We'll then rebalance the portfolio by running the same screen we used to get these 17 stocks, selling any of the 17 that no longer meet the criteria and replacing them with stocks that do.

For the six months ending June 30, 1991 this crude emulation of CGM was up 24.9 percent, with Scimed Life recording the best performance of up 114.7 percent and Procter & Gamble doing the worst, down 9.7 percent. For the same period, CGM itself was up 40.7 percent. (I obtained all performance figures for our model's stocks using Compuserve's stock price return program that allows you to calculate return with dividends reinvested.)

On June 30 we run the screen again and rebalance our portfolio. This time, only nine stocks meet all the criteria, and only

Table 4-4. 9 Stocks Meeting the Model's Criteria as of June 30, 1991

Ticker	Stock	Industry
MRK	Merck & Co.	Drug
AMGN	Amgen	Drug
SYN	Syntex	Drug
SMLS	Scimed Life Systems	Medical supply
BMET	Biomet	Medical supply
MSFT	Microsoft	Computer software
ADBE	Adobe Systems	Computer software
FISV	Fiserv, Inc.	Computer software
MO	Philip Morris	Tobacco

three of them (Merck, Scimed Life, and Biomet) were in the original portfolio of 17 stocks. We'll therefore sell the 14 stocks that no longer meet the criteria and replace them with the new list of nine, again equally weighted. Table 4-4 lists the nine stocks.

For the six months ending December 31, 1991, the nine stocks in the CGM clone were up 56.8 percent, with Biomet turning in the best performance (up 134.2 percent) and Syntex turning in the worst performance (up 27.4 percent). For the same six-month period, CGM itself was up 41.4 percent. Thus, for the year, our first crude emulation of CGM that was rebalanced only once during the year was up 95.84 percent, compared to a gain of 99.08 percent for CGM itself.

The Need for a More Stable, Simple Model

Not bad for a first go-around, but not good enough. The 15-factor model isn't desirable for several reasons. First, the model returns a different number of stocks each time you use it, depending on prevailing market conditions. On January 1, 1992, the model returned a list of 22 stocks whereas on June 30, 1992, it recommended only three. This is not an acceptable variance. We *don't* want a model that might recommend just three stocks. We *do* want to design a model that recommends a fairly fixed number of stocks, so that we don't face a huge variance when rebalancing the portfolio. We also want to assure proper diversification.

Second, this model has too many factor screens. After you've reached a certain number, each factor you add to a model tends to "muddy" the model. You never want a model that has more then a dozen factors. The 15-factor model is simply too complicated. The more streamlined and elegant a model, the better its overall performance and the lower its variance in performance. When designing quantitative models, follow the rule, "Keep it simple, stupid." This is very important, yet it goes against our innate desire to see things as more complex than they are and to find the more complex answer superior to the simple one, even if the more complex answer is wrong!

A wonderful study done by Professor Alex Bavelas demonstrates these phenomena. Two subjects, Mr. A and Mr. B, sit facing a projection screen. The two have a partition between them, so that they can't see or communicate with each other. The moderator tells them that the purpose of the experiment is to learn how to recognize the difference between healthy and sick cells. They must learn to distinguish the two by trial and error. In front of each are buttons marked "Healthy" and "Sick," along with two signal lights marked "Right" and "Wrong." Every time a slide of a cell is projected, they have to guess if it's healthy or sick by pressing the button so marked. After they guess, their signal light will flash right or wrong, informing them if they have guessed correctly.

Here's the hitch. Mr. A gets true feedback based on his guess. If he's right, his light flashes correct; if he's wrong, his light flashes wrong. Since he gets true feedback, Mr. A is soon getting around 80 percent right, with just 20 percent of his guesses wrong, since it's a matter of simple discrimination.

Poor Mr. B's situation is entirely different. He doesn't get true feedback based on his guesses. Instead, the feedback he sees is based on Mr. A's guesses! It doesn't matter if he's right or wrong about a particular slide, he's told he's right if Mr. A guessed right and wrong if Mr. A guessed wrong. Of course, Mr. B doesn't know this. He's been told there is a true order that he can discover by making guesses and getting feedback. He ends up searching for an order when there is no way that he could discover it.

The moderator then asks Mr. A and Mr. B to discuss the rules they use for judging which cells are healthy and which are sick. *Mr. A, who got true feedback, offers rules that are simple, concrete, and to the point. Mr. B's rules, on the other hand, are out of necessity subtle, very complex, and highly adorned.* After all, he had to base his decisions on contradictory guesses and hunches.

The amazing thing is that Mr. A doesn't think Mr. B's explanations are absurd, crazy, or unnecessarily complicated. More, he's impressed by the "brilliance" of Mr. B's methods and tends to feel inferior and vulnerable because of the pedestrian simplicity of his rules. The more complicated and ornate Mr. B's explanations, *the more likely they are to convince Mr. A!*

Before the next test with new slides, the two are asked to guess who will do better than in the first test. All Mr. Bs tested and most Mr. As say that Mr. B will do better. In fact, Mr. B shows no improvement at all. Mr. A, on the other hand, does significantly worse than the first time because he now makes guesses based on some of the complicated and subtle rules he learned from Mr. A.

As Yogi Berra said, "Sometimes you can see a lot just by looking." That's our mission here. We want to examine what factors made CGM the best performing mutual fund in 1991, and then use them as screens in our model. The *simplest* way to do that is to concentrate only on the highest deviations and use them as our screens.

Designing an Alternate Model

Before we start designing the next model, we need to decide how many stocks we want to own. It is foolish to own a one- or two-stock portfolio. When you buy stocks, you face two distinct forms of risk. One is called *market risk,* or the risk common to all securities, while the other is called *nonmarket risk,* or the risk specific to a given company or industry. When you own just one or two stocks, you take an extremely high nonmarket risk that is usually not compensated.

You can reduce nonmarket risk nearly to zero simply by holding a portfolio of approximately ten stocks. According to a study that J. L. Evans and S. H. Archer published in the *Journal of Finance,* almost all benefits of diversification occur as you move from one to ten stocks, with virtually no risk reduction occurring after you reach 15 stocks.

We'll therefore want to focus on developing emulations that hold around ten stocks. At this number, you'll face virtually no nonmarket risk, yet you'll still be able to hold a concentrated number of the best stocks of any given strategy. As mentioned earlier, one of the reasons that the pros don't do better is that government regulation and portfolio size conspire and force them to buy more stocks than they might ideally want to hold, causing returns to suffer. Since none of the professionals we'll be learning from can concentrate their portfolios to just the ten top stocks, this is a potentially *huge* advantage for the individual investor. We'll want to take maximum advantage of it.

Designing the Model

We could use innumerable factor combinations to design a portfolio whose underlying factor profile matched CGM's. We could use only Value Line ranks and relative strength, or any combination of the key and secondary factors we found when analyzing CGM. Yet these suggestions aren't as intuitive as simply developing an emulation based just on CGM's top four deviations from the database.

The top four, in order of the level of their deviation from the database, are:

1. 12-Month EPS % Change.

2. Excellent relative strength.

3. Last Quarter EPS % Change.

4. Estimated percentage changes for the coming fiscal year.

The First Factor

CGM's factor with the highest deviation from the database is 12-month earnings per share percentage gains; so we'll make it the first factor in our model. The question is how high should we set it? When you consider that the stocks in CGM's portfolio had 12-month earnings gains that were 1010 percent higher than the database average, you might be tempted to use some extraordinarily large figure. That would be a mistake. You definitely want to set the number high enough that the stocks in the port-folio will have extraordinary gains, but low enough that you'll still have ten or more stocks to invest in after adding the other three factors.

The first thing we'll try is setting this number so that only stocks with 12-month earnings gains 50 percent greater than the market will make the cut-off. On January 1, 1991, the average stock in the database had a 12-month earnings per share per-centage change of 6.3 percent. Adding 50 percent to 6.3 percent gives us 9.45 percent, and this is the number we enter into Value/Screen as our minimum for 12-Month EPS % Change. (The entry would look like this in Value/Screen: 12-Month EPS % Change ≥ 9.45%.)

Screening on that factor alone, we would reduce the number of acceptable stocks to 537 out of the 1600. Looking at the 12-Month EPS % Change histogram under the *Analysis of Screened List* section, we'd find they had an average 12-Month EPS % change of 42.9 percent, 581 percent higher than the average stock in the database. While dramatically higher, we should con-sider two things at this point: First, it's not 1010 percent higher. Second, if earnings gains are very low for the average stock in the database, as they are here, we might be allowing too many stocks to make the cut if we only require that 12-Month EPS % Changes be 50 percent above the mean, *whatever it may be.*

A floor or a minimum is the most obvious choice. By estab-lishing an absolute number as a floor, we assure that, when earnings gains are low, the floor will still provide a very high cut-off for our model. How high should we set the minimum? Given that CGM's earnings gains are so high, we might simply want to establish a number that allows roughly the top 20 per-cent of stocks in the database through the screen. Some experi-mentation shows that, if you set the 12-Month EPS % Change number to allow only stocks with gains of 20 percent or better, you reduce the number of stocks that pass the screen to 303, or roughly the top 20 percent of the database. You also find that, by examining the 12-Month EPS % Change histogram, the average gain for these 303 stocks was 64.7 percent, some 926 percent higher then the database average. This is certainly within strik-ing distance of the original CGM number, and since we still have three factors to add, it seems like a good fit. Therefore, we'll set the first factor screen in our model to: 12-month EPS %

Change must be greater than 20 percent or the mean plus 50 percent, *whichever is greater.*

The Second Factor

Now that we've found an acceptable value for our first factor, note that we're working with a smaller group of stocks than we started with. Instead of 1600 stocks, we've reduced our list to just 303 stocks, all with 12-month EPS percentage changes greater than 20 percent. If you did a factor analysis of this list, you'd find significant deviations in all the other factors, not just the 12-month EPS percentage change.

Now we'll reduce the list further by adding our second factor screen to the model: positive relative strength. Looking at the histogram for 26-week percentage price gains for our list of 303 stocks, you'll find that they *already* have positive relative strength, since they were down 9.6 percent, compared to the larger loss of 16.1 percent for the full database.

CGM's portfolio had a 26-week price percentage gain almost 450 percent higher than the database. We therefore want to set a high minimum for this figure so that we continue to narrow down the stocks making the cut. Since we've already established a minimum of 20 percent for the 12-month earnings gains, we'll try the same number here. The CGM portfolio had a minimum of 21.40 percent, but that was when the database average was up 9.6 percent, not down 16 percent. It may seem as though we are moving away from the CGM model by setting this figure so high. And that is exactly what we are doing. Our goal is to do better than CGM; so we need not restrict ourselves to duplicating their factor profile.

As you analyze more of the best pros of the growth school, you'll see that extraordinary relative strength often leads to continued outstanding performance. As Damon Runyon said, "It may be that the race is not always to the swift, nor the battle to the strong—but that's the way to bet." Since we're not constrained to create a model that exactly mimics CGM, we'll make our second factor screen: 26-week price percentage change must be equal to or greater than 20 percent or 50 percent plus the mean, *whichever is greater.* (In the Value/Screen database, this entry would read: 26-Wk. % Price Chng. ≥ 20.)

In a year when the market is down substantially, such a high relative strength figure will wipe out all but a handful of stocks. That's what happens here, with our 303 stocks being reduced to just 22. We're building a powerful yet elegant model that insists not just on outstanding earnings, but on outstanding market validation as measured by how well the stocks have performed versus the market. For a growth strategy, it's good to have strong market validation of the earnings gains for the stocks. So we're narrowing down our stocks to just those outstanding few that managed to buck a down market by over 36 percent, going up 20 percent or more when the market was down 16 percent.

The Third Factor

The third highest deviation in the CGM portfolio was last quarter EPS percentage changes. In the CGM portfolio, they were 285 percent higher than the database. Without even using the factor as a screen, the 22 stocks we have left already have last quarter EPS percentage changes 498 percent greater than the database, almost twice the CGM number. Yet we want to do better than CGM and we have the luxury of quantitative tools that let us accept only the best stocks that meet *all* our criteria. Therefore, we should add continuity to the model and use the same 20 or 50 percent greater than the database mean figure for last quarter EPS percentage changes as well. Because we're getting our "edge" from quantitative modeling, we'll continue to use what we've learned from the CGM analysis and make it better by insisting on far more stringent criteria.

Since the average earnings per share percentage change for the last quarter stood at 13 percent for the database on January 1, 1991, we'll use the 20 percent figure. (In the Value/Screen program, your entry would read: Last Qtr EPS % Chg $\geq$ 20.)

The Fourth Factor

Look at what we've accomplished with just three factors. We've reduced the database of 1600 stocks to just 18, all of which have rapidly growing earnings per share when measured on a quarterly and a 12-month basis. All 18 are also outstanding price gainers, with their average 26-week percentage gain an extraordinary 30.8 percent, compared to a *loss of over 16 percent for the average stock in the database.* Clearly, the factor profile of this group is significantly different from the database!

Before we add the last active screening factor, we need to make sure that Value Line ranks all our stocks for Timeliness. We do this because, when you set relative strength numbers so high, you might get a stock that has gone up a lot because it's being taken over by another company. Obviously, if the deal is done we aren't going to get any gains from buying it after the fact. So we can avoid allowing those stocks on the list by either setting Timeliness rank to 5 or less, or by saying that we don't want stocks without Timeliness ranks included in the screen. (Which one you use depends on the version of the software you are using.) In both cases, this lets us avoid takeover stocks because Value Line suspends a stock's Timeliness rank when it is involved in a takeover.

That done, we can add our fourth and final factor. This factor is estimated percentage changes for earnings per share over the next fiscal year. Now what should we set it at? The average for our 18 stocks is approximately 150 percent higher than the database, compared to the CGM portfolio's 265 percent advantage. Since we've seen that we should hold around 10 stocks, the easiest thing to do is make this final factor a relative one, setting the minimum to whatever number leaves us with ten stocks.

We can find the minimum by going to the *Tabular Reports* section and getting a report on Est % Chg EPS Fis Yr. Have the program list them in descending order. Next, simply count down to the tenth number. We find that it's 29.3, so we go back to the main program and set our fourth factor screen to a minimum of 29.3 percent, leaving us with a ten-stock portfolio. Table 4-5 shows what your screen would look like after running this four-factor model.

Table 4-5. Value/Screen Database Screen after Running the Four Active Factor Model

Variable	< = >	Value	Number of stocks
12-Month EPS % Chg	≥	20	303
26-Wk % Price Chg	≥	20	22
Last Qtr EPS % Chg	≥	20	18
Timeliness rank	≤	5	18
Est % Chg EPS Fis Yr	≥	29.3	10

Reviewing the Portfolio

Using just four factors, we've managed to reduce 1600 stocks to ten outstanding growth stocks. Setting minimums for the factors lets us narrow down our selections to just ten stocks with outstanding earnings gains over the last quarter and year, *and* outstanding relative strength over the last six months, *and* a forecast for a continuation of outstanding earnings gains. Using a quantitative process gives us the luxury of insisting that *each* stock meet *all* our criteria, not just a few. It lets us take a "no compromises" position that will give us a factor profile even more outstanding than CGM's, yet based on the same top four factors.

Despite using only four factors and using them in a different year, you still find a striking similarity in the underlying factor profiles of CGM and our ten-stock portfolio. Tables 4-6 and 4-7 compare CGM's key factors and secondary factors with our portfolio. The two portfolios are near replicas of each other in every important respect. Under the key factors, our ten-stock portfolio has a considerable advantage in both relative strength and last quarter earnings per share percentage gains. It is extremely close to CGM's profile for 12-month earnings per share percentage changes and estimated percentage change for

Table 4-6. Comparison of CGM's Key Factors and 10-Stock Portfolio

Factor	CGM's difference from database	10-stock portfolio's difference from database
12-Month EPS % Chg	1010% higher	982.54% higher
26-Wk % Price Chg	448% higher, with a low of 21.4%	NA, due to positive versus negative number. Average of 33.6% gain versus a loss of 16% for the database
Last Qtr EPS % Chg	285% higher	828% higher
Est % Chg EPS Fis Yr	266% higher	253% higher
Timeliness rank	Low, high of 2	Low, high of 2

Table 4-7. Comparison of CGM's Secondary Factors and 10-Stock Portfolio

Factor	CGM's difference from database	10-stock portfolio's difference from database
Price-to-book ratio	182% higher	180% higher
Current PE ratio	16% higher, maximum of 39	39% higher, maximum of 33
Return on net worth and percentage retained to common	Both high	Both high
Projected 3- to 5-year growth in EPS and book value	Both high, with projected book value average more than double database mean	Both high, with projected book value average more than double database mean
Price-to-cash flow	High, low of 12	High, low of 8
Price-to-sales ratio	256% higher than database	124% higher than database
Margins	175% higher than database	43% higher than database

earnings per share for the coming fiscal year. Under the secondary factors, we find virtually the same variations from the database mean in both portfolios.

Thus, we find that we can duplicate all of CGM's important underlying factors using an elegant and simple four-factor model. More, we've improved our portfolio's underlying factor profile by using quantitative methods that require each stock in the portfolio to meet *all* our specific criteria.

Examining Performance

Table 4-8 lists our ten stocks and their industries. As we did with our first emulation, we'll review how this portfolio performed over the first six months of 1991. Again, we'll hold these ten stocks for six months, until June 30, 1991. We'll then rebalance the portfolio by running the same screen we used to get these ten stocks, selling any of the ten that no longer meet the criteria and replacing them with stocks that do.

For the six months ending June 30, 1991, this model—

Table 4-8. 10 Stocks Recommended by the Four-Factor
Model for First Half of 1991

Ticker	Stock	Industry
SFDS	Smithfield Foods	Food processing
CQB	Chiquita Brands	Food processing
APCC	American Power Conversion	Computer/peripherals
GPS	Gap Stores	Specialty retail
HF	House of Fabric	Specialty retail
AFL	American Family Insurance	Life insurance
USHC	U.S. Healthcare	Medical services
BMET	Biomet	Medical supply
CORD	Cordis Corp.	Medical supply
USS	U.S. Surgical	Medical supply

designed using the best of CGM's factors—was up 50.5 percent,
with Smithfield Foods turning in the best performance of up 105
percent and American Family Insurance doing the worst with a
gain of 14.6 percent! This is quite a difference from our first
crude emulation and better than CGM's return of 40.7 percent.
Because we need not own more than ten stocks and can insist
that the stocks we own meet all the criteria we've selected, we
have managed to do around 10 percent better than the CGM
portfolio.

On June 30 we'll again run the screen we used to get these ten
stocks. Only two stocks from the preceding portfolio, U.S.
Healthcare and U.S. Surgical, still make the list. Thus, we'll sell
the eight that no longer meet our criteria and replace them with
the new stocks that meet the criteria as of June 30, 1991. We'll
again equal-weight the portfolio. Table 4-9 lists the new ten-
stock portfolio for June 30 through December 31, 1991.

Now let's look at the six-month performance ending on
December 31, 1991. For the six months ending December 31,
1991, these ten stocks were up 63.8 percent! Amgen turned in
the best performance for the six months of up 92.7 percent and
Playboy did the worst, going up 18.7 percent. For the same six-
month period, CGM itself was up 41.4 percent.

For the year, our ten-stock portfolio was up 146.52 percent! By

Table 4-9. 10 Stocks Recommended by Four-Factor Model for Second Half of 1991

Ticker	Stock	Industry
WSAU	Wasau Paper	Paper/forest products
PLA	Playboy Ent "B"	Publishing
AMGN	Amgen	Drug
AIZ	Amcast Ind.	Metal fabricating
SCH	Schwab(Charles)	Brokerage
CNC	Conseco	Life insurance
USHC	U.S. Healthcare	Medical services
USS	U.S. Surgical	Medical supply
HDYN	Healthdyne	Medical supply
UNIH	United Healthcare	Unclassified

comparing this to a gain of 99.08 percent for CGM, we know we're on the right track!

Looking Backward and Moving Forward

Our one-year results show that we certainly have a model that picks high-performing growth stocks. Yet the results we have are for only one year. Maybe they are a fluke. After all, the model we built didn't create an exact clone of the CGM portfolio. The model uses CGM's four highest factor deviations (all having to do with momentum) in a more aggressive way than CGM does, so much so that we can name this model the *Momentum Growth Model.* Maybe the model's aggressiveness is why we did so much better in 1991, and it might mean that we'll do significantly *worse* in years when the overall market heads down.

The only way to know is to test the model back as far as possible. I have Value Line data going back to the end of 1985. These additional five years include the great crash of 1987 and a bear market year in 1990, so we'll be able to get a much better feel for how the model performs in a variety of market environments. Also, many market professionals look at five years as one complete market cycle, which gives a clear picture of the benefits and liabilities of any given strategy.

Since we are insisting on a rigorous implementation of the model, the results we see in our test should also mirror the results you would have gotten if you had actually bought the model's recommendations. We'll do the same thing we did for our test of 1991. We'll use the model to screen the database once on December 31 and again on June 30. Other than those two periods, we will not make trades in the portfolio, and we'll always own ten stocks.

Tables 4-10 and 4-11 show the results of testing the strategy back to the end of 1985. Wow! This is an incredible model for picking growth stocks: $10,000.00 invested on December 31, 1985 would have been worth $82,235.70 on December 31, 1991! Our four-factor model beat CGM's return in each year of our test because it had the luxury of owning just the 10 stocks that *always met the highest standards according to what we found when we examined CGM's portfolio.* CGM itself did outstandingly well over the same period, gaining 264.86 percent, but this model did considerably better because it faced none of CGM's constraints.

Table 4-10. Performance Results of the Momentum Growth Model December 31, 1985 through December 31, 1990

Period	Portfolio performance (%)
December 31, 1985–June 30, 1986	+47.1
June 30, 1986–December 31, 1986	−7.26
1986, full year	**36.42**
December 31, 1986–June 30, 1987	33.65
June 30, 1987–December 31, 1987	−9.90
1987, full year	**20.42**
December 31, 1987–June 30, 1988	6.0
June 30, 1988–December 31, 1988	21.99
1988, full year	**29.31**
December 31, 1988–June 30, 1989	21.8
June 30, 1989–December 31, 1989	9.47
1989, full year	**33.33**
December 31, 1989–June 30, 1990	14.8
June 30, 1990–December 31, 1990	2.60
1990, full year	**17.78**

Table 4-11. Summary Performance Statistics for CGM, Morningstar's Average Growth Fund, the S&P 500, and Stocks from Momentum Growth Model (December 31, 1985–December 31, 1991)

Fund	$10,000 grows to:	Cumulative percentage change (%)	Compounded average annual change (%)
CGM	$36,485.78	264.86	23.71
S&P 500	$25,364.40	153.64	16.53
Average growth fund	$23,095.71	130.96	14.75
Momentum Growth Model	$82,235.70	722.36	42.07

SOURCE: Morningstar Mutual Fund OnDisc and Compuserve.

We never bought or held a stock that wasn't in the top ten for all four of our factors. We never had to own more than ten stocks because of a government regulation or because of the size of our portfolio. Most importantly, we did well because we consistently bought and sold the stocks that the model recommended, *never deviating from the program.*

In reality, few investors, amateur or professional, could have held on during the crash without blinking. Many investors might have been tempted to "close their books" on 1991 after the first half's performance put them so far ahead of the pack. Had they done so, they would still have done better than almost all the aggressive growth mutual funds covered in Morningstar, but they would have left an additional 63 percent on the table!

We did so well because we allowed a superior investment strategy to be superior. We allowed no second guessing or emotional decision making: That would have only fouled things up. David Faust, in *The Limits of Scientific Reasoning,* enumerates the many tests showing that human judges—whether they are clinical psychologists making predictions about patient outcome, college admissions officers making predictions about how well new students will do, or stock market analysts making projections for a stock's earnings—almost always show inferior predictions in the face of empirically derived actuarial formulas based only on a few attributes known to be associated with outcome. Intuitive forecasters are not only worse than optimal regression equations, they usually do worse than *any* simple formula. Intuitive forecasters don't lose to simple formulas because they apply invalid weights, but rather *because they apply them unreliably—once using a piece of data, another time rejecting it, depending on how they feel or the current circumstances.* If there is any "secret" to investing, it's the will to consistently execute an excellent strategy.

1992 Performance

Our historical test shows that 1991's performance wasn't a fluke. We designed a model that did beautifully both in 1991 and in the preceding five years. Now we'll see how it did more recently.

One of the most difficult years for growth investors during the last decade was 1992. At mid-year, many of the aggressive growth and growth managers that had been at the top of Morningstar's performance list at the end of 1991 found themselves at the bottom for the first six months of 1992. Many were down over 15 percent as growth stocks fell out of favor with investors who began pouring their money into small-cap stocks, cyclical, and other "value" stocks.

The market also hit our ten stocks very hard, with the portfolio falling 15.5 percent in the first six months of the year. Using history as our guide, we'd know not to abandon the program and we would rebalance on June 30, 1992 to again hold the ten stocks that met all our criteria. The portfolio rebounded during the second half of 1992, showing a gain for the period of 18.2 percent, ending a very difficult year for growth stocks almost unchanged, or −0.12 percent for the year. CGM, on the other hand, showed a gain of 17.47 percent for the year, beating our ten-stock portfolio for the first time since the beginning of our test.

Our Momentum Growth Model's cumulative return dwarfed that of every mutual fund in the Morningstar database. Starting on December 31, 1985, $10,000 invested using this strategy would have been worth $82,137 on December 31, 1992. That's a cumulative gain of 721.37 percent, or an average annual gain of 35.10 percent a year. Table 4-12 shows the performance of the model for every year of our test.

The Portfolio for 1993

The ten stocks that meet the model's criteria as of December 31, 1992 are listed in Table 4-13. The ten stocks show the same dra-

Table 4-12. Performance Results of the Momentum
Growth Model December 31, 1985–December 31, 1992

Period	Portfolio performance (%)
December 31, 1985–June 30, 1986	+47.1
June 30, 1986–December 31, 1986	−7.26
1986, full year	**36.42**
December 31, 1986–June 30, 1987	33.65
June 30, 1987–December 31, 1987	−9.90
1987, full year	**20.42**
December 31, 1987–June 30, 1988	6.0
June 30, 1988–December 31, 1988	21.99
1988, full year	**29.31**
December 31, 1988–June 30, 1989	21.8
June 30, 1989–December 31, 1989	9.47
1989, full year	**33.33**
December 31, 1989–June 30, 1990	14.8
June 30, 1990–December 31, 1990	2.60
1990, full year	**17.78**
December 31, 1990–June 30, 1991	50.50
June 30, 1991–December 31, 1991	63.80
1991, full year	**146.52**
December 31, 1991–June 30, 1992	−15.50
June 30, 1992–December 31, 1992	18.20
1992, full year	**−0.12**

matic deviations from the database as all our other selections.
Last quarter earnings per share gains were 155.4 percent, 740
percent higher than the database average of 18.5 percent.
Earnings per share gains for the last 12 months are 187.4 percent, 574 percent higher than the database. Relative strength, as
measured by the 26-week price percentage change, was
extremely strong, with the ten stocks showing an average six-
month gain of 34.3 percent, some 662 percent higher than the
database average of 4.5 percent. Finally, the estimated change
for earnings for the coming fiscal year is 592 percent higher
than the database average, coming in at 214.4 percent.

Using history as our guide, we can assume the model will
continue to be an excellent performer. Indeed, as of April 1993,
the first quarter results of the portfolio bode well: It gained 15.1

Table 4-13. 10 Stocks Recommended by Momentum Growth Model for First Half of 1993

Ticker	Stock	Industry
LPX	Louisiana-Pacific	Paper/forest products
BGEN	Biogen	Drug
JSTN	Justin Ind.	Building material
LUV	Southwest Air	Air transport
QVCN	QVC Network	Specialty retail
BK	Bank of New York	Bank
PGR	Progressive	Insurance: P/C
KZ	Kysor Ind.	Diversified
SRV	Service Corp.	Diversified
VRLN	Varlen Corp.	Diversified

percent compared to a gain of 3.6 percent for the S&P 500, and just 2.78 percent for the average growth fund. More, its 15.1 percent return beat every growth fund in the Morningstar database. If you extend the list to include aggressive growth funds as well, only one—American Heritage—did better, returning 18.58 percent.

Ever Onward

To create this performance, we had to understand that CGM was the best performing mutual fund in 1991 for a reason and that we could find that reason by looking at the factors that CGM's manager liked in stocks. By understanding that a portfolio's underlying factors are responsible for its performance, we have a tremendous edge on people who refuse to see the obvious.

We'll see, as we analyze other funds throughout the book, that those that do extraordinarily well for more than one year do so because they possess a superior strategy for selecting stocks and as well as the will to implement it. Managers with a superior performance record who use the same style will also have highly similar factor profiles. All we need to do is *look at the portfolio to see what that strategy is, and then design a model that uses it better than the mutual fund or funds themselves!* You'll move beyond the masters by using quantitative techniques that require stocks to meet *all* your criteria. When you do this, as we've seen from the CGM example, you gain a tremendous performance advantage over the original fund because you've improved on their ideas. If you are willing to take these simple steps, you'll design models and pick portfolios that tear up the average mutual fund.

5

The Common Characteristics of Growth Managers

In this chapter, we look at other top aggressive growth portfolios and learn more about their underlying factor structures. We'll do the same as we did with CGM—find the most consistent performers in the Morningstar database and analyze their portfolios. Always keep a journal of your analysis and emulation results. A review of this journal will show which factors the best managers share and point you toward the factors that are most effective when designing a model. As we proceed, we'll find that the top funds may buy different stocks, but their underlying factor profiles are very similar to one another and their key factors are virtually indistinguishable.

Looking at Morningstar's Top Performers

The aggressive growth manager with the best performance for 1991 was the American Heritage Fund, up 96.04 percent for the year. (CGM did better, but Morningstar covers them in the growth section of the database.) That's a great return, but when we look back in time we see that the fund's five-year record puts it at the *bottom* of all the aggressive growth funds, with a total return of just 9.15 percent, compared to a gain of 103 per-

Table 5-1. American Heritage Fund's Five-Year
Performance Record, 1987–1991

Year	Total return	S&P 500 total return	Difference
1987	−18.82	5.23	−24.04
1988	1.90	16.51	−14.61
1989	−2.80	31.68	−34.48
1990	−30.77	−3.1	−27.67
1991	96.04	30.4	64.64

cent for the S&P 500. (See Table 5-1.) Such a huge inconsistency suggests that the fund has changed managers or gotten extremely lucky. My guess is that a new manager came on board, but since Morningstar is silent on that point, we'll reject this fund as inconsistent and move on.

The Kaufmann Fund

The second best performing aggressive growth fund in 1991 was the Kaufmann Fund, with a gain of 79.43 percent. Over the previous five years, the fund had a rocky 1987 and a loss in 1990, yet it still managed a five-year gain of 146 percent, better than the S&P 500 and in line with other aggressive growth managers. Next, read what the analyst has to say about the fund in Morningstar's write-up. Here you can often find managers' rules of thumb for buying stocks and translate them into factors to use in your model. With the Kaufmann Fund, you learn that they like to buy stocks with earnings gains of at least 25 percent a year (sound familiar?) that also have positive cash flows. While we learned about high earnings-per-share gains looking at CGM's portfolio, the positive cash flow rule-of-thumb might be useful. So note it in your journal and go to the portfolio holdings section.

Kaufmann's Stocks

Table 5-2 lists Kaufmann's ten top stock holdings as of June 30, 1991. As you search the Value/Screen list for these companies, you'll find that not one of Kaufmann's top ten holdings shows up in Value Line's database. We've run into a wall. Since Kaufmann specializes in stocks that are outside the Value Line

Table 5-2. Kaufmann Fund's 10 Top Stock Holdings as of June 30, 1991

Ticker	Stock
KNCI	Kinetic Concepts
EQP	Health Equity Properties
EPTO	Epitope
CYS	Cycare Systems
KRB	MBNA
NHP	Nationwide Health Properties
TANK	Tanknology Environmental
EBPI	Employee Benefit Plans
CS	Cabletron Systems
ASZ	Amsco International

database, we'll have to move on to the next manager. We've nevertheless gained a rule to test and found another growth manager who relies on high 12-month earnings per share percentage gains. Note these two things in your journal: (1) the similar use of high 12-month EPS, and (2) the positive cash flow rule (mentioned previously).

The Delaware Trend Fund

The third best performing aggressive growth fund in 1991 was the Delaware Trend Fund, with a gain of 74.49 percent. Checking the fund's five-year performance, we find that it gained about 130 percent. It did better than the S&P 500, but it also had a bad 1990, falling almost 25 percent. Such a large loss in a single year would normally disqualify the fund from consideration. Yet an idea from the Morningstar analyst's write-up of the fund is worth noting: The fund sells any stock when its price-to-earnings ratio exceeds it earnings per share growth rate. While value investors usually focus on P/E levels, perhaps Delaware Trend is generating good performance using a hybrid of the growth and value schools of investing. This is something worth knowing about, so let's go ahead with the analysis.

Table 5-3. Delaware Trend Fund's 10 Stock Holdings Covered by Value Line as of June 30, 1991

Ticker	Stock
BBY	Best Buy
RDA	Reader's Digest Class A
RBK	Reebok International
HUF	Huffy
SBL	Symbol Technologies
CPY	CPI
CHRS	Charming Shoppes
IRF	International Rectifier
RYAN	Ryan's Family Steak House
SPLS	Staples

The Delaware Trend Fund's Stocks

Following the procedure covered in Chap. 3, we'll go to the Value Line database and look up the stocks held by Delaware Trend. After looking for their top 30 stocks in Value/Screen, we find only ten out of the 30 in the Value Line database. (See Table 5-3.) A 33 percent representation doesn't sound promising, but it's enough for us to get a useful picture of the fund's underlying factor profile.

Delaware Trend's Underlying Factors

Enter Delaware Trend's stocks in Value/Screen and go step by step through the factor screens in the database, noting all substantial deviations. Tables 5-4, 5-5, and 5-6 show the results of our factor analysis.

While Delaware Trend shares CGM's exposure to stocks with big forecasted earnings gains and good relative strength, there are several key differences between the portfolios. First, Delaware Trend's portfolio has very good short-term (13-week) relative strength, with only an ordinary figure for 6-month performance. More, Delaware Trend's stocks don't show huge recent earnings gains: In the most recent quarter, the stocks in Delaware Trend's portfolio showed an earnings gain 31 percent

Table 5-4. Results of Delaware Trend's Factor Analysis
Using Data from December 1991

Variable	High	Low	Mean	Value Line mean	Difference (%)
Timeliness rank	4	2	3	3	0
Safety rank	5	3	3	3	0
Financial strength	C	A	B	B+	Lower
Industry rank	92	29	56	46	21.3
Price stability	55	5	20	52	−61
Beta	1.5	1.1	1.32	1.05	26
Current EPS	2.31	.48	1.15	1.88	−38.62
Current dividend	0.6	0	0.21	0.77	−73.38
Technical rank	4	1	3	3	0
Recent price	28.75	5.13	14.66	23.94	−38.74
52-week high	34.38	8.5	19.83	32.09	−38.22
52-week low	23.5	3.88	10.38	18.88	−45
Current PE	26	6	14	13	6
Current yield	2.9	0	1.07	3.1	−66
Price-to-book ratio	5.67	.64	2.66	2.12	25.28
13-week % price change	79.2	−28.1	23.46	4.6	410
26-week % price change	16.2	−53.9	−15.13	−16.1	−6.02
Market value ($ mill)	3432	42.4	686	2076	−67

less than the Value/Screen database. The fund's stocks also have a much lower market capitalization than either the CGM portfolio or the Value Line database. Finally, we find the difference that caused us to originally pursue this analysis: the average Delaware Trend stock has a price-to-sales ratio 51 percent *below* the database and a price-to-earnings ratio equal to the database. That's very unusual for an aggressive growth fund with such high expected earnings gains. CGM's average price-to-sales ratio, in contrast, was 256 percent *higher* than the database average.

Table 5-7 lists Delaware Trend's key factors. Like CGM, Delaware Trend owns stocks with great relative strength and very high anticipated earnings gains. Unlike CGM, it focuses on volatile, smaller-cap stocks that are "cheap" based on their

Table 5-5. Delaware Trend's Factors from December 1991

Variable	High	Low	Mean	Value Line mean	Difference (%)
Sales ($ mill)	2009	182	683	2969	−77
% ret net worth	27.8	6.8	15.23	15.5	−1.74
% retained to common	21.4	6.8	13.17	10.8	22
Book value per share	11.15	1.88	6.63	15.4	−57
Debt as % of capital	85	0	20	33	−40
Last qtr EPS % chg	30	−18.2	9.01	13	−31
12-month EPS % chg	34.1	−15.3	13.11	6.3	109
*5-yr EPS growth	47	17.5	28	9.6	188
*5-yr div growth	10.5	.5	5.5	9	−39
5-yr bk val growth	97	−14	31	9.2	237
Est. % chg EPS qtr 1	650	−5	93	22	327
Est. % chg EPS qtr 2	300	1.6	49	23	112
Est. % chg EPS fis yr	289	1.3	47	17.3	172
Prj 3-5 yr apprec %	339	13	141	133	6
Prj EPS growth	28	11	15	14.8	1.77
Prj div growth	23.5	0	8.2	8.3	−1.20
Prj book val growth	30.5	7.5	15.7	10.1	55.45
Prj 3-5 yr av return	45	5	23.9	24	−0.42

Table 5-6. Delaware Trend's Factors from December 1991

Variable	High	Low	Mean	Value Line mean	Difference (%)
Cash flow per share	7	0	1.63	3.61	−55
% institutional	72	23	44	41	6.8
Shares outstanding	119	8.2	41	65	−37
Price-to-cash-flow ratio	26	4	10.3	7	46
Earnings yield	16.7	3.8	8.7	5.45	59.6
Margins	9.6	1	5.69	5.56	2.3
Price-to-sales ratio	1.71	0.08	0.87	1.76	−51

price-to-sales and price-to-earnings ratios. Aggressive growth portfolios normally have high price-to-sales ratios, because investors usually pay a premium for such outstanding earnings growth. Delaware Trend also differs from CGM in that its stocks have no great *recent* earnings gains; only their *projections* are high. In short, Delaware Trend buys bargain-priced, volatile, small-cap stocks that have huge forecasted earnings gains and short-term relative strength.

Table 5-7. Delaware Trend's Key Factors

Key Factors

1. *Strong short-term relative strength:* 13-week price gains are 410% higher than the database.
2. *Very high estimated earnings gains:* The estimated change for the first quarter is 326% higher than the database, and the estimated change for the fiscal year is 171% higher than the database.
3. *Average market capitalization is 67% lower than the database, with a high of $3.4 billion.*
4. *Average price stability is 60% lower than the database average.*
5. *Average price-to-sales ratio is 51% below the database average, with a high of 1.71.* Average price-to-earnings ratio is just 6% higher than the database, with a high of 26.

Building a Model to Emulate Delaware Trend

As we did with CGM, let's build a model using only Delaware Trend's key factors, as listed in Table 5-7. Simply go down the list to make a model, starting with 13-week percentage price change. For simplicity's sake, let's require that all our stocks' 13-week percentage gains be equal to or greater than the Value Line database *or* greater than zero.

Next, let's capture the small-cap, volatile nature of Delaware Trend's stocks by creating a maximum level for market value and price stability. Delaware Trend's portfolio has a maximum market value of $3.43 billion; so we'll round that up to $3.5 billion and use it as a ceiling. The average price stability rank for a Delaware trend stock is 21, with a maximum of 55. We'd first experiment with the 55 figure and find that it doesn't give us a low enough overall stability rank. Some experimentation with the number shows that a maximum of 40 gives us an overall stability rank close to Delaware Trend's.

The next two factors limit the price-to-sales and price-to-earnings ratios. We'll use the numbers we found in the Delaware Trend factor analysis as our ceiling, requiring price-to-sales ratios to be equal to or less than 1.71, and price-to-earnings ratios to be equal to or less than 26.

Our final factor is the estimated change in earnings per share for the coming fiscal year. As we did with CGM, we'll make this factor relative, setting its minimum at the number that leaves us with ten stocks.

Testing the Model

We now have the model listed in Table 5-8. Running it on December 31, 1990 produces the ten stocks listed in Table 5-9. As we did with CGM, compare the key factors of each portfolio. The portfolios are skewed along the same factors, but with a great difference in the amounts by which they vary from the database. Estimated earnings gains for the coming year for our ten-stock model are 1930 percent greater than the database average, compared to an advantage of just 171 percent for the Delaware Trend portfolio. Table 5-9 shows the other differences.

Now let's run a historical test of this model. As we did with CGM, we'll check performance and rebalance the portfolio every six months. Table 5-10 shows the results of our test.

Our model and the Delaware Trend portfolio show significant performance differences. To begin with, 1990 wasn't nearly as hard on our model as it was on Delaware Trend. The model was down just 3.6 percent for the year, compared to a loss of over 24 percent for the Delaware Trend fund. Yet 1989 shows just the opposite, with the Delaware Trend fund scoring a gain of over 49 percent and our model turning in a modest 3.63 percent gain for the year. Our results are so different because we're using a model that has stricter requirements than the Delaware Trend fund, even if the underlying factors are the same. More, using a quantitatively consistent approach reduces our volatility substantially. For the seven years between 1985 and 1992, the stan-

Table 5-8. The Value/Screen Database Screen after Running Our First Model Using Delaware Trend's Key Factors on December 31, 1990

Variable	<=>	Value	Number of stocks
13-wk % price chg	≥	4.6	842
Market value ($ mill)	≤	3500	701
Price stability	≤	40	275
Profit-to-sales ratio	≤	1.71	224
Current PE ratio	≤	26	191
Est % chg EPS fis yr	≥	188.9	10

Table 5-9. 10 Stocks Meeting the Model's Criteria on December 31, 1990

Ticker	Stock
SCIS	SCI Systems
BSIM	Burnup & Sims
GH	General Host
OHM	OHM, Inc.
CAO	Carolina Freight
IRF	International Rectifier
YELL	Yellow Freight
KSF	Quaker State
BC	Brunswick Corp.
RELL	Richardson Electronics

A Useful Shortcut

I recommend a shortcut when you are first testing the historical performance of the model emulating Delaware Trend. Instead of going to Compuserve's return network, simply save the ticker list of selected stocks and change to the Value Line database six months hence. Open the saved ticker list, and look at the histogram for the 26-week price percentage change. Although it doesn't include dividends, this is a quick and accurate method for getting the six-month performance figures.

After you have refined your model to the point that it might be used for actual trades, double-check all performance via Compuserve.

---

dard deviation of return on our ten-stock portfolio was just 22.43 percent, considerably less than Delaware Trend's 31.34 percent. Yet, because we used a disciplined quantitative method, the model showed a seven-year gain of 381 percent, considerably higher than Delaware Trend's total return of 197 percent (Table 5-11). Our advantage came from our ability to

Table 5-10. Contrasting Key Factors of 10-Stock Portfolio and Delaware Trend Portfolio

Factor	10-stock portfolio	Delaware Trend
13-wk % price chg	354% higher	410% higher
Market value ($ mill)	87% lower	67% lower
Price stability	52% lower	60% lower
Profit-to-sales ratio	60% lower	51% lower
Current PE ratio	10% higher	6% higher
Est % chg EPS fis yr	1930% higher	171% higher

Table 5-11. Performance Results of the 6-Factor Delaware Trend Model from December 31, 1985 through December 31, 1992

Time period	Portfolio performance (%)
December 31, 1985–June 30, 1986	47.5
June 30, 1986–December 31, 1986	−1.9
1986, full year	**44.7**
December 31, 1986–June 30, 1987	36.4
June 30, 1987–December 31, 1987	−14.8
1987, full year	**16.21**
December 31, 1987–June 30, 1988	16.2
June 30, 1988–December 31, 1988	7.5
1988, full year	**24.92**
December 31, 1988–June 30, 1989	14.9
June 30, 1989–December 31, 1989	−9.8
1989, full year	**3.63**
December 31, 1989–June 30, 1990	19.3
June 30, 1990–December 31, 1990	−19.2
1990, full year	**−3.6**
December 31, 1990–June 30, 1991	17.3
June 30, 1991–December 31, 1991	41.0
1991, full year	**65.39**
December 31, 1991–June 30, 1992	8.8
June 30, 1992–December 31, 1992	27.3
1992, full year	**38.5**

hold a concentrated portfolio of stocks that meet *all* the criteria that we found were important to Delaware Trend.

Experimenting with the Model

If this hybrid growth-value style focusing on small-cap stocks appeals to you, use this first model as a starting point. Continue to experiment with the variables and see what might happen if you refine a factor screen, even slightly. For example, strong 13-week price performance was the top factor deviation in Delaware Trend's portfolio. We set this factor so that all stocks making the screen were greater than the database average or zero during bear markets. What if we refined this to reflect the 13-week price performance of the volatile, small-cap stocks in the database that traded at bargain price-to-sales and price-to-earnings ratios? Different styles have different underlying factors. Maybe volatile, small-cap companies did much better or worse than the database average. By setting our 13-week price gains *relative* to this group, we might improve the model's performance.

To do this, all you need do is separate the factors. Start with the following list:

1. Price-to-sales ratios under 1.71
2. Price-to-earnings ratios under 26
3. Price Stability under 40
4. Market Value under $3.5 billion

When you run this model you're left with 393 stocks. Now go to the *Tabular Reports* section and get a report on 13-week price changes, from the best to the worst. Let's refine this factor screen slightly by focusing on the 100 best 13-week performers from the list of 393 stocks that meet the four criteria. You find that setting 13-week percentage gains equal to or greater than 19.8 percent leaves you with 100 stocks. From here, we'd again choose the ten with the highest estimated change for earnings per share for the coming fiscal year. This may seem like a small change (in many years it is), but it lets you focus more on price momentum and less on expected gains in earnings. You'll still have tremendous forecasted earnings gains, but they will be on stocks also showing market price movements that indicate investors *believe* those gains will occur.

Table 5-12. 10 Stocks Meeting the Model's Criteria on December 31, 1990 after Modifying the 13-Week Percentage Gain Screen

Ticker	Stock
IRF	International Rectifier
YELL	Yellow Freight
BC	Brunswick Corp.
SFDS	Smithfield Foods
RAUT	Republic Automotive
CNR	Conner Peripherals
USHC	U.S. Healthcare
MU	Micron Technology
WYL	Wyle Labs
GHW	General Housewares

Making this small change on December 31, 1990 changes our model's stocks and their factor profile considerably. The new ten-stock list appears in Table 5-12. Because of the new model's higher 13-week percentage gain, it has only three stocks in common with the first model. The first list had much higher estimated earnings gains because the 13-week percentage gain hurdle was much lower. Here we've tightened up our requirements, as Table 5-13 shows. It's amazing how just a slight variation in one factor screen can dramatically change the outcome. Yet at other times the change won't affect the recommended stocks at all. In 1992, for example, you'd have ended up with almost the same stocks in both models.

Table 5-13. Contrasting Key Factors of 10-Stock Portfolio and Delaware Trend Portfolio

Factor	First 10-stock portfolio	Revised 10-stock portfolio	Delaware Trend
13-wk % price chg	354% higher	617% higher	410% higher
Market value ($ mill)	87% lower	78% lower	67% lower
Price stability	52% lower	59% lower	60% lower
Profit-to-sales ratio	60% lower	40% lower	51% lower
Current PE ratio	10% higher	4.6% higher	6% higher
Est % chg EPS fis yr	1930% higher	835% higher	171% higher

The next step is to see if you'd gain an important performance advantage by making this change. In 1991, for example, we'd increase the return from 66 percent to 94.77 percent, a gain of almost 29 percent for the year! In 1992, however, our returns were virtually the same: This variation of the portfolio had a gain of 38.75 percent, the same as the first version. Experiment and look at the results. You'll learn which factors have the greatest influence on portfolio performance and how best to unite them in a model. Over a market cycle, many of these small variations are fairly meaningless, with one variation of a model being a hit in one year and a miss in the next one. For example, in 1987, this new version of our strategy had a gain of just 0.28 percent for the year. That's almost 16 percent less than the first version. Since most of these small changes have little effect on the multiyear returns of a strategy, incorporate just those that make sense and show empirical superiority.

Changing the Order of the Factors

The only way to learn more about the best underlying factor structure is experimentation. There are six factors to test at various levels. Try making 13-week price percentage changes the last and relative factor. Set the old relative factor, estimated change in earnings per share for the coming fiscal year, to equal the mean or better. Then buy the top ten performing stocks, using 13-week price performance as your guide.

In 1992, the return for the year dropped from 38.5 percent to 11.26 percent. Not great. Do a few more years to see if this was a fluke. If not, make sure that you include this test in your journal. You sometimes learn more *from what doesn't work than from what does work when doing factor analysis.*

Looking at the Longer Term

CGM was unique in that not only was it the best performing mutual fund in 1991, it also had the best ten-year performance record. None of the preceding funds can make that claim. Now let's look at the longer term to see if any funds differ substantially from those we've already studied.

Pacific Horizon Aggressive Growth Fund

Looking at the longer term, we find that Pacific Horizon Aggressive Growth Fund (PHAG) has the best five-year record of Morningstar's aggressive growth funds. It was up 177 percent, compared to the S&P 500's gain of 104 percent and CGM's return of 175 percent. Its performance was also consistent, with the fund ranking number one over the last three years and in the top ten for 1991.

Thus, the Pacific Horizon fund is an ideal prospect for factor analysis. Following our procedure, we'll read what the Morningstar analyst says about the fund. Here, we find that "the fund relies in part on a computer model that screens stocks based on their growth potential and on their valuation vis-a-vis that potential." That's a convoluted way of saying that they don't care about a stock's PE, as long as its growth in earnings is outstanding.

The write-up does not tell us much more. So we go to the stocks. Table 5-14 shows the stocks in Pacific Horizon fund's portfolio also in Value/Screen. After loading the stocks into the

Table 5-14. Pacific Horizon Aggressive Growth Fund's Stock Holdings Covered by Value/Screen as of August 31, 1991

Ticker	Stock
AMGN	Amgen
RBK	Reebok International
CNTO	Centocor
HD	Home Depot
CORD	Cordis
COST	Costco Wholesale
TOY	Toys 'R' Us
LES	Leslie Faye
USHC	U.S. Healthcare
RYC	Raychem
RML	Russell
KR	Kroger

Value/Screen database, we again would follow the step-by-step factor analysis we outlined in Chap. 3.

PHAG Fund's Underlying Factors the Same as CGM

To spare you several more tables showing each of Pacific Horizon's factor differences from the market, refer to Table 5-15. Pacific Horizon's key differences from the database are virtually identical to CGM's, but the order is different. Pacific Horizon's top factor difference is estimated percentage changes in earnings per share for the coming year, whereas CGM's was 12-month earnings per share percentage gains. However, the top four differences are *the same for both CGM and Pacific Horizon Aggressive Growth!*

On the surface, these funds have little but their extraordinary performance in common. Morningstar lists Pacific Horizon under the "aggressive growth" category, whereas CGM resides in "growth." They hold different stocks, describe their investment process differently, and claim to be interested in different segments of the market. Yet at the factor level, the two are virtually indistinguishable. The model that we developed for CGM would also fit Pacific Horizon's factor profile. Perhaps we could change the focus of the model to demand higher overall projections for earnings per share gains, since Pacific Horizon's are substantially higher than CGM's. Yet once you have the basic "factor mix" established, these changes are just refinements. You'd want to continue experimenting to find the best mix, but the basic factor package is the same as CGM's.

Table 5-15. Key Factors of Pacific Horizon's Portfolio as of January 1, 1991

Key Factors
1. Est % change EPS fiscal year 915.40% is higher than database.
2. Strong relative strength. The 26-week percentage change is a positive 4.98% compared to a loss of 16.1% for the database; the 13-week percentage change is 472% higher than the database.
3. The 12-month EPS % change is 386% higher.
4. The last quarter EPS % change is 230% higher than the database.

An Underlying Structure to Top Performers

This isn't a coincidence. Examining the second best performer over the last five years, AIM Constellation, you find that it too shares the same key factors. Its top difference from the market is, like CGM's, 12-month earnings per share percentage gains. The next difference, like the others, is very strong relative strength. The third difference is last quarter earnings per share percentage gain, just like CGM and Pacific Horizon. Finally, as the fourth, we find that the projected book value growth rate had just edged out the estimated change in earnings per share for the coming fiscal year, giving us something new to consider. Yet the *basic structure of the fund is the same.* Any portfolio built using these factors will have quite similar returns.

Take 1991, for example. Use the projected book value growth rate figure found in AIM Constellation and build a model such that:

1. *Annual earnings per share gains exceed mean.* Twelve-month earnings per share percentage gains were greater than the database mean.

2. *Strong quarterly earnings gains.* Last quarter's earnings per share percentage gains were greater than the database mean.

3. *High estimated earnings gains.* Estimated percentage gains in earnings per share for the coming fiscal year are greater than the database mean.

4. *High 3- to 5-year gains projected.* Projected book value growth rates were greater than the database mean.

Suppose we then limit the portfolio to the ten stocks with the best 26-week price percentage gains. We'd end up with the stocks listed in Tables 5-16 and 5-17. The stocks were up 52 percent for the first six months and 47 percent for the last half of the year, for a total gain of 124 percent in 1991. While that's not as good as CGM's model, it's close because we are using a similar factor mix.

Continue to study great managers and see if they show you the way to a better factor combination. As you continue to analyze the best performers from a particular style, a handful of factors will emerge as the dominating or defining factors of that style.

Table 5-16. 10-Stock Portfolio as of
December 31, 1990

Ticker	Stock
CMH	Clayton Homes
USHC	U.S. Healthcare
APCC	American Power Conversion
USS	United States Surgical
SFDS	Smithfield Foods
CORD	Cordis Corp.
FSS	Federal Signal Corp.
BMET	Biomet
CQB	Chiquita Brands
NOVL	Novell, Inc.
RML	Russell
KR	Kroger

Table 5-17. 10-Stock Portfolio as of
June 30, 1991

Ticker	Stock
GGUY	The Good Guys
IGT	International Game Technology
CNC	Conseco
GNT	Green Tree Acceptance
GDX	Genovese Drug Stores
SMLS	SCI Med Life Systems
PHSY	Pacificare Health Systems
CCR	Countrywide Credit
SCH	Charles Schwab & Co.
DOLR	Dollar General Corp.
RML	Russell
KR	Kroger

You'll find the same factor structure as you go down the list of the best performing aggressive growth funds. Metlife-State Street Capital was the third best performing aggressive growth fund for the five years ending December 31, 1991, with an average annual gain of 20.36 percent. As of December 31, 1991, its top deviations from the database were:

1. *Positive relative strength.* A positive 26-week percentage change contrasts with a loss of 16 percent for the database, and 13-week gains were some 410 percent higher than the database average.

2. *High estimated earnings gains.* The estimated change for earnings per share for the coming fiscal year were 364 percent greater than the database average.

3. *Annual earnings per share gains exceed mean.* Twelve-month earnings per share percentage gains were 233 percent greater than the database average.

4. *Strong quarterly earnings gains.* Last quarter earnings per share percentage gains were 190 percent greater than the database average.

Looking at the fourth best five-year performer, Keystone American Omega fund, you find more of the same: great relative strength and 12-month earnings per share gains over 300 percent higher than the database. Estimated earnings aren't as high, but you get the idea: These funds all have an incredibly similar underlying factor structure.

What about the longer term? Looking at the best ten-year performer, Putnam Voyager, which turned in a decade-long performance of 477.18 percent, almost double that of the average aggressive growth fund, you see more similarities. Doing an analysis on December 31, 1991, you find that:

1. *Annual earnings per share gains exceed mean.* Twelve-month earnings per share percentage gains are 459 percent higher than the database average.

2. *Positive relative strength.* Thirteen-week price gains are 374 percent greater than the database average with positive 26-week gains, versus a 16-percent loss for the average stock in the database.

3. *Strong quarterly earnings gains.* Last quarter earnings per share percentage gains are 243 percent higher than the database average.

4. *High estimated earnings gains.* Estimated change in earnings per share for the coming fiscal year are more than 236 percent greater than the database average.

5. *High five-year growth rates.* Five-year earnings per share growth rates are 156 percent higher than the database average.

Again, you see all the familiar factors with the addition of five-year earnings per share growth rates. This didn't show up with the other managers primarily because the number of stocks with a figure for five-year earnings gains was too low to include in the analysis. You'll see these minor variations all the time. Many times a fund will have a market cap bias, or it will stress an additional factor along with the ones we see regularly in the best aggressive growth funds.

What All the Top Aggressive Growth Funds Have

The top aggressive growth funds invest in different stocks, but the underlying structure of their portfolios—their factor profiles—are virtually identical. With a few exceptions, all the top aggressive growth funds have:

- Exceptional 12-month earnings per share percentage gains.

- Outstanding relative price performance.

- Extremely high estimated gains for earnings per share percentage changes over the coming fiscal year.

These are the *core factors* of a successful aggressive growth strategy. You can use many variations. You can give the portfolio a big-cap or a small-cap tilt. You can attempt to dampen quarterly volatility by concentrating on stocks with a higher score on the price stability index or a lower rank for safety. Yet the *core factors* should always be included for maximum performance.

Learning More

If you're an aggressive investor, you'll want to learn more. You can never experiment too much. Try using Value Line's Timeliness rank with the common factors we identified in this chapter. See if you can reduce volatility yet still get great returns by adding a high five-year earnings per share growth rate, a high stability index number, or a high market cap to your model. Narrow down your list to ten stocks by experimenting with different final relative factors. The more you experiment, the better you'll become at identifying the best factors for each school of investing.

6
Building
a Winning
Growth Portfolio

Henrik Ibsen said that heroes of finance are like beads on a string: When one slips off, the rest follow. The same is true of mutual funds, with the best performing funds in the growth category slipping into the same factor profiles as their aggressive growth brethren.

The torturously named Fidelity Advisor Equity Portfolio: Growth, Institutional Class had the best five-year performance of the 381 growth funds in Morningstar, gaining 281.43 percent, compared to gains of 126.53 percent for the S&P 500 and 119.05 percent for the average growth fund. This achievement is worth emulating. But when you look at the portfolio's underlying factors, you see very few differences from other top-performing growth and aggressive growth funds. Tables 6-1 and 6-2 show the close similarity between this fund and CGM. It's just not worth building a new model to capture the small differences.

Institutional Managers Share
Primary Factors

Mutual funds are not the only ones that share similar underlying factor profiles. The same is true of the top private managers who invest for pension funds and wealthy individuals. For sev-

Table 6-1. Comparing Two Funds' Key Factors

Key factor	CGM Capital	Fidelity Advisor: Growth
12-month EPS % gain	1010% higher than database average	1367.57% higher than database average
Strong relative strength	26-week % gain 448% higher than database average	26-week % gain 443.94% higher than database average
Last quarter EPS % gain	285% higher than database average	281% higher than database average
Estimated change EPS fiscal year	265.8% higher than database average	157.59% higher than database average

Table 6-2. Comparing Two Funds' Secondary Factors

Secondary factor	CGM Capital	Fidelity Advisor: Growth
Price-to-book ratio	182% higher than database average	240% higher than database average
PE ratio	16% higher, high of 39	46% higher, high of 53
Return on net worth and plowback ratio	Both high	Both high
Projected 3-5 year growth in EPS and book value	Both high, projected book value growth double database average	Both high, projected book value growth more than double database average
Price-to-cash flow	High	High
Price-to-sales ratio	256% higher than database average	351% higher than database average
Margins	175% higher than database average	45% higher than database average

eral years, I've profiled the top managers in *Nelson's Directory of Investment Managers*, an annual guide that reviews over 1700 investment management firms. Here's a selection of their factor profiles over the last few years:

Norman L. Yu & Company. This growth manager's gain of 105.80 percent was one of the best in 1991. The key factors of the manager's top ten stock holdings on January 1, 1991 were:

1. *Annual earnings per share gains exceed mean.* The 12-month earnings per share percentage gains were 611 percent above the database mean.

2. *Big-cap stocks.* Market value was 398 percent above database mean, with a $887 million minimum.

3. *Strong quarterly earnings gains.* Last quarter earnings per share percentage gains were 276 percent above the database mean.

4. *Large number of shares outstanding.* This figure, 24 million, was 271 percent above the database mean.

5. *Positive relative strength.* Thirteen-week percentage gains 267 percent higher than the database mean.

6. *High estimated earnings gains.* The forecasted earnings per share gains for the next quarter are 258 percent higher than the database mean.

Insight Capital Management. This was one of the best performing growth managers of 1989, gaining 41.30 percent. The key factors of the manager's top ten stock holdings on January 1, 1990 were:

1. *Positive relative strength.* The 26-week price percentage gain was extremely high, at 44 percent, compared to a *loss* of 0.8 percent for the average stock in the database.

2. *Annual earnings per share gains exceed mean.* The 12-month earnings per share percentage gains were 492 percent higher than the database mean.

3. *Strong quarterly earnings gains.* Last quarter earnings per share percentage gains were 463 percent higher than the database mean.

4. *High estimated earnings gains.* The estimated change in earnings per share for the coming fiscal year is 289 percent higher than the database mean.

5. *High five-year growth rates.* Earnings per share growth rates over the last five years were 244 percent higher than the database mean.

6. *Excellent Timeliness ranks.* All Value Line Timeliness ranks were below 2.

Beacon Investment Company. For this, another of 1989's best performing growth managers, gaining 49.60 percent, the key differences from the database on January 1, 1990, were:

1. *Positive relative strength.* The 26-week price percentage gains were 10.08 percent, compared to a *loss* of 0.8 percent for the average stock in the database.

2. *Big-cap stocks.* Market values were 342 percent higher than the database average.

3. *High annual sales.* These were 217 percent higher than the database average.

4. *Large number of shares outstanding.* Shares outstanding was 240 percent higher than the database average.

5. *Strong quarterly earnings gains.* Last quarter earnings per share percentage gains were 191 percent higher than the database average.

6. *Annual earnings per share gains exceed mean.* The 12-month earnings per share percentage gains were 143 percent higher than the database average.

Provident Investment Counsel. Provident's return of 46.90 percent in 1989 made them the number one money manager with more than $1 billion under management. Its key factor differences from the database on January 1, 1990 were:

1. *Positive relative strength.* The 26-week price percentage gains were 20.60 percent, compared to a loss of 0.8 percent for the database.

2. *Big-cap stocks.* Market value was 387 percent higher than the database mean.

3. *Large number of shares outstanding.* Shares outstanding were 292 percent higher than the database mean.

4. *Strong quarterly earnings gains.* Last quarter earnings per share percentage gains were 287 percent higher than the database mean.

5. *Annual earnings per share gains exceed mean.* The 12-month earnings per share percentage gains were 197 percent higher than the database mean.

6. *High estimated earnings gains.* Estimates for the coming fiscal year expect earnings to grow at rates 143 percent higher than the database mean.

The pattern continues, with each of the top growth managers in recent years showing the same key factor deviations from the database. Clearly, the profiles aren't identical and have many small differences. Some managers have a large-cap bias. Others buy only stocks with a Timeliness rank of 2 or better. Still others insist on very high returns on net worth. The list of secondary differences is endless and will give you many ideas for testing. Yet the underlying consistency of the best growth managers should not be forgotten.

Testing Two Models

Let's now test two new growth models. The first is based on the big-cap bias that the previously mentioned money managers share, and the second is based on another private manager that I emulated several years ago. We'll also learn about risk-adjusted return, a better way to determine how well a strategy performs.

Adding a Big-Cap Bias

Many of the best performing managers in 1989 had a big-cap bias. They shared the same commitment to stocks with great earnings gains and relative strength as CGM and the other top-performing growth managers, but the stocks they bought were much larger and had greater trading liquidity than the database average. Let's create a growth model that adds these factors. Table 6-3 shows the model.

Table 6-3. Value/Screen Database Screen after Running a Big-Cap Growth Model on January 1, 1993 Data

Variable	<=>	Value	Number of stocks
Market value	≥	800	805
Shares outstanding	≥	30	731
12-month EPS % chg	≥	20	174
26-wk % price chg	≥	20	59
Est % chg EPS fis yr	≥	80.50	10

The minimums for market value and shares outstanding were set rather arbitrarily, borrowing figures from a big-cap, high-yield model. Requiring market values above $800 million and shares outstanding above 30 million eliminates more than half of the database. Thus, we're now applying growth factors to a larger, more mature group of stocks than we did with the CGM model. We'll borrow the next three factors from the CGM model:

1. All 12-month earnings per share percentage gains must be above 20.

2. The 26-week percentage price gain must be above 20, *or a number that leaves you with ten stocks.* (Many big-cap stocks fail to make such a high relative strength cut-off, forcing you to make this the relative factor that leaves you with ten stocks.)

3. The estimated percentage gain for earnings per share for the next fiscal year will be a relative number, using whatever figure leaves you with ten stocks. In some cases, you will not need this factor because the 26-week percentage price gain served as the final factor.

That's all there is to this model. In essence, we're grafting a large capitalization profile onto the Momentum Growth Model. Table 6-4 shows the ten-stock portfolio on January 1, 1993.

Table 6-4. 10 Stocks Recommended on January 1, 1993

Ticker	Stock	Industry
BGEN	Biogen	Drug
BK	Bank of New York	Bank
CTX	Centex Corp.	Homebuilding
CRFC	Crestar Financial	Bank
EMC	EMC Corp.	Computer
LPX	Louisiana-Pacific	Paper
MRV	Marvel Entertainment	Publishing
ORCL	Oracle Systems	Computer software
PGR	Progressive	Insurance
LUV	Southwest Air	Air Transport

The portfolio's key differences from the database average are:

1. Twelve-month earnings per share percentage gains are 806 percent higher than the database average.
2. Last quarter earnings per share percentage gains are 650 percent higher than the database average.
3. The estimated percentage change in earnings per share for the next quarter is 431 percent higher than the database average.
4. The estimated percentage change in earnings per share for the coming fiscal year is 412 percent higher than the database average.
5. Relative strength is high, with 26-week percentage gains 410 percent higher than the database average.

Figures 6-1 and 6-2 show some additional deviations from the database. Note that market value and shares outstanding fail to make the list. The average market value for the ten stocks is a little over $2 billion, *26 percent lower than the average stock in the database.* The same is true for shares outstanding. The high minimums for earnings gains and relative strength kept the market

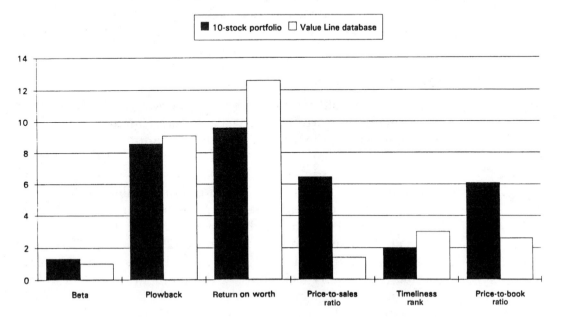

Figure 6-1. Factor profiles of 10-stock portfolio and Value Line database.

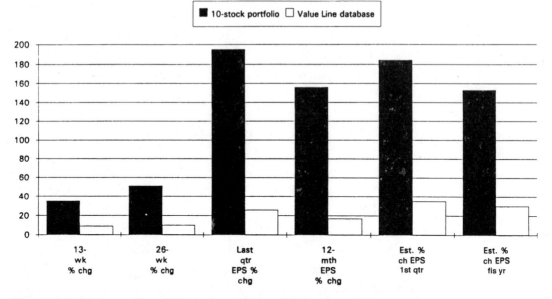

Figure 6-2. Factor profiles of 10-stock portfolio and Value Line database.

cap of the stocks in the portfolio lower since really big-cap stocks rarely have huge earnings gains. Making $800 million your cut-off, however, assures that any company on the list is *not* a small-cap stock and has a great deal of liquidity and market presence. Let's test it out.

Historical Performance Results

Do the same historical test as before, checking performance and rebalancing the portfolio every six months. The 26-week relative strength was the final, relative factor three times: on December 31, 1986, December 31, 1987, and December 31, 1990. That's not surprising since each six-month period before these dates saw broad market declines. Table 6-5 shows the results of our test.

For the seven years between December 31, 1985 and December 31, 1992, the model had a cumulative gain of 477.94 percent, or an average annual return of 28.48 percent. That beat every mutual fund in the Morningstar database over the same period, but it falls well short of the momentum model developed in Chap. 4, which had a return of 721.37 percent during the same period.

Table 6-5. Performance Results of the Model from
December 31, 1985 through December 31, 1992

Time period	Portfolio performance (%)
December 31, 1985–June 30, 1986	43.3
June 30, 1986–December 31, 1986	−3.9
1986, full year	**36.75**
December 31, 1986–June 30, 1987	41.62
June 30, 1987–December 31, 1987	−16.50
1987, full year	**18.25**
December 31, 1987–June 30, 1988	4.34
June 30, 1988–December 31, 1988	4.2
1988, full year	**8.73**
December 31, 1988–June 30, 1989	21.26
June 30, 1989–December 31, 1989	11.27
1989, full year	**34.93**
December 31, 1989–June 30, 1990	7.2
June 30, 1990–December 31, 1990	−6.94
1990, full year	**−0.24**
December 31, 1990–June 30, 1991	29.6
June 30, 1991–December 31, 1991	49.9
1991, full year	**94.27**
December 31, 1991–June 30, 1992	−6.4
June 30, 1992–December 31, 1992	34.3
1992, full year	**25.70**

Using Standard Deviations to Compare
Risk-Adjusted Returns

One of the reasons the Momentum Growth Model did so much better was that it wasn't restricted to larger stocks. Very often, great earnings gains come from small, volatile companies. You might intuitively guess that a portfolio made up of larger-cap and more mature stocks would be less risky than a portfolio without such restrictions. Let's test this by looking at the strategy's *standard deviation of return, spread, and risk-adjusted return,* common measurements of an investment's risk.

The standard deviation of return is the positive square root of the variance and one of the most commonly used measures of dispersion. This sounds difficult, but it's easily calculated using any computer spreadsheet's preprogrammed function. Simply enter the returns and use the spreadsheet's built-in function to arrive at the standard deviation. Generally, the higher the standard deviation, the riskier the strategy is.

You use the standard deviation to arrive at the strategy's spread, or the range of returns that can be expected from a strategy. You establish a strategy's spread by:

1. Multiplying the standard deviation by 2.
2. Adding this number to the strategy's mean return to get the maximum expected return.
3. Subtracting this number from the strategy's mean return to arrive at the minimum expected return.
4. Finally, subtracting the minimum from the maximum to get the overall spread.

Assuming that stock returns are normally distributed, 95 percent of all returns will fall between the two extremes and within the overall spread figure. You can therefore use this information to forecast a strategy's worst expected loss to its best expected gain.

This works in reality: The S&P 500's mean return over the last 64 years was 11.47 percent, with a standard deviation of 20.29 percent. With normally distributed returns, you can safely say that 95 percent of all returns from the S&P 500 should fall between −29.12 percent and 52.05 percent. [The mean return, 11.47%, minus (2 × 20.29%) gives you the low figure, whereas the mean plus (2 × 20.29%) gives you the high.] Reviewing the S&P's actual returns for the 64 years shows that only three periods, or 4.69 percent of all returns, were outside that spread, with 95.31 percent of all returns within the spread.

You also use the standard deviation to derive a strategy's risk-adjusted return, which measures how well it did after volatility is taken into account. To get this number, divide the mean return by the standard deviation of return. This figure shows whether the risk a strategy took was justified.

Table 6-6 compares the semiannual returns from four strategies: the Momentum Growth Model based on CGM, the larger-cap version just reviewed, CGM mutual fund, and a Vanguard fund that duplicates the return of the S&P 500. (*Note:* I used semiannual rather than annual returns to increase the accuracy of the standard deviation of return.)

Table 6-6. Contrasting Returns Using Standard Deviations

Time period	Momentum Model based on CGM (%)	Big-cap growth model (%)	CGM Mutual Fund (%)	Vanguard S&P 500 Index Fund (%)
December 31, 1985–June 30, 1986	47.1	43.30	35.81	20.53
June 30, 1986–December 31, 1986	−7.26	−3.39	−5.42	−2.06
December 31, 1986–June 30, 1987	33.65	41.62	32.38	27.27
June 30, 1987–December 31, 1987	−9.90	−16.50	−12.45	−17.73
December 31, 1987–June 30, 1988	6.0	4.34	0.95	12.48
June 30, 1988–December 31, 1988	21.99	4.20	−1.25	3.33
December 31, 1988–June 30, 1989	21.8	21.26	10.59	16.44
June 30, 1989–December 31, 1989	9.47	11.27	6.44	12.83
December 31, 1989–June 30, 1990	14.80	7.20	16.65	2.98
June 30, 1990–December 31, 1990	2.60	−6.94	−13.0	−6.12
December 31, 1990–June 30, 1991	50.50	29.60	40.70	14.15
June 30, 1991–December 31, 1991	63.80	49.90	41.48	14.09
December 31, 1990–June 30, 1991	−15.50	−6.40	−6.98	−0.77
June 30, 1991–December 31, 1991	18.20	34.30	26.30	8.23
Average	18.38	15.23	12.30	7.55
Standard deviation	22.80	20.61	19.12	11.34
Maximum expected return	63.97	56.45	50.54	30.23
Minimum expected return	−27.22	−25.98	−25.94	−15.14
Spread	91.19	82.43	76.47	45.38
Risk-adjustment (mean ÷ standard deviation)	0.81	0.74	0.64	0.67

Our intuition about the larger-cap fund proved correct, but not by much. Its standard deviation is 2.19 percent lower than the Momentum Growth Model, but its mean return was 3.15 percent lower, translating into a *lower* risk-adjusted rate of return.

Vanguard's S&P 500 clone is decidedly less risky than either the Momentum or big-cap models—its standard deviation is just 11.34 percent—yet it also has a much more limited maximum and much lower minimum expected return. The lower the risk, the lower the potential reward there is on an *absolute basis*. By looking at the risk-adjusted return (the mean divided by the standard deviation), you can see whether the additional risk of investing in more volatile securities is justified. Generally, the higher the risk-adjusted rate of return, the more you are being compensated for the risk you're taking. For example, the Momentum Growth Model's risk-adjusted return of 0.81 is much higher than the S&P 500's 0.67, suggesting that the investor will be well compensated for assuming additional risk.

If you're a longer-term investor (five years or more), a good rule of thumb is to choose the strategy with the largest spread and a high risk-adjusted return. For example, the momentum model has a spread of 91.19 percent between high and low [63.97% − (−27.22%)] *and* a risk-adjusted return of 0.81. That's better than the bigger-cap strategy's spread of 82.43 and risk-adjusted return of 0.74.

Numerous studies I've done show that the best strategies have a risk-adjusted return of at least 0.80 when measured over 14 semiannual periods. The longer the time horizon, however, the lower the acceptable risk-adjusted return is. A strategy that I tested back to 1928—buying the five lowest-priced members of the top ten yielding stocks in the Dow Jones Industrial Average—had a risk-adjusted return of 0.64 for a 64-year period, compared to the S&P 500's rating of 0.57. Yet the strategy still managed to turn a hypothetical $10,000 invested on December 31, 1928 into $29,071,395 as of December 31, 1992. The same $10,000 invested in the S&P 500 would be worth just $3,266,476, proving that a little risk-adjusted advantage can go a long way.

If you can't focus on the long term, or may need to liquidate your investments at any given time or simply can't emotionally tolerate volatility, choose the strategy that has the narrowest spread but a high risk-adjusted return rating. You'll face much lower volatility and still hold a portfolio with high risk-adjusted returns.

Tested on Mutual Funds

These methods are also useful in deciding which mutual fund to invest in. Using risk-adjusted return to test the 14 aggressive growth funds in Morningstar with records going back to 1976, I used the returns generated between 1976 and 1983 to determine which funds *should* do the best over the next seven years. Table 6-7 shows the results.

Each of the first four funds had a high spread, but their risk-adjusted rates of return were below 0.80, indicating too much risk was taken for the reward achieved. The first fund with a high spread *and* a risk-adjusted return above 0.80 was Alliance Quasar, which went on to turn in the best annual returns for the next seven-year period.

Dreyfus Capital Growth had the lowest spread *and* a good risk-adjusted return, making it the choice for investors who couldn't make a long-term commitment. Its 15.63 percent average annual return over the subsequent seven-year period was quite respectable considering the fund's low spread and standard deviation.

Obviously, these numbers are always changing and should simply serve as an additional guide after you've determined that a strategy makes sense and has consistently good returns.

The Importance of Multiyear Studies

Looking at returns over a number of years is also important. When you get past seven years, you can make reliable assumptions about a strategy, particularly whether it's something worth using. Some pension consultants make use of a branch of statistics called *reliability mathematics* to analyze past performance and to make predictions about future performance. They've found that analyzing performance over at least 14 periods (in this case, we used semiannual returns over seven years to get our 14 periods) helps you predict which manager will do better than the market in the future. Such predictions are 83 percent accurate and help identify managers or strategies that took excessive risk or had all of their return advantage come from one or two periods.

Table 6-7. Standard Deviations of Return, Spreads, and Risk-Adjusted Returns on 14 Aggressive Growth Mutual Funds for the 7 Years Between December 31, 1975 and December 31, 1982 Along with Subsequent 7-Year Performance Figures, Ranked by Spread

Fund	Average semiannual return (1975–1982, %)	Standard deviation (%)	Spread (%)	Risk-adjusted return	Average annual return (1982–1989, %)
AIM Constellation	13.05	23.71	94.85	0.55	16.08
Keystone Custodian	11.83	22.96	91.85	0.52	7.93
Security Ultra	14.70	21.76	87.03	0.68	8.12
Seligman Capital	12.66	18.44	73.76	0.69	11.40
Alliance Quasar	16.0	18.40	73.61	0.87	17.42
Steinroe Capital	12.61	17.91	71.62	0.70	9.65
Value Line Special Situation	14.35	17.30	69.21	0.83	3.75
Founders Special	11.21	16.88	67.51	0.66	14.09
Keystone Omega	8.21	16.01	64.04	0.51	16.63
Putnam Voyager A	11.01	14.88	59.51	0.74	16.61
Delaware Trend	10.47	11.73	46.93	0.89	14.92
Value Line Leveraged	15.34	11.24	44.96	1.36	12.20
Financial Dynamics	10.04	11.17	44.70	0.90	8.57
Dreyfus Capital Growth	8.94	10.31	41.26	0.87	15.63

A Mediocre Manager Masquerading as a Star

To see how useful these tools are, let's look at an emulation of a private growth manager whose returns were mediocre for several years and yet who *looked outstanding because of one great year.*

The manager's key factors were:

1. Five-year earnings per share growth rates were 310 percent higher than the database average.

2. Market capitalization was 238 percent higher.

3. All stocks had a Value Line Timeliness rank of 1 or 2.

4. Last quarter earnings per share percentage gains were 160 percent higher than the database average.

5. The 12-month earnings per share percentage gains were 149 percent higher than the database mean.

This looks like a promising strategy, and translates easily into the multifactor model in Table 6-8.

Limiting Timeliness to 2 or better eliminates 1204 stocks, or 75 percent of the database. Next, require that market capitalization, last quarter earnings per share percentage change, and 12-month earnings per share percentage change figures be equal to or greater than the mean. Finally, make the relative factor five-year earnings per share growth rates, picking as the minimum the number that leaves ten stocks. Table 6-9 lists the stocks making the cut on January 1, 1993, and Table 6-10 compares this ten-stock portfolio's key factors with the manager's portfolio.

Table 6-8. Value/Screen Database Screen after Running 5-Factor Big-Cap Growth Model on January 1, 1993

Variable	<=>	Value	Number of stocks
Time	≤	2	396
Market value	≥	2825.8	104
Last qtr EPS % chg	≥	26	30
12-month EPS % chg	≥	17.2	20
5-yr EPS growth	≥	25	10

Table 6-9. 10 Stocks Recommended on January 1, 1993

Ticker	Stock	Industry
ABX	American Barrick	Gold/silver mining
CTB	Cooper Tire	Tire/rubber
GLK	Great Lakes Chemical	Chemical
HD	Home Depot	Building supply
IGT	International Game Tech.	Hotel/gaming
MCCS	Medco Containment	Medical supply
MSFT	Microsoft	Computer software
NOVL	Novell	Computer software
ORCL	Oracle Systems	Computer software
UNH	United Healthcare	Medical services

Table 6-10. Comparison of Private Manager's Key Factors and Our 10-Stock Portfolio

Factor	Private manager's difference from database	10-stock portfolio's difference from database
5-year EPS growth rates	310% higher	490% higher
Market capitalization	238% higher	186% higher
Timeliness ranks	1 or 2	1 or 2
Last quarter EPS percentage gain	160% higher	136% gain higher
12-month EPS percentage gain	149% higher	250% higher

Looking at Historical Results

Now that we've replicated the manager's key factors, we'll do the same six-month rebalancing historical performance test we've done on all the other models. Table 6-11 shows the results.

The model had a seven-year return of 278.93 percent, or 20.96 percent on an average annual basis. Over the last five years, between December 31, 1987 and December 31, 1992, the strategy

Table 6-11. Performance Results of 5-Factor Model
from December 31, 1985 through December 31, 1992

Time period	Portfolio performance (%)
December 31, 1985–June 30, 1986	41.90
June 30, 1986–December 31, 1986	−15.80
1986, full year	**19.48**
December 31, 1986–June 30, 1987	57.70
June 30, 1987–December 31, 1987	−35.70
1987, full year	**1.40**
December 31, 1987–June 30, 1988	12.60
June 30, 1988–December 31, 1988	−5.10
1988, full year	**12.60**
December 31, 1988–June 30, 1989	12.70
June 30, 1989–December 31, 1989	10.30
1989, full year	**24.31**
December 31, 1989–June 30, 1990	26.20
June 30, 1990–December 31, 1990	−12.40
1990, full year	**10.55**
December 31, 1990–June 30, 1991	37.45
June 30, 1991–December 31, 1991	51.0
1991, full year	**107.55**
December 31, 1991–June 30, 1992	−15.90
June 30, 1992–December 31, 1992	22.10
1992, full year	**2.70**

had an average annual gain of 25.63 percent. This is a great record, considering only eight nonspecialty funds in the Morningstar database did better in those five years and that, of those, only two did better over the full seven-year period.

However, on closer inspection, you see that this is a mediocre strategy that takes far too much risk and owes *all* of its glow to a good 1990 and an outstanding 1991. Between 1985 and 1990, this strategy had a total return of 77.80 percent, which is 4.66 percent *less* than a fund that mimics the S&P 500. More, it delivered less on both an absolute *and* relative basis. The strategy's standard deviation for the 1985–1990 period was 26.55 percent, more than double the 12.82 percent figure for Vanguard's S&P 500 fund.

We see the same lessons on a risk-adjusted basis that we see looking at absolute returns. Table 6-12 compares the strategy's

Table 6-12. Contrasting Returns on Risk-Adjusted Basis

Time period	Momentum Growth Model based on CGM (%)	First big-cap growth Model (%)	"Mediocre" growth model (%)	Vanguard S&P 500 Index Fund (%)
December 31, 1985–June 30, 1986	47.1	43.30	41.90	20.53
June 30, 1986–December 31, 1986	–7.26	–3.39	–15.80	–2.06
December 31, 1986–June 30, 1987	33.65	41.62	57.70	27.27
June 30, 1987–December 31, 1987	–9.90	–16.50	–35.70	–17.73
December 31, 1987–June 30, 1988	6.0	4.34	12.60	12.48
June 30, 1988–December 31, 1988	21.99	4.20	–5.10	3.33
December 31, 1988–June 30, 1989	21.8	21.26	12.70	16.44
June 30, 1989–December 31, 1989	9.47	11.27	10.30	12.83
December 31, 1989–June 30, 1990	14.80	7.20	26.20	2.98
June 30, 1990–December 31, 1990	2.60	–6.94	–12.40	–6.12
December 31, 1990–June 30, 1991	50.50	29.60	37.45	14.15
June 30, 1991–December 31, 1991	63.80	49.90	51.0	14.09
December 31, 1991–June 30, 1992	–15.50	–6.40	–15.90	–0.77
June 30, 1992–December 31, 1992	18.20	34.30	22.10	8.23
Average	18.38	15.23	13.36	7.55
Standard deviation	22.80	20.61	26.92	11.34
Maximum expected return	63.97	56.45	67.20	30.23
Minimum expected return	–27.22	–25.98	–40.49	–15.14
Spread	91.19	82.43	107.69	45.38
Risk-adjustment (mean ÷ standard deviation)	0.81	0.74	0.50	0.67

risk-adjusted return and spread with some other strategies and funds. The strategy had a huge spread of 107.69 percent and a risk-adjusted return of 0.50, one of the lowest seen thus far.

This is very important information to use when comparing strategies, since it is the only way to understand if risk is being compensated. As we learned in Chap. 1, almost any fund with a growth bias did well in 1991. This strategy was "in the right place at the right time" for its 1991 gain of 107.55 percent, but only investors using multiyear reviews and risk analysis would know, to paraphrase Cole Porter, that even though it was in the right place at the right time, this strategy had the wrong face. There's no way to know if a strategy is truly superior by looking at just one or two years of performance data. Even three-year returns can mislead: between December 31, 1989 and December 31, 1992, this strategy had an average annual gain of 33.07 percent, with only two funds in Morningstar doing better.

Always Do a Multiyear Review of Risk-Adjusted Returns

Thus, after you've designed a strategy that makes sense and has both logical and intuitive appeal, make sure to:

1. Test several years of the strategy's performance to see if it owes all of its performance advantage to one or two years.

2. Look at the standard deviation, spread, and risk-adjusted returns. Generally, an aggressive investor would choose strategies with large spreads and high risk-adjusted returns (over 0.80 for 14 measurement periods, less for longer ones). Risk-averse investors would look for low spreads that still had good risk-adjusted returns.

3. Keep a record of all your findings. You'll see that the same factors keep turning up in strategies with high risk-adjusted returns *and* in strategies with low risk-adjusted returns. Use this information as feedback when designing additional models.

Identifying the Worst Potential Performers

Factor profiles and risk-adjusted returns also help to identify strategies that will do poorly. Using mutual funds again as an example, searching Morningstar for funds that did worse than the average fund over the last five and ten years turns up a sorry group.

One is a growth fund that actually beat the S&P 500 between 1975 and 1982—providing a 15.02 percent average annual return compared to the S&P 500's 11.81 percent—only to turn in the *worst* ten-year performance of all the growth funds, gaining a paltry 34.11 percent when the S&P 500 gained 358.58 percent. You certainly couldn't use the fund's absolute prior performance to forecast this performance, since it had beaten the S&P 500 between 1975 and 1982. The only way to forecast this type of trouble back in 1982 would have been to look at the fund's risk-adjusted return and factor profile. While it managed to beat the S&P 500 between 1975 and 1992, its high standard deviation and very low risk-adjusted return of 0.50 were warnings to stay away from the fund.

Factor Analysis Confirms Risk-Adjusted Analysis

Doing a factor analysis of the fund's current stocks shows that they haven't gotten any better. Whereas the top performers have consistently skewed portfolios, this fund's factors are all over the map. Two of its top deviations from the database indicate a large-cap bias, with the third (positive relative strength) indicating a momentum strategy. Yet *all earnings changes are negative, from last quarter to five-year growth rates.* More, only one of the earnings forecasts is above the database mean, with all others flat or below it.

This might lead you to guess that they use a value strategy, but once again you'd be wrong. The price-to-sales ratio average is actually 305 percent higher than the database (normally a secondary factor for stocks with huge earnings gains). Price-to-earnings ratios are similar to the database and the yield is slightly below. It's not a "quality" style since the portfolio's financial strength rating is B+ (the same as the database), and its price stability is 20 percent lower, indicating slightly riskier stocks. The portfolio is also "distinguished" in owning *no* stocks with a Value Line Timeliness rank of 1! The portfolio has *no underlying factor consistency. It's neither fish nor fowl and has no thematic, understandable unifying factor profile that would indicate a well thought-out strategy.*

When you see a portfolio without a highly defined factor profile and a very low risk-adjusted return, you can almost always guarantee that it will do substantially worse than the market in the future.

Continually Testing the Style

An old joke says that there are more money management *styles* than money managers. Indeed, there are innumerable ways to build a growth portfolio. Yet if you use factor modeling, coupled with a statistical test of risk-adjusted return, spread, and reliability analysis, you can see that very *few* growth styles or models provide superior returns on a risk-adjusted basis. Our method lets you see that what might appear conservative on the surface is actually a less profitable, riskier portfolio and vice versa.

For example, take a conservative growth investor who holds 20 stocks and rebalances the portfolio once a year. Assume that each of his or her stocks must meet the following criteria:

1. Financial strength greater than A, thus excluding all but the most financially secure companies

2. Cash flows above the Value Line mean

3. Return on net worth greater than the Value Line mean

4. 26-week price percentage gain above the Value Line mean

5. Estimated change in earnings per share for the coming fiscal year set to the number that leaves you with 20 stocks

Table 6-13 shows the portfolio as of January 1, 1993. It's filled with companies that are household names like Quaker Oats, Nike, and Procter & Gamble. All meet the highest financial standards and have excellent earnings prospects for the coming year. This portfolio is indistinguishable from hundreds of other growth-oriented funds. Yet even a brief comparative look at its historical performance shows that you could do much better at the same level of risk. From 1988 on, this strategy did better than the S&P 500 only in 1990 and 1991. It turned in a *loss* of 1.2 percent in 1992, compared to a *gain* of over 7.0 percent for the S&P 500. Our momentum growth model also turned in a flat performance in 1992, but that was after a gain of 145 percent in 1991! This strategy returned just 39.9 percent in 1991.

Table 6-13. 20 Stock Conservative Growth Portfolio on January 1, 1992

Ticker	Stock	Financial strength
OAT	Quaker Oats	A
GCI	Gannett	A+
MDT	Medtronic	A+
SGP	Schering Plough	A+
SONO	Sonoco Products	A
NKE	Nike	A+
TMX	Telefonos De Mexico	A
UNP	Union Pacific	A+
BOL	Bausch & Lomb	A+
WLA	Warner Lambert	A+
ROK	Rockwell International	A+
TR	Tootsie Roll	A
UVV	Universal Corp.	A
PG	Procter & Gamble	A++
IFF	International Flavors & Frag	A++
SBC	Southwestern Bell	A+
WIN	Winn Dixie Stores	A++
INTC	Intel	A+
BL	Blair Corp.	A
ESY	E-Systems	A+

Putting It All Together

Superior models for growth investing share similar underlying factors. Several of the models we tested show that most models, even those that do much better than the market on an absolute basis, offer mediocre results on a risk-adjusted return basis. It's vital to use risk-adjusted returns when selecting a stock market strategy because we don't invest historically but in "real time." The impulse when reviewing a model's performance is to choose the one with the highest absolute return, whatever its standard deviation. Yet history is bloodless, and the "obvious" always looks it because it's unclouded by emotions. Portfolios with high standard deviations are likely to go down more during market breaks—causing great emotional jitters at precisely the time you're most likely to abandon the strategy, leaving you with a larger loss. Volatility is a two-edged sword. You can use it to decide whether you want a portfolio that lets you eat well or sleep well. In "real time," your emotions are ever-present. So you *must* understand the implications of a high standard deviation.

Additionally, many strategies achieve great absolute returns by hitting a homerun in one or two years and striking out in the rest—something that only risk-adjusted return can tell you. Thus, it's vital to look at the whole picture before embarking on any investment course.

7

Emulating a Top Value Investor

There are two main types of investors.

First is the aggressive investor who might identify with a quote from the legendary Jim Fiske, a robber baron and Wall Street speculator who wreaked havoc in his attempt to corner the gold market and who forced the U.S. government to flood the market with gold, foiling Fiske's scheme. To the hue and cry that resulted from his actions, Fiske replied, "A fellow can't have a little innocent fun without everyone raising a halo and going wild." To him, the only sensible market position was full exposure to risk to maximize capital gains.

The second type is a very different sort: These investors would find far more truth in Mark Twain's observation of the stock market: "October. This is one of the peculiarly dangerous months to speculate in stocks. The others are July, January, September, April, November, May, March, June, December, August, and February." To these investors, taking a plunge on growth stocks would cause anxiety and sleeplessness. They want a portfolio of reliable stocks that deliver high income with some potential for capital gain. They play the tortoise to the aggressive investor's hare.

Let's focus now on the market's tortoises. Buying big, safe stocks with high yields is the dominant investment theme among the equity-income tortoises. Searching for a manager to emulate, we'll scan the Morningstar on two criteria: First, we'll limit our funds to the equity-income category; second, we'll require that they yield more than 4 percent.

On January 1, 1993, only 16 funds in the Morningstar database met these two requirements. The 16 funds, as a group, had an average yield of 5.37 percent, much higher than the S&P 500's. Yet their average annual five-year total return was just 12.46 percent, well below the S&P 500's 17.45 percent. The search for high yields leads investors to slow growth industries such as natural resources, finance, and electric utilities, whose companies, heavily regulated and rarely showing impressive earnings gains, are bought strictly for their yield and not their capital appreciation potential.

Since the equity-income style is so conservative, it's sensible to focus on five-year performance rankings and find the steady performer that does well year-in and year-out. The fund with the best five-year total return is the Shearson Premium Total Return B fund. The fund was the only one of the 16 to beat the S&P 500 over the last five years, gaining 137.34 percent compared to the S&P 500's 126.53 percent.

In the analyst's commentary, however, we find a problem. She says: "There is one area … where the fund pales in comparison to its peers—yield. Although the fund pays a high distribution, it's rarely pure income…." She states that Shearson pays out a lot, even if it must come from capital appreciation. Thus, even though the fund made our dividend cut-off, we see it's not purely from yield. Since an investor looking for a high-yield portfolio wouldn't consider a payout from capital to be a dividend, we'll skip this fund and move on to the next.

USAA Mutual Income Stock Fund

The second best-performing fund is the USAA Mutual Income Stock Fund. It had a total return of 112.60 percent for the five years ending December 31, 1992. While underperforming the S&P 500, it still ranks above the average equity-income fund.

In the analyst's commentary, we find that USAA boasts a 5.1 percent distributed yield, 1.3 percent higher than its average rival. The analyst says: "Credit for the fund's yield success goes to Miller's [the fund manager] strict buy criteria. By charter, he can't buy stocks that yield less than the S&P 500, and the portfolio as a whole must pay out 200 basis points [2%] more than the broad market." This comment should go right in your journal, since it's more than just the manager's rule of thumb, it's an iron-clad buy rule that you can easily transfer into a factor screen.

USAA's Stocks

In the Stock Report section, we see that the $480 million portfolio is invested in 45 stocks across several industries. Investments are of roughly equal weight, with Bristol-Myers Squibb, the fund's top holding, accounting for 3.84 percent of the portfolio and UST, the fund's smallest holding, accounting for 0.13 percent of the portfolio. Table 7-1 shows the portfolio's stocks covered in the Value/Screen database.

Following the method in Chap. 3, we enter these stocks into the Value Line database and proceed with a factor analysis. Tables 7-2 through 7-4 show the results.

USAA's Key Factors

Tables 7-5 and 7-6 list USAA's key and secondary factors. In many respects, this portfolio is the opposite of our growth funds: All earnings per share percentage gains are substantially below the database average, as are most forecasted earnings. Relative strength is negative. The two largest deviations from the database highlight the enormous market capitalization of the stocks in the portfolio. The average sales of the stocks in USAA's portfolio are over $14 billion dollars, 314 percent higher than the database. The *smallest* annual sales figure is $865 million. The average stock in USAA's portfolio has a market capitalization of $11.5 billion, 305 percent higher than the average stock in the Value Line. The smallest stock in the portfolio has a market capitalization of $908 million. *These are huge companies when compared to the average stock in the database.* The third largest deviation concerns liquidity. Besides being among the biggest market cap stocks in the database, they also have the most shares outstanding. The average number of shares outstanding for the USAA portfolio is 234 million, almost 200 percent higher than the database. The minimum is 30 million shares.

Yield is the next important factor. The average stock in the portfolio has a yield of 5.31 percent, with a minimum yield of 3.20 percent, *142 percent higher* than the database average. Finally, we see that USAA's stocks have strong cash flows per

Table 7-1. USAA Mutual Income Fund's Stocks Also in the Value/Screen Database on January 1, 1993

Ticker	Company	Industry
AMB	American Brands	Tobacco
BT	Bankers Trust	Bank
BBI	Barnett Banks	Bank
BMY	Brist-Myers Squibb	Drug
CMB	Chase Manhattan	Bank
CI	Cigna Corp.	Insurance
CIC	Continental Corp.	Insurance
DOW	Dow Chemical	Chemical
FTX	Freeport-McMoran	Copper
GTE	GTE Corp.	Telecommunications
HPC	Hercules	Chemical
HOU	Houston Ind.	Electric utility
IBM	International Business Machines	Computer
LYO	Lyondell Petrochemical	Chemical
NFG	National Fuel Gas	Natural gas
GAS	Nicor	Natural gas
NU	Northeast Utilities	Electric utility
NYN	NYNEX Corp.	Telecommunications
OXY	Occidental Petroleum	Petroleum
PCG	Pacific G&E	Electric utility
MO	Philip Morris	Tobacco
PSR	Public Service	Electric utility
SCE	SCE Corp.	Electric utility
SO	Southern Co.	Electric utility
TX	Texaco	Petroleum
TXU	Texas Utilities	Electric utility
TIC	Travelers Corp.	Insurance
XRX	Xerox Corp.	Office equipment

Table 7-2. Results of USAA Mutual Income's Factor Analysis on January 1, 1993

Variable	High	Low	Mean	Value Line mean	Difference (%)
Timeliness rank	5	2	3	3	0
Safety rank	4	1	2	3	−33
Financial strength	B	A++	B++	B+	Higher
Industry rank	97	10	57	48	18
Price stability	100	30	81	52	55
Beta	1.5	0.65	0.92	1.02	−10
Current EPS	8.89	−2.12	3.14	1.71	84
Current dividend	4.64	1	2.28	.7	226
Technical rank	4	2	3	3	0
Recent price	84	17.13	45.04	29.28	54
52-week high	100.38	22.44	50.68	33.84	50
52-week low	69.5	15.75	37.69	22.05	71
Current PE	45	7	16	17.8	−11
Current yield	7.3	3.20	5.31	2.2	142
Price-to-book	16.09	0.57	2.56	2.62	−2.15
13-week % price change	30	−38.4	2.24	9.1	−75
26-week % price change	22.3	−49.4	3	10	−70
Market value ($ mill)	71,633	908	11,467	2828.5	305

share: The minimum is $2.03, and the average of $6.90 is 128 percent above the database.

Building a Model

USAA's factors are very straightforward: They buy huge companies with strong cash flows and high yields. Now design the factor model using the same technique used with our growth managers. Go down the list of key factor deviations found in Table 7-5 and make them the criteria for this model.

1. *Annual sales.* Use USAA's minimum by requiring that all

Table 7-3. USAA Mutual Income Factors on January 1, 1993

Variable	High	Low	Mean	Value Line mean	Difference (%)
Sales ($ mill)	64,792	865	14,134	3415	314
% ret net worth	35.5	2.7	12.96	12.6	2.85
% retained to common	67.2	0.4	7.83	9.1	−13.9
Book value per share	81.93	1.53	28.47	14.97	90.16
Debt as % of capital	85	2	43	32	34
Last qtr EPS % chg	43.1	−92.6	−6.76	26	−126
12-month EPS % chg	99.2	−88.6	−0.37	17.2	−102
5-yr EPS growth	25.5	−26	.26	8.2	−97
5-yr div growth	33	−4.5	6.02	9.6	−37.3
5-yr bk val growth	19.5	−11	2.35	9.3	−75
Est. % chg EPS qt. 1	1000	−40	43.46	34.7	25.2
Est. % chg EPS qt. 2	233.3	−91.7	18.52	41.9	−56
Est. % chg EPS fis yr	145.8	−89.2	5.2	29.9	−83
Prj 3-5 yr apprec %	212	−10	40.61	74	−45.1
Prj EPS growth	50.5	1.5	10.56	15.3	−31
Prj div growth	17	−10	3.3	6.6	−50
Prj book val growth	36	−2.5	5.80	9.3	−38
Prj 3-5 yr av return	36	3	12.57	16	−21.4

Table 7-4. USAA Mutual Income Factors on January 1, 1993

Variable	High	Low	Mean	Value Line mean	Difference (%)
Cash flow per share	17.42	2.03	6.90	3.02	128.4
% institutional	77.9	22.3	49.6	43.2	15
Shares outstanding	919.14	28.65	234	79.14	196
Price-to-cash-flow ratio	15.46	3.20	7.33	10.42	−30
Earnings	12.8	0	6.61	5.38	23
Yield margins	18.4	3.2	7.85	9.6	−18.3
Price-to-sales ratio	3.19	0.34	1.14	1.4	−19

Table 7-5. USAA Mutual Income Fund's Key Differences from the Value/Screen Database on January 1, 1993

1. The average sales (in millions) are 314% higher than the database average, with a minimum average sales of $865 million.
2. The average market value (in millions) is 305% higher than the database average, with a minimum market value of $908 million.
3. The average number of shares outstanding is 196% higher than the database average, with a minimum of 30 million.
4. The average current yield (in percent) is 142% higher than the database average, with a minimum of 3.20%.
5. The average cash flow per share is 128% higher than the database mean, with a minimum of $2.03.

Table 7-6. USAA Mutual Income Fund's Secondary Differences from the Value/Screen Database on January 1, 1993

1. All earnings per share percentage gains are substantially below the database average.
2. All forecasted earnings, book value, and dividend growth rates, with the exception of the forecasted gain in earnings for the first quarter, are substantially below the database mean.
3. Relative strength is negative.
4. Value ratios, such as price-to-earnings and price-to-sales, are lower than the database average, but not by a substantial margin.
5. The average price stability is high and the average beta is low, indicating a low volatility level for the portfolio.

stocks making it into the portfolio have annual sales equal to or above $865 million.

2. *Market capitalization.* Again, use USAA's minimum as the cutoff, requiring all stocks to have market caps at or above $908 million.

3. *Shares outstanding.* Use USAA's minimum and require that all stocks have at least 30 million shares outstanding.

4. *Cash flow per share.* Using the $2.03 per share figure from USAA's portfolio leaves us with a cash flow per share figure that's not as high as we'd like. Remedy this by requiring that

Table 7-7. Value/Screen Database Screen after Running the 5-Factor Model

Variable	<=>	Value	Number of stocks
Sales	≥	865	710
Market value	≥	908	548
Shares outstanding	≥	30	525
Cash flow per share	≥	3.03	320
Current yield	≥	7	10

cash flow be above the database mean, whatever that might be when running the model. Experimenting with data from January 1, 1993, we find that this gives us the higher cash flow per share we want. So we'll make that our fourth factor: Cash flow per share must be equal to or greater than the mean.

5. *Yield.* Make this important factor relative, using a number that eliminates all but ten stocks from the portfolio. Doing this also ensures compliance with USAA's rule never to buy a stock with a yield below the S&P 500. Remember, to find the figure that will leave you with ten stocks, go to the *Tabular Reports* section and request a report on yield, from highest to lowest. Doing this on January 1, 1993, you'd find that using a yield cut-off of 7.0 percent would leave you with ten stocks.

Table 7-7 shows the model as it would appear in Value/Screen.

Industry Concentration

Table 7-8 shows that 70 percent of the stocks in the model portfolio as of January 1, 1993 are utility companies. Requiring a yield above 7.0 percent almost assures this result; so we must decide whether or not this is acceptable. Utility stocks can be an excellent investment, yet they are more sensitive to interest rate movements than most other industry categories. Allowing 70 percent of your portfolio to be concentrated in the industry reduces diversification, increases your industry risk, and places you in the position of having a bet on interest rates. Also, if you

Table 7-8. 10 Stocks Meeting the Criteria on January 1, 1993

Ticker	Stock	Industry	Yield (%)
PEG	Public Service Enterprise	Electric utility	7.0
CWE	Commonwealth Edison	Electric utility	7.1
TXU	Texas Utilities	Electric utility	7.1
AEP	American Electric Power	Electric utility	7.3
LYO	Lyondell Petrochemical	Chemical	7.3
OGE	Oklahoma Gas & Electric	Electric utility	7.7
PPW	Pacificorp	Electric utility	7.7
CX	Centerior Energy Corp.	Electric utility	8.1
ICI	Imperial Chemical Industries	Chemical	8.4
BRG	British Gas Plc	Foreign diversified	9.3

were interested in a utility portfolio, it would be more appropriate to study a sector fund that invests only in utility companies.

Removing the Utilities

Therefore, vote for diversification by *excluding utility companies from the screen.* To do this, you must exclude the utility industry using its industry code. Clear the current screen and screen on the variable *market price* > 0, which gives you all the stocks in the database. Go to the *Tabular Reports* section and choose *Industry Name* and *Industry Code* as the report variables and choose *Industry Code* as the sort variable. After you press Go, you'll see all the industries sorted by their code. Scroll down to *Electric Utility: East.* Note that its industry code is 4911. Next is *Electric Utility: Central.* Its code is 4912. Finally, you see that *Electric Utility: West* has an industry code of 4913. Return to the main screening menu and reenter our earlier screen, but this time include the following:

Industry code < > 4911

Industry code < > 4912

Industry code < > 4913

This bars the electric utilities from the screen. Run the model again, and go to the tabular reports section to see what figure to use as a cut-off for current yield. Now we see that using 5.8 per-

Table 7-9. Stocks Meeting the New Criteria on
January 1, 1993

Ticker	Stock	Industry	Yield (%)
RD	Royal Dutch Petroleum	Petroleum	5.8
SC	Shell Transport	Petroleum	5.9
PZL	Pennzoil Co.	Petroleum	6.0
PGL	Peoples Energy	Natural gas	6.0
BCT.T	B.C. Telephone	Foreign telephone	6.1
B.TO	BCE, Inc.	Foreign telephone	6.4
SUN	Sun Co.	Petroleum	6.5
LYO	Lyondell Petrochemical	Chemical	7.3
ICI	Imperial Chemical	Chemical	8.4
BRG	British Gas Plc	European diversified	9.2
Average yield			6.80

cent leaves us with ten stocks. This figure is lower because the high-yield utility stocks have been eliminated. Table 7-9 lists the stocks.

There is still some industry concentration, with 40 percent of the portfolio invested in the petroleum industry, but it's not as severe as the utility concentration. The ten-stock portfolio is concentrated into five industries, and the 6.8 percent average yield is more than double that of the market.

Comparing Key and Secondary Factors

Tables 7-10 and 7-11 compare our ten-stock portfolio to USAA's using USAA's key and secondary factors. On a factor level, the portfolios are extremely similar. Our ten-stock portfolio has higher figures for annual sales and average yield, but its factor profile is virtually the same as USAA's, right down to having negative forecasted earnings for every period except the first quarter!

Now look at the stocks that met the model's criteria for 1992, to see if they are similar to our current group. As Tables 7-12 and 7-13 show, the stocks and their average yield for 1992 are very similar to the list on January 1, 1993. So we'll go ahead and test the model's performance.

Table 7-10. Comparison of USAA's Key Factors and Our 10-Stock Portfolio

Factor	USAA's difference from database	10-stock portfolio's difference from database
Average sales ($ mill)	314% higher, low of $865 million	788.5% higher, low of $1.1 billion
Average market value ($ mill)	305% higher, low of $908 million	341% higher, low of $995 million
Shares outstanding	196% higher, low of 30 million	199% higher, low of 33 million
Average current yield	142% higher, low of 3.20%	209% higher, low of 5.8%
Cash flow per share	128% higher, low of $2.03	146% higher, low of $3.29

Table 7-11. Comparison of USAA's Secondary Factors and Our 10-Stock Portfolio

Factor	USAA's difference from database	10-stock portfolio's difference from database
Earnings per share percentage gains	All below the database mean	All below the database mean
Forecasted earnings, book value, and dividend growth rates, except the first quarter	Much lower than the database, in many cases, negative	Much lower than the database, in many cases, negative
Relative strength	Negative	Negative
Price-to-earnings ratio	Lower, but not by substantial margin	Higher, but not by substantial margin
Price-to-sales ratio	Lower	Lower
Price stability index	High, indicating low volatility	High, indicating low volatility

Table 7-12. 10 Stocks in the Portfolio as of December 31, 1991

Ticker	Stock	Yield (%)
RCM	Arco Chemical Company	6.3
BP	British Petroleum PLC	6.8
DCN	Dana Corp.	5.8
F	Ford Motor Co.	5.7
FTX	Freeport-McMoran	6.4
ICI	Imperial Chemical PLC	6.0
LYO	Lyondell Petrochemical	8.0
SNT	Sonat, Inc.	6.1
SUN	Sun, Inc.	5.9
WX	Westinghouse Electric	7.8
Average		6.48

Table 7-13. 10 Stocks in the Portfolio as of June 30, 1992

Ticker	Stock	Yield (%)
BCT	British Columbia Tel	6.0
BRG	British Gas PLC	6.4
BP	British Petroleum	9.8
ICI	Imperial Chemical PLC	5.9
LYO	Lyondell Petrochemical	8.1
NYN	NYNEX Corp.	5.9
PZL	Pennzoil Co.	6.7
NZT	Telecom Co. New Zealand	6.6
SUN	Sun, Inc.	7.0
MRO	USX Marathon	6.6
Average		6.90

The Model's Performance History

As we've done before, rebalance the portfolio every six months, and begin the test on December 31, 1985.

Since this is a high-yield strategy, it's also interesting to compare the strategy's average yield over time with that of long-term government bonds, a competing source for yield-hungry investors. On December 31, 1985, for example, the ten stocks in this portfolio had an average yield of 8.60 percent, which was 0.71 percent *higher* than the yield on long-term government bonds! Throughout the years of the test, the average yield on this model's portfolio was usually lower than the long bond's yield, but rarely by more than 1 or 2 percent. Thus, this strategy offers an excellent yield *plus* a chance at capital appreciation. Table 7-14 shows the model's total returns for the last seven years. (These returns were found using Compuserve's return program.)

Table 7-14. Performance Results of the Income Model December 31, 1985 Through December 31, 1992

Time period	Portfolio performance (%)
December 31, 1985–June 30, 1986	6.27
June 30, 1986–December 31, 1986	9.49
1986, full year	**16.36**
December 31, 1986–June 30, 1987	22.64
June 30, 1987–December 31, 1987	−9.65
1987, full year	**10.81**
December 31, 1987–June 30, 1988	20.19
June 30, 1988–December 31, 1988	4.6
1988, full year	**25.72**
December 31, 1988–June 30, 1989	13
June 30, 1989–December 31, 1989	15.2
1989, full year	**30.18**
December 31, 1989–June 30, 1990	3.1
June 30, 1990–December 31, 1990	−10.9
1990, full year	**−8.14**
December 31, 1990–June 30, 1991	34.5
June 30, 1991–December 31, 1991	11.4
1991, full year	**49.83**
December 31, 1991–June 30, 1992	12.9
June 30, 1992–December 31, 1992	2.2
1992, full year	**15.38**
Average return	**9.64**
Standard deviation	**11.60**
Projected maximum 6-month return	**32.83**
Projected minimum 6-month return	**−13.56**
Spread	**46.39**
Risk-adjusted return	**0.83**

Returns Better Than the Other 16 Funds

Score another one for the advantage of quantitative development and rigorous rebalancing over normal hit-and-miss investing! The seven-year total return (excluding commissions and management fees) for the model was 235 percent. That's almost double the average equity-income fund's return of 121.14 percent, and the average annual gain works out to be 18.85 percent. The performance is also well ahead of the top-performing higher-yielding equity-income funds. Of the 16 funds we looked at, Shearson Premium Total Return B fund had the best return over the same period, with a gain of 134 percent. (USAA's record only goes back to the end of 1987.) The model also beat the S&P 500, which returned 176 percent over the same period.

More impressive is the model's risk-adjusted return of 0.83—the strategy's standard deviation of return was virtually the same as the S&P 500, yet its average return was more than 2.0 percent higher. That translates into a higher expected maximum gain and a lower expected maximum loss than the S&P 500 with a much higher average return. The spread of 46.39 percent is also quite low, making this strategy suitable for the most conservative investor.

What about costs? The returns for our model don't include costs, and they subtract from performance. If we assumed that you faced the same average expense ratio as these 16 funds of 1.14 percent a year, your seven-year return would drop to 209 percent. Yet that's *still* way ahead of the closest competitor and the S&P 500. It beats *all* the funds in the equity-income category. If you dropped the requirement of a 4-percent yield and looked at *all* the equity-income funds, you'd *still* be on top. The best, United Income, had a return of 194.87 percent over the same period, yet it pays a paltry yield of 2.30 percent and, according to the Morningstar analyst, takes more risk than the average equity-income fund. Indeed, this model's returns were better than the average return for all funds in the Morningstar database, from aggressive growth to equity-income.

This is certainly a usable model for the income-oriented investor. By insisting on big-cap stocks with strong cash flows and high yields, we've designed a model that offers a high yield—just 1 or 2 percent lower than long-term government bonds. Nevertheless it shows historical performance better than all other funds in the equity-income category.

Learning More

If you're a tortoise and want to beat the hare, use this model just as a starting point. As we did with the aggressive growth models, test a variety of additional factors to see if you can improve performance, reduce volatility, or both. Always look at a strategy's variability, spread, and risk-adjusted return to determine its suitability for your investment needs. Experiment with including Value Line's Safety Rank as a factor, or buying only stocks with financial strength rankings above A+. Maybe limiting price-to-earnings or price-to-sales would help the overall return. What about a hybrid model that isolates stocks with high yields *and* good earnings per share? The possibilities are limitless. Keep trying experiments, and see where they lead.

8

The Most Profitable Value Factors

USAA and the model that emulated it used factors often appearing in value portfolio's factor profiles. Windsor Fund, a well-known mutual fund, uses a value approach. Four of Windsor's top five key deviations are the same as the USAA portfolio. Further, if you compared USAA's model with a compiled factor analysis of four leading value managers done in 1991, you would again find that the managers' had four of the same five key factors. Yet there are also several other very popular value approaches, and we'll compare some of these new tortoises to the ones found in Chap. 7.

What About Low Price-to-Earnings Ratios?

Voltaire said that, when it comes to making money, we're all of the same religion. Many on Wall Street believe that buying stocks with low price-to-earnings ratios is the one true faith, since many studies show that these stocks outperform those with high price-to-earnings ratios. So it's somewhat surprising that the top-performing funds in the value category aren't more highly defined by low price-to-earnings ratios. Even among those funds with the lowest price-to-earnings ratios, the factor profiles of the best performers are similar to USAA Mutual's.

On January 1, 1993, the 100 mutual funds with the lowest price-to-earnings ratios in the Morningstar database showed an average annual five-year return of 9.39 percent. That's much less than the market, and shows that low PE and value investing were out of favor over the period. Of the 100 funds with the lowest PE, MAS Pooled Value Fund had the best five-year record, with an average annual gain of 16.93 percent, some 7.54 percent higher than its peers. Between December 31, 1985 and December 31, 1992, the fund had an average annual gain of 15.15 percent, slightly lower than the S&P 500's 15.39 percent, but well ahead of even the average growth fund, which showed a 13.87 percent gain.

No Morningstar analyst's comment is available, but the fund's stated investment objective is to seek above-average total returns over a market cycle of three to five years by investing in stocks with market capitalizations usually greater than $300 million. The fund buys undervalued dividend-paying stocks with relative value determined by price-to-earnings and price-to-book ratios.

MAS Pooled Value's $448.3 million dollar portfolio is invested in 80 stocks, the top 30 of which appear in Table 8-1. Entering the stocks into the Value/Screen database, we quickly see that MAS Pooled Value fund's five key factor differences from the database are exactly the same as USAA Mutual Income. Tables 8-2 and 8-3 list its key and secondary factors. The fund's price-to-earnings ratio doesn't even make it on the secondary list since it's just 27 percent lower than database average, along with only moderately lower price-to-book and price-to-cash flow ratios. That's because a low price-to-earnings ratio is helpful only *after* a variety of other criteria are met, such as market capitalization, price stability, adequate liquidity, and other indicators of good financial strength.

Low PE Alone Can Be Dangerous

As Chap. 13 covers in detail, using *any* single factor to screen the broad Value Line database is a big mistake, but using "value" factors alone is even a bigger gamble. That's because a low price-to-earnings ratio *by itself* can lead you to stocks on their way to bankruptcy and the market graveyard, especially if you are narrowing your selections down to just ten stocks. When selecting just a handful of stocks, it's best to apply low price-to-earnings ratios or price-to-book ratios to mature, stable big-cap stocks.

Table 8-1. MAS Pooled Value Fund's
Top 30 Stocks

Ticker	Stock	Value ($ 000)
AMB	American Brands	9926.2
LTR	Loews	9834.8
RBK	Reebok	9522.1
BT	Bankers Trust	9362.6
GPU	General Public Utilities	9345.0
MCIC	MCI Communications	9033.5
PD	Phelps Dodge	8985.0
PIN	PSI Resources	8632.6
ITT	ITT	8317.9
BAC	BankAmerica	7961.8
DH	Dayton Hudson	7798.0
STPL	Saint Paul Co.	7797.6
EK	Eastman Kodak	7547.2
CI	Cigna	7540.0
ETR	Entergy	7432.2
KM	K Mart	7381.6
PE	Philadelphia Electric	7239.9
PMI	Premark International	7225.4
S	Sears	7146.6
BNI	Burlington Northern	7021.5
BDX	Becton Dickinson	7009.2
ML	Martin Marietta	6880.4
LIL	Long Island Lighting	6727.7
TAN	Tandy	6442.2
UTX	United Technologies	6374.9
HSC	Harsco	6351.0
CSX	CSX	6172.3
UPJ	Upjohn	6058.9
FFM	First Financial Management	5960.8
TX	Texaco	5822.5

Table 8-2. MAS Pooled Value Fund's Key Factors

1. Annual sales are 235% higher than the database average.
2. Average cash flow is 115% higher than the database average.
3. Market capitalizations are 113% higher than the database average.
4. Average number of shares outstanding are 75% higher than the database average.
5. Average yield is 59% higher than the database average.

Table 8-3. MAS Pooled Value Fund's Secondary Factors

1. 12-month earnings per share percentage gains are 111% lower than the database average.
2. Last quarter earnings per share percentage gains are 99% lower than the database average.
3. All estimated earnings gains are substantially lower than the database average.
4. Price-to-sales ratios are 39% lower than the database average.
5. 13-week relative strength is negative.

Looking at a Down Year

A good example of a down year is 1990, because the market really punished value-oriented strategies. If you screened the database using factors associated with value investing, buying smaller-cap stocks with low multiples—like the model listed in Table 8-4—you'd really be courting danger. Applying the criteria in Table 8-4 to the Value Line database on December 31, 1989 and June 30, 1990 would leave the ten stocks featured in Tables 8-5 and 8-6.

For all of 1990, this portfolio lost a stunning 65.78 percent because using the "value" criteria alone led you to stocks on the brink of bankruptcy. You *must* use additional factors that require larger, more financially stable stocks when using a value strategy to avoid these results. My research suggests that you need a larger market capitalization, even with stocks that have high ranks for financial strength and stability.

Consider the model in Table 8-7. It looks for stocks with excellent financial strength, high price stability, a Value Line Safety

Table 8-4. Naive Value Strategy

1. Market value ≤ Value Line mean
2. Price-to-book ratio ≤ Value Line mean
3. Price-to-sales ratio ≤ Value Line mean, allowing those that are not available
4. Price-to-earnings ratio ≤ number that leaves you with 10 stocks

Table 8-5. 11 Stocks Meeting the Model's Criteria as of December 31, 1989

Ticker	Stock	Price-to-book ratio	Price-to-sales ratio	Price-to-earnings ratio
BKNE	Bank New Eng.	0.36	N/A	3.1
NVR	Nvryan L.P.	1.14	0.10	3.9
SPF	Standard Pac.	1.83	0.80	4.0
MNCO	Michigan Nat.	1.31	N/A	4.1
MIDL	Midlantic Corp.	0.91	N/A	4.7
AMX	Amax	1.11	0.50	4.8
FEXC	First Executive	0.64	N/A	4.8
GLN	Glenfed	0.44	N/A	4.8
CBK	Continental Bank	0.85	N/A	4.9
HOV	Hovnanian	1.35	0.50	4.9
WND	Windmere	1.40	0.70	4.9
Price change, December 31, 1989– June 30, 1990		−33.34%		

Table 8-6. 10 Stocks Meeting the Model's Criteria as of June 30, 1990

Ticker	Stock	Price-to-book ratio	Price-to-sales ratio	Price-to-earnings ratio
FEXC	First Executive	0.33	N/A	2.3
GLN	Glenfed	0.37	N/A	3.1
HFD	Homefed	0.44	N/A	3.3
GGC	Georgia Gulf	0.67	0.20	3.4
NVR	Nvryan L.P.	0.56	0.10	3.4
SPF	Standard Pac.	1.27	0.70	3.4
ENST	Enstar	0.30	0.10	4.0
DME	Dime Savings	0.24	N/A	4.1
PHM	PHM Corp.	0.74	0.20	4.7
PD	Phelps Dodge	1.46	0.70	4.8
Price change, June 30, 1990– December 31, 1990		−48.66%		

Table 8-7. Value Model Based on Financial
Stability Factors

1. Financial strength ≥ Value Line mean

2. Price stability ≥ Value Line mean

3. Price-to-book ratio ≤ Value Line mean

4. Safety rank ≤ 2

5. Price-to-earnings ratio ≤ number that leaves 10 or 11 stocks
   (7.2 in 1989)

rank of 1 or 2, and low price-to-book and price-to-earnings ratios, with price-to-earnings ratio serving as the final and relative factor. Applying the criteria to the database on December 31, 1989 leaves you with the 11 stocks featured in Table 8-8. (The model buys more than ten stocks if there is a tie in price-to-earnings ratios.) The underlying factors of the stocks certainly show financial strength and stability, as the cross-section of factors in Table 8-9 demonstrates. Yet this model, with a June 30 rebalancing, lost 33.29 percent for the year. That's because a market capitalization minimum, a vital addition to this type of strategy, is missing. Simply adding a requirement that all stocks have market capitalizations above the database mean to this model

Table 8-8. 10 Stocks Meeting the Model's Criteria on
December 31, 1989

Ticker	Stock	Price-to-earnings ratio
F	Ford	4.4
MIDL	Midlantic Corp.	4.7
SNC	Shawmut National	5.4
GD	General Dynamics	5.9
MNC	MNC Financial	6.2
WFC	Wells Fargo	6.2
FFB	First Fid Bancorp	6.3
FABK	First American Bank	6.8
SOCI	Society	7.1
DMBK	Dominion Bankshares	7.2
MNTL	Manufacturers National	7.2

Table 8-9. Cross Section of Relevant Factors on December 31, 1989

Factor	Level	Percentage difference from database mean
Financial strength	A	Higher
Price stability	85	63% higher
Beta	0.93	9% lower
Price-to-book ratio	1.14	58% lower
Yield	5.6	115% higher
Dividend growth rate	16.4	119% higher

would replace all but two of the stocks from the first list with larger-cap selections. Yet it significantly alters only one factor—market capitalization. Table 8-10 shows the new stocks making the list after the addition of a minimum market capitalization, and Table 8-11 contrasts the underlying factors of the larger-cap list with our first list. The only thing that's changed is average market capitalization, with the new list sporting an average of $8.6 billion, 175 percent higher than the first list's $3.1 billion.

Table 8-10. 11 Stocks Meeting the Model's Criteria on December 31, 1989 After Adding Minimum Market Capitalization

Ticker	Stock	Price-to-earnings ratio
F	Ford	4.4
WFC	Wells Fargo	6.2
GM	General Motors	7.3
PNC	PNC Financial	7.5
FTU	First Union	7.6
FNG	Fleet Norstar	7.7
RTN	Raytheon	8.2
NCC	National City	8.4
TD	Toronto Dominion Bank	8.4
AGC	American General	8.5
BRG	British Gas	8.5

Table 8-11. Cross Section of Relevant Factors Compared on December 31, 1989

Factor	Without minimum market capitalization	With minimum market capitalization
Financial strength	A	A+
Price stability	85	86
Beta	0.93	0.92
Price-to-book ratio	1.14	1.40
Yield	5.6	5.4
Dividend growth rate	16.4	17.5

The performance difference, however, is amazing. For the first half of 1990, the first strategy *lost* 17.54 percent, whereas the second larger-cap group *gained* 3.2 percent. The first strategy lost 33.29 percent for the year, whereas the larger-cap group lost just 5.16 percent, an improvement of over 28 percent.

A Full Test of the Strategy

A loss of just 5.16 percent in 1990 makes this an interesting value strategy, since even the best value strategies got hammered that year. So let's do a full seven-year test of the strategy. As usual, we'll rebalance the portfolio on December 31 and June 30 of every year. Table 8-12 shows the results of the seven-year test. The strategy's average annual return of 15.99 percent beat all the 100 funds with low price-to-earnings ratios in the Morningstar database, and it did so buying conservative, big-cap stocks. Yet, in a comparison of its performance with the income model from the last chapter, the nod goes to the income model, since it beat this model both on absolute return (with an average annual gain of 18.85 percent) and on risk-adjusted return (sporting a 0.83 to this model's 0.73).

Comparing High Yield and Low Price-to-Earnings Strategies

While many think that high yield and low price-to-earnings ratio strategies are interchangeable, history suggests otherwise.

Table 8-12. Performance Results of Low Price-to-Earnings Ratio Model from December 31, 1985 through December 31, 1992

Time period	Portfolio performance (%)
December 31, 1985–June 30, 1986	25.30
June 30, 1986–December 31, 1986	2.40
1986, full year	**28.30**
December 31, 1986–June 30, 1987	15.40
June 30, 1987–December 31, 1987	−18.50
1987, full year	**−5.95**
December 31, 1987–June 30, 1988	15.40
June 30, 1988–December 31, 1988	10.10
1988, full year	**27.06**
December 31, 1988–June 30, 1989	14.40
June 30, 1989–December 31, 1989	8.70
1989, full year	**24.36**
December 31, 1989–June 30, 1990	3.20
June 30, 1990–December 31, 1990	− 8.10
1990, full year	**−5.16**
December 31, 1990–June 30, 1991	20.90
June 30, 1991–December 31, 1991	19.60
1991, full year	**44.60**
December 31, 1991–June 30, 1992	2.60
June 30, 1992–December 31, 1992	5.30
1992, full year	**8.03**
Cumulative return	**182.48**
Average annual return	**15.99**
Average 6-month return	**8.34**
Standard deviation of return	**11.36**
Projected maximum 6-month return	**31.05**
Projected minimum 6-month return	**−14.38**
Spread	**45.44**
Risk-adjusted return	**0.73**

For while almost all big-cap, high-yielding portfolios *also* have low price-to-earnings ratios, not all big-cap, low price-to-earnings ratios have high yields. History gives the nod to choosing the high-yield approach over the low price-to-earnings ratio strategy when applying them as relative factors to large companies.

Using a preselected database like the Dow Jones Industrial Average as a proxy for well-known, big-cap stocks and comparing a high-yield approach with buying the Dow stocks with the lowest price-to-earnings ratios, you find that buying the high-yielding stocks has the edge. For the 33 years between June 30, 1959 and June 30, 1992 (the June-to-June period was used by a Lord Abbett study from which part of these figures come), buying the ten Dow stocks with the lowest price-to-earnings ratios, holding them a year, and then rebalancing the portfolio to again hold the ten Dow stocks with the lowest price-to-earnings ratios would have shown an average annual gain of 6.55 percent—on a *capital appreciation basis only, not taking into account any dividends.* Buying the ten highest-yielding Dow stocks would have returned 7.58 percent on an average annual basis, more than a full percentage point higher, again only on a capital appreciation basis. Both strategies beat the Dow Jones Industrial Average's return of 5.75 percent.

Taking dividends into account, the gap widens considerably, since the ten highest-yielding Dow stocks usually yield about 1 percent more than the low price-to-earnings ratio Dow stocks. Table 8-13 shows that, over the past five years, the average yield of the ten highest-yielding Dow stocks was 1.32 percent higher than that of the ten Dow stocks with the lowest price-to-earnings ratios. Assuming a return that's just 1 percent higher than the high-yield stocks, reinvesting the gains would have added an additional 808 percent over the 33-year period.

Why yield works better is fairly simple. It's almost impossible to monkey around with a dividend yield, since the company

Table 8-13. Comparing Average Dividend Yields on 2 Dow Jones Industrial Average Portfolios

Year	10 low-PE portfolio yield (%)	10 highest-yielding portfolio yield(%)	Difference (%)
1988	3.6	5.3	1.7
1989	4.0	5.1	1.1
1990	4.6	6.4	1.8
1991	4.4	5.3	0.90
1992	3.5	4.6	1.1
Average	4.02	5.34	1.32

must either pay, defer, or cancel it. Earnings aren't so simple. Their stated level is sometimes more a function of the creativity of the company's chief financial executive than of any resemblance to reality. The old joke about a firm looking for a new accountant puts it well: As each prospective candidate sits down, they are asked what 2 plus 2 equals. All answer 4—all, that is, except the person who got the job. His reply was, "What number did you have in mind?" You can't manipulate yield that way, so it often gives you a more accurate picture of the company's health than earnings. Further, many times a low price-to-earnings ratio is quite warranted, with the company having very limited prospects for the future. High yield, on the other hand, at least compensates the patient investor with an excellent dividend income.

A Graham and Dodd Approach

USAA Mutual Income Stock Fund and MAS Pooled Value Fund's underlying factor profiles reflect many of the criteria outlined by Ben Graham in *The Intelligent Investor*. Graham was the dean of modern stock analysis, and his nuts-and-bolts value approach has been popular for almost half a century. In his book he called for buying medium to large firms with strong financial conditions, earnings stability, high dividend yields, and low price-to-book and price-to-earnings ratios.

A benefit to this type of investing is the ability to hold the stocks for much longer periods, since you are basing your selections not on hot earnings gains, but on basic values like strong balance sheets and high dividend yields. Thus, if you like to buy stocks and lock them in your safety deposit box, you're probably better off using a value strategy. Table 8-14 shows a model that is a modified version of some of Ben Graham's criteria. Earnings yield is essentially a restatement of a low price-to-earnings ratio screen.

Applying the model to the database on December 31, 1985 and buying only nonutility stocks would have left you with the seven stocks in Table 8-15. If you held those seven stocks for the seven years of our test, without ever selling or rebalancing, you'd have a gain of 194.7 percent—very close to the low price-to-earnings ratio model just tested. Yet this model would have

Table 8-14. Model Based on Some of
Ben Graham's Investing Criteria

1. Market capitalization ≥ Value Line mean
2. Annual sales ≥ Value Line mean
3. Earnings yield ≥ 14
4. Price-to-book ratio ≤ 1.1
5. Yield ≥ 4.8%

Table 8-15. 7 Nonutility Stocks Meeting Graham's
Criteria on December 31, 1985 and Subsequent 7-Year
Performance.

Ticker	Stock	December 31, 1985–December 31, 1992 price change (%)
SC	Shell Trans. & Trading	295.9
RD	Royal Dutch	264.7
TX	Texaco	237.1
F	Ford	222.3
P	Phillips Petroleum	186.5
BP	British Petroleum	116.4
GM	General Motors	39.8
Average		194.7

ultimately provided higher returns since you didn't incur any additional transaction costs or taxes after the initial trade. Its return is also better than the S&P 500 and the majority of mutual funds in Morningstar's database. If you aren't the type to rebalance a portfolio, this is the type of strategy you should use.

A Simple Way to Create an Excellent Utility Portfolio

Most successful value strategies use the factors discussed in this chapter, but there are many other successful ways to create a value portfolio, some surprisingly simple and effective. Until now, we've purchased only nonutility stocks in our value portfolios to get a better chance at capital appreciation, but many very conservative investors might desire a stable, high-yield utility portfolio. A simple way to create such a portfolio is to require that the stocks have a Value Line Safety rank of 1 and then buy the ten stocks with the highest yields. The result is a portfolio that usually has 80 percent or more of its stocks in the big-cap power utility industry, since they are the most likely stocks to have the highest Safety rank coupled with the highest yield.

Value Line bases a stock's Safety rank, as you will recall from Chap. 2, on the stability of its price. The Safety rank reflects the stock's sensitivity to the overall market as well as its inherent volatility (adjusted for trend) and other factors, including company size, the penetration of its markets, product market volatility, the degree of financial leverage, earnings quality, and the overall condition of the balance sheet. In essence, Safety rank is a multifactor model.

Table 8-16 shows the ten stocks making the grade on December 31, 1992. The portfolio's underlying factors—Table 8-17 lists a cross section—are extremely conservative and would appeal to the most conservative investors. The minimum market cap of the stocks is over $1 billion, and all the value factors are quite low. Indeed, it should come as no surprise that this portfolio's top five key deviations from the database are the same as all of the other successful value strategies we've analyzed: big-cap, financially secure companies with strong cash flows and

Table 8-16. 10 Stocks Meeting the Model's Criteria on December 31, 1992

Ticker	Stock	Industry	Yield (%)
BRG	British Gas	Petroleum	9.2
SPS	Southwestern Public Sr.	Utility	6.9
AYP	Allegheny Power	Utility	6.8
POM	Potomac Electric	Utility	6.7
HAN	Hanson Plc.	European diversified	6.6
BCE	BCE, Inc.	Utility	6.4
SCE	SCE Corp.	Utility	6.4
UEP	Union Electric	Utility	6.3
CIP	Cipsco, Inc.	Utility	6.2
SDO	San Diego Gas	Utility	6.2

Table 8-17. Cross Section of Relevant Factors on
December 31, 1989

Factor	Level	Percentage difference from database mean
Financial strength	A+	Higher
Price stability	95	64% higher
Beta	0.68	33% lower
Price-to-book ratio	1.61	37% lower
Price-to-earnings ratio	12.4	33% lower
Yield	6.8%	209% higher
Market capitalization	$7.2 billion	155% higher

high yields. Yet since it's concentrated in utility companies, we could say that this is the portfolio version of the Civil War ship *Ironsides*—it can take many hits without sinking, but it's not expected to go very fast.

Yet Table 8-18 shows that its performance clipped right along, beating the S&P 500 and all the mutual funds in Morningstar specializing in power utility stocks. Its seven-year average annual return of 16.51 percent not only topped all the utility funds, it did better than the average nonspecialized funds as well. Its risk-adjusted return of 0.91 and low spread would make this portfolio appeal to the most risk-averse investor. More, its average yield of 6.8 percent was higher than all the utility funds in the Morningstar database, so it appeals to those who need a steady income as well.

Learning More

If you are a conservative investor, or simply want to diversify your style bets, you can use these value techniques to design value portfolios that are *extremely* safe, yet whose returns trounce the average value fund. And you can delve deeper than we have here, experimenting with a variety of factor combinations that may deliver greater performance at lower levels of risk.

Table 8-18. Performance Results of the Utility Model from December 31, 1985 through December 31, 1992

Time period	Portfolio performance %
December 31, 1985–June 30, 1986	30.3
June 30, 1986–December 31, 1986	4.80
1986, full year	**36.55**
December 31, 1986–June 30, 1987	5.41
June 30, 1987–December 31, 1987	−5.80
1987, full year	**−0.70**
December 31, 1987–June 30, 1988	9.76
June 30, 1988–December 31, 1988	3.0
1988, full year	**13.05**
December 31, 1988–June 30, 1989	10.60
June 30, 1989–December 31, 1989	12.96
1989, full year	**24.93**
December 31, 1989–June 30, 1990	−2.20
June 30, 1990–December 31, 1990	3.10
1990, full year	**0.83**
December 31, 1990–June 30, 1991	11.0
June 30, 1991–December 31, 1991	22.90
1991, full year	**36.42**
December 31, 1991–June 30, 1992	1.70
June 30, 1992–December 31, 1992	8.80
1992, full year	**10.65**
Cumulative return	**191.49**
Average annual return	**16.51**
Average 6-month return	**8.31**
Standard deviation of return	**9.11**
Projected maximum 6-month return	**26.53**
Projected minimum 6-month return	**−9.91**
Spread	**36.44**
Risk-adjusted return	**0.91**

9

Factor Profiles
of the Rich
and Famous

You'll find very few of the most famous mutual funds in the number one position on our performance lists. Ironically, many of the best-known funds become victims of their own success: Their tremendous track records entice investors to pour money into them, leaving managers with too much money to successfully employ the stock-picking style that fueled their fine records in the first place.

The Janus Twenty Fund

Thankfully, this isn't *always* true. One of the fastest growing funds that still maintains a sizzling performance is the Janus Twenty Fund. Morningstar's analyst calls it one of the best growth funds around. Through December 1992, Janus Twenty had a five-year average annual return of 25.53 percent, beating all but four funds in Morningstar's growth category. The fund also attracted loads of money: During the same period, assets soared from $13 million to over $2 billion, making it one of the hottest, fastest growing funds in the country.

Janus Twenty's name is instructive. The fund invests in just 20 to 30 stocks (listed in Table 9-1) that are selected on the basis of an evaluation of factors indicating the fundamental investment value of the stock. Now let's do a factor analysis, and see if all

Table 9-1. Stocks in Janus Twenty's Portfolio as of September 30, 1991

Stock	Value ($ 000)	% net assets
Glaxo	38,223.7	4.82
Amgen	38,085.2	4.80
Medco Containment	34,906.6	4.40
FNMA	33,528.6	4.23
Synergen	31,736.2	4.00
Philip Morris	31,523.4	3.94
Telefonos De Mexico	29,714.3	3.75
Waste Management	28,876.9	3.64
Chambers Development A	28,535.5	3.60
Gap	27,691.7	3.49
Home Depot	27,270.4	3.44
Pfizer	26,924.3	3.39
Duracell	26,670.2	3.36
Wal-Mart	26,247	3.31
US Surgical	25,247	3.19
BankAmerica	21,689.2	2.73
Kroger	21,638.9	2.73
Mid-America Waste	18,989.3	2.39
Merck	18,274.8	2.30
Circus Circus	17,386.2	2.19
Liz Claiborne	14,575.1	1.84
Staples	11,373.8	1.43
Saint Jude Medical	11,247.6	1.42
Marion Merrell Dow	10,301.8	1.30

the investors pouring money into the fund are going to be happy with their investment.

Janus Has the Same Key Factors as CGM

After doing a factor profile, you see that, although they only have three stocks in common, Janus Twenty and CGM have the same key factors, the exception being Janus Twenty's average market capitalization. Janus Twenty is simply a big-cap version of CGM's style, with Janus Twenty's portfolio sporting a minimum market capitalization of $1.7 billion. Other than that, Janus Twenty has the same key factor differences, along with similar magnitudes of deviation, that we found with CGM and almost every other top-performing growth manager. Figures 9-1

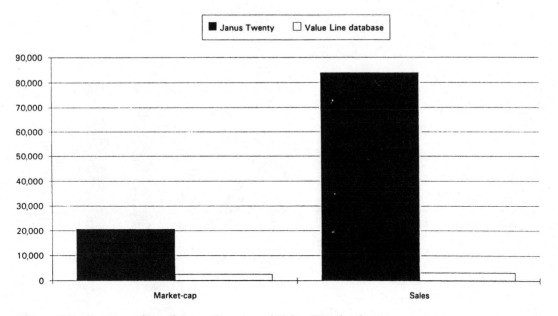

Figure 9-1. Factor profiles of Janus Twenty and Value Line database.

through 9-3 illustrate the portfolio's underlying factors, and Tables 9-2 and 9-3 list the fund's key and secondary factor differences.

Janus Twenty's investors, it appears, were right to pour their money into the fund and should be well served in the future.

The Windsor Fund

Another fund that shares key factors with its top-performing peers is the Windsor Fund. Windsor is perhaps the best-known equity-income fund, with its highly disciplined Graham and Dodd approach to investing: buying high-yielding large companies that also have low price-to-earnings and price-to-book ratios. This leads to a long-term performance that only a handful of rivals can beat. Over the past fifteen years, Windsor has outperformed 95 percent of the funds in the equity-income group. Morningstar's analyst says that, while Windsor's portfolio "may not always be a pretty sight, it has paid off nicely over time … due to its intense and highly disciplined application of the classic rules of value investing." As a matter of fact, Windsor paid off so well that it's closed to new investors.

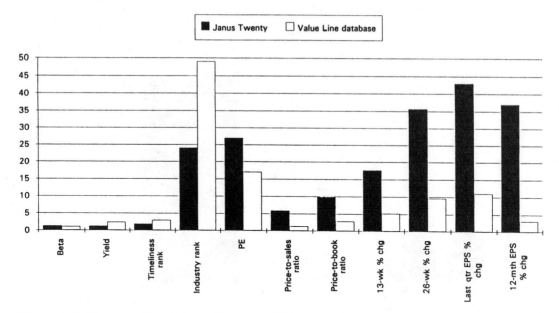

Figure 9-2. Factor profiles of Janus Twenty and Value Line database.

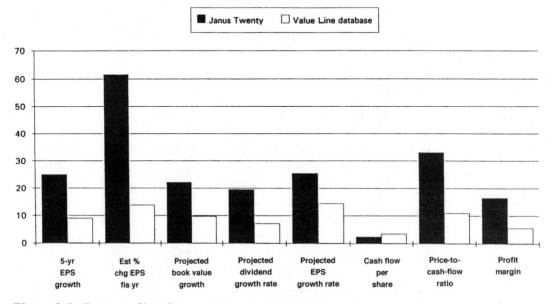

Figure 9-3. Factor profiles of Janus Twenty and Value Line database.

Table 9-2. Janus Twenty's Key Factors

Key Factors

1. 12-month earnings per share percentage gains are 1085% higher than the database.
2. Market capitalization is 677% higher than the database with a minimum of $1.69 billion.
3. Average number of shares outstanding is 381% higher than the database.
4. Estimated earnings per share percentage change for the coming fiscal year is 346% higher than the database.
5. Last quarter earnings per share percentage gains are 294% higher than the database.
6. 26-week price percentage gains are 271% higher than the database average.

Table 9-3. Janus Twenty's Secondary Factors

Secondary Factors

1. Average price-to-sales ratio is 347% higher than the database.
2. Average price-to-book ratio is 247% higher than the database.
3. Average price-to-cash flow ratio is 216% higher than the database.
4. Average retained to common equity is 98% higher than the database.
5. Average return on net worth is 76% higher than the database.
6. Average yield is 50% below the database average.
7. 26-week price percentage gains are 271% higher than the database average.

Windsor's Key Factors Similar to USAA Mutual Income

A factor analysis of Windsor's stocks, featured in Table 9-4, reveals the profile found in Figs. 9-4 through 9-6. Windsor's key factors, listed in Tables 9-5 and 9-6, along with its secondary factors featured in Table 9-7, are the same as those of USAA Mutual Income and MAS Pooled Value. All of Windsor's key positive factors are the same as the other top-performing value funds we've analyzed.

Table 9-4. Windsor Fund's Top 30 Stock Holdings as of June 30, 1992

Stock	Value ($ 000)	% net assets
Citicorp	454,025.4	5.38
Alcoa	435,241.8	5.15
Burlington Resources	399,243.8	4.73
Aetna Life	372,821.3	4.42
Cigna	345,978.9	4.10
Bankers Trust	323,208.4	3.83
USX-Marathon	294,627.7	3.49
BankAmerica	284,641.9	3.37
Golden West Financial	289,588.3	3.07
Chrysler	250,446.4	2.97
Commonwealth Edison	244,746.4	2.90
UAL	240,526.0	2.85
Telefonica De Espana	236,884.6	2.81
Bayer	215,670.6	2.55
Great Western Financial	186,987.7	2.21
HF Ahmanson	173,783.7	2.06
Union Carbide	157,379.7	1.86
Phillips Petroleum	128,813.6	1.53
Bethlehem Steel	111,683.0	1.32
Amax	103,683.8	1.23
Pennzoil	99,000.4	1.17
Lyondell Petrochemical	98,040.0	1.16
Enserch	90,645.0	1.07
Reynolds Metals	86,337.9	1.02
Akzo	55,449.5	0.66
Hoechst	52,546.2	0.62
Baybanks	49,700.2	0.59
Travelers	49,276.4	0.58
Ultramar	44,965.1	0.53
Owens-Corning	44,180.1	0.52

Windsor has the same secondary factors as well. One difference is Windsor's price stability, which is the same as the database mean. (Normally, equity-income funds have much higher price stability ranks; so this is worth minor note.) But because of the great similarities between Windsor and other top equity-income funds, we can draw the same conclusions we did with Janus Twenty: Windsor's investors have their money in a fund that should perform well in the future.

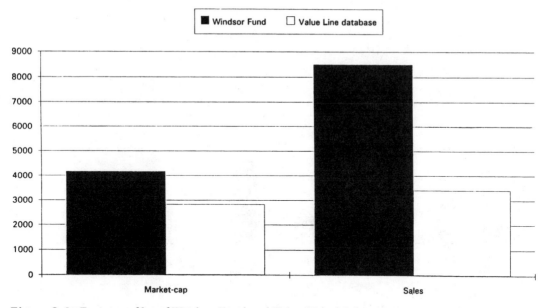

Figure 9-4. Factor profiles of Windsor Fund and Value Line database.

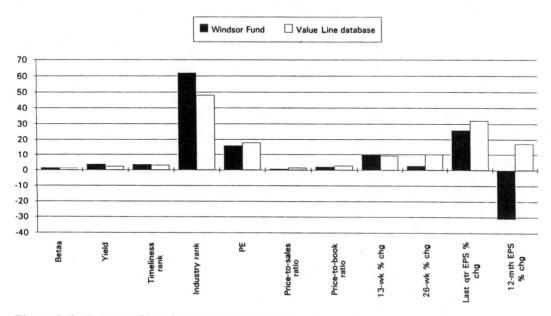

Figure 9-5. Factor profiles of Windsor Fund and Value Line database.

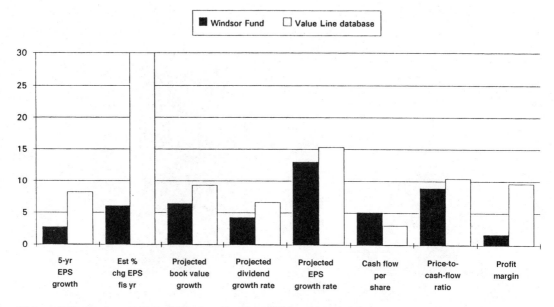

Figure 9-6. Factor profiles of Windsor Fund and Value Line database.

Table 9-5. Windsor Fund's Key Positive Factors

Key Positive Factors

1. Average annual sales are 149% higher than the database.
2. Average number of shares outstanding is 67% higher than the database
3. Average cash flow per share is 66% higher than the database.
4. Average current yield is 61% higher than the database.
5. Average market capitalization is 47% higher than the database.

Table 9-6. Windsor Fund's Key Negative Factors

Key Negative Factors

1. Average price-to-sales ratio is 54% below the database average.
2. Average price-to-book ratio is 27% below the database average.
3. Average price-to-earnings ratio is 11% below the database average.

Table 9-7. Windsor Fund's Secondary Factors

Secondary Factors
1. 12-month earnings per share percentage gains are negative and 278% below the database average.
2. Five-year earnings per share growth rates are 67% below the database average.
3. All earnings estimates except for the first quarter are substantially below the database average.
4. Return on net worth is 35% below the database average.

The Magellan Fund

I've saved the best-known mutual fund in America for last because it proves once again that it's the underlying factor profile that determines what performance to expect, not a name brand.

Fidelity Magellan is the largest mutual fund in America. Its assets of over $20 billion led the Morningstar analyst to quip that if Magellan were permitted to issue junk bonds, it could buy any company on the stock market—or a few countries. The analyst also said that, even without debt, Magellan could buy up *every* non-Fidelity entrant in Morningstar's aggressive growth and equity-income categories. Magellan's performance is also mind-boggling. Over the last 17 years, Magellan has swamped the S&P 500, returning an eye-popping 5450 percent, or 26.55 percent on an average annual basis. Over the same period, the S&P 500 returned just 887.93 percent (14.42 percent compounded annually), while the average growth fund showed a gain of 1121.51 percent (15.86 percent compounded annually).

A critic might say that this performance number is misleading, since Magellan wasn't open to the public until 1981. Also, its best relative performance occurred between 1976 and 1981, when it sported an annual return of 35.65 percent compared to the S&P 500's 10.37 percent. Nevertheless, its record as a fund open to the public is still formidable. Since 1981 Magellan has returned 21.53 percent a year, well ahead of the S&P 500 and average growth fund, which returned 16.29 percent and 14.72 percent respectively. More, in the category of nonspecialty mutual funds, Magellan's performance is second only to CGM Capital Development over the last decade.

For the bulk of the period, Fidelity had Peter Lynch to thank. While he ran the fund, Magellan had a highly defined, classic big-cap growth profile. The 12-month earnings per share percentage gains were almost always well above the market, as was relative strength and all the other factors found in high-performing big-cap growth funds. Given the fund's size, that's a remarkable achievement.

But Lynch retired from the fund in May 1990, and only those looking at underlying factors would know that change was afoot. Lynch's successor, Morris Smith, moved the fund to an even stronger growth profile, removing as many as 400 stocks in an effort to tighten up the fund's commitment to growth stocks. The fund might still possess a classic growth profile if Smith had stayed on, but he resigned just a year after being hired. Figures 9-7 through 9-9 show a factor profile of Magellan in December of 1991, when the fund was still under Smith's management.

You see a classic growth fund, with 12-month earnings per share percentage gains almost 350 percent higher than the market, excellent 26-week relative strength, and a host of other growth factors. Its secondary factors were also those of a classic growth fund, with price-to-sales ratios more than 100 percent higher than the market, price-to-book ratios almost 70 percent higher, and a current yield almost equal to the market. All told, the fund's profile remained highly similar to the one that Peter Lynch had successfully used to keep the fund well ahead of the pack.

The man who replaced Smith was Jeff Vinik, who previously ran Fidelity's Growth and Income Fund—a fund with much more of a value bent than Magellan. It wasn't long before Vinik made his mark on Magellan, shifting the investment focus away from growth towards value. So, although Magellan is still shorthand for a high-quality growth fund, the *actual* fund—whose factor profile can be found in Figs. 9-10 through 9-12—now looks very much like a big-cap value fund. The size and quality of stocks continue to be the same as before—big-cap stocks with enormous amounts of shares outstanding and strong cash flows—but the other factors are considerably different. The 12-month earnings per share percentage changes are now 251 percent *lower* than the average stock in the database, 26-week relative strength is *negative*, price-to-book and price-to-sales ratios

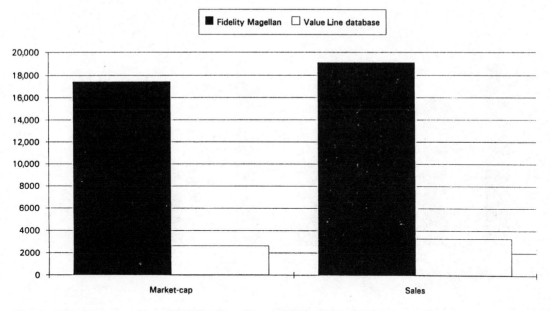

Figure 9-7. Factor profiles of Fidelity Magellan and Value Line database.

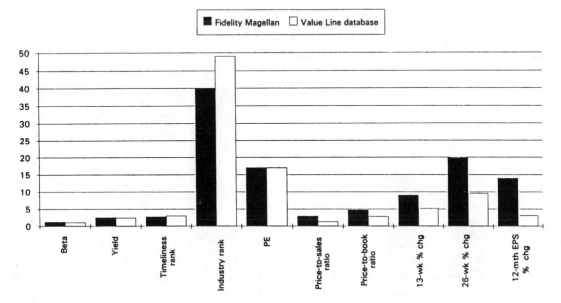

Figure 9-8. Factor profiles of Fidelity Magellan and Value Line database.

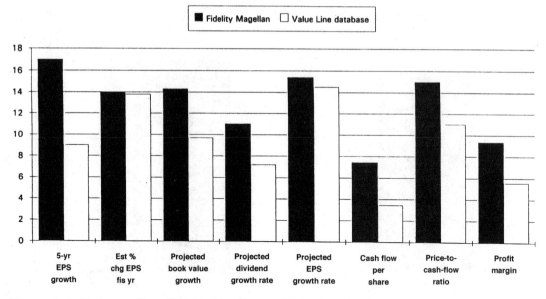

Figure 9-9. Factor profiles of Fidelity Magellan and Value Line database.

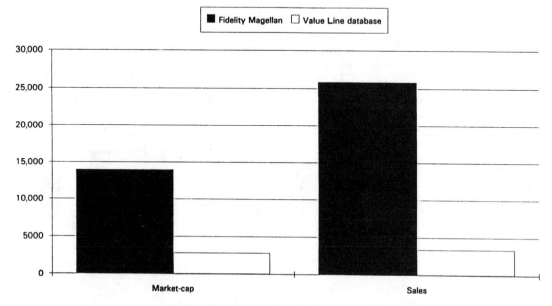

Figure 9-10. Factor profiles of Fidelity Magellan and Value Line database.

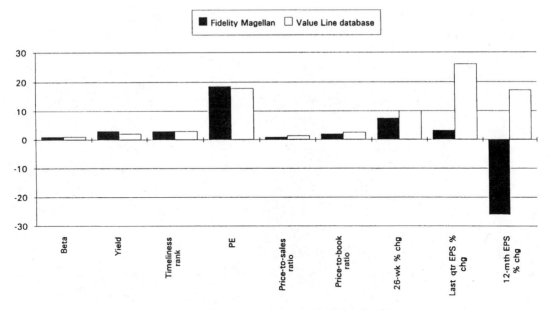

Figure 9-11. Factor profiles of Fidelity Magellan and Value Line database.

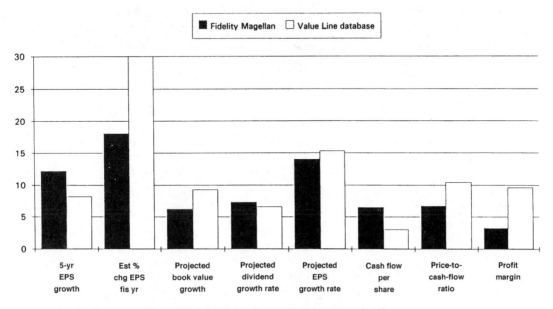

Figure 9-12. Factor profiles of Fidelity Magellan and Value Line database.

are now considerably *lower* than the market, and the average current yield of the funds top 30 stocks is 41 percent *greater* than the database mean. The only remaining growth factor is estimated change in earnings per share for the next quarter, with this considerably higher than the market. So, while many investors continue to equate the Magellan fund with a high-quality growth fund, its underlying factor profile has *radically* shifted from classic growth to classic value.

Vinik has, in reality, changed the fund radically. While his moves might be right on for the coming market, you can see that the only way to know what style a fund manager employs is to pay attention to its factor profile, not its name.

Strong Similarities Between Factors

As Table 9-8 demonstrates, all Magellan needs to do to share *all* its key factors with top-performing value funds is to bump up its average dividend yield. This is fascinating! In all the funds we've studied, we've seen that the best-known, most sought-after funds share the same underlying factor profile with the top performers in their category. This is true not just generally, but specifically and closely. The lesson is clear: If all the top-performing funds from each school of investing share similar underlying factors, we can improve on them by using factors that replicate the top factor deviations, and then use the most relevant factor (perhaps yield for equity-income and estimated earnings or relative strength for growth) to reduce the portfolio

Table 9-8. Magellan's Key Factors on December 31, 1992

1. Average sales are 657% higher than the database average.

2. Average market capitalization is 393% higher than the database average.

3. Average number of shares outstanding is 254% higher than the database average.

4. Estimated change in earnings per share for the next quarter is 232% higher than the database average.

5. Average cash flow is 114% higher than the database average.

to a manageable number of stocks. Finally and most importantly, rebalance your portfolio often enough to keep the factor profile highly defined and strongly associated with the factor profiles of top-ranking funds.

A Consistent Pattern

The list could go on, but you'd continue to find that a fund's
performance is based less on its famous name and more on its
underlying factor profile. The best-known funds that continue
to turn in eye-popping results do so by consistently keeping the
fund's portfolio tilted to the best factors for their style. Other
famous funds, like Magellan, may be changing their styles from
growth to value—a change that may be perfect for the coming
market environment—yet a change that's definitely something
anyone interested in the fund will want to know about.

Thus, if you'd prefer to invest in a well-known fund, first do a
factor profile and contrast what you *thought* about the fund's
style with the actual profile your factor analysis reveals. Next
compare the fund's key factor differences from the database
with those that we've found the best managers employ. If all
this looks good, test the fund's risk-adjusted return and contrast
it to that of a model based on the fund's key factors. If the fund
can pass all these tests, you can be far more confident than the
casual investor that it will probably continue its winning ways.

10
Seeing Through a Broker's Advice

Oscar Wilde said that, dressed in an evening coat and white tie, even a stockbroker could gain a reputation for being civilized. Of all the professions, only lawyers are more maligned and subjected to a greater barrage of jokes about their motivation and intentions. People regularly dismiss stockbrokers as little more than untrustworthy salespeople. Many feel brokers don't care *what* you buy or sell, as long as you *do* buy and sell. In short, to most people the most satisfying killing they could make in the market is shooting their broker.

Yet many full-service brokers have done well for their clients by recommending good stocks. Just as importantly, they help clients hold on through nervous market spells when many unsupported amateur investors let their emotions take over and sell at exactly the wrong time. However, like money managers, only one broker in a hundred is going to be good at finding the best stocks. Factor analysis lets you separate the top-performing brokers from the pack.

Ask the Right Questions

Warren Buffet, the legendary investor from Omaha, uses the story of a sports fisherman trying to buy a lure to describe Wall Street. The sales clerk offers the fisherman a great variety of colorful, expensive lures. Unable to choose, the fellow asks, "Do fish *really* like these things?" To which the clerk curtly replies, "I don't sell to fish."

To determine if a prospective broker knows the fish as well, you've got to ask the right questions. Most full-service brokerage houses provide similar services. Individual brokers compete with one another on two points: individualized attention and quality of investment ideas.

After you're satisfied that a broker will give you a high degree of personal service (i.e., you'll be able to get him on the phone when the markets are falling or running wild; his calls don't *always* concern your selling or buying something), you'll need to judge the quality of his or her investment advice by asking very specific questions. Unlike money managers or mutual funds, most individual brokers have no year-to-year performance record, since they rarely have full trading discretion over their accounts. They simply make recommendations and the client decides whether to follow the advice. Therefore, even if the advice is outstanding, you may still find a mediocre performance in several of the broker's accounts because the client failed to take the advice. If a broker *does* show you a performance record, you can bet it's one of his or her *best-performing* accounts, and doesn't reflect an average client's results.

Pin Them Down

Therefore, your best course of action is to analyze a broker's list of current stock recommendations. Ask concrete, direct questions. Ask if he or she is comfortable making both conservative and aggressive investment recommendations, and get a list of stocks he or she is currently recommending. Thus, on January 1, 1993, you might hear:

YOU: What do you recommend for conservative investors?

BROKER: We like solid, well-run blue chip companies for our conservative clients.

YOU: Which ones, specifically?

BROKER: Well, there are hundreds of excellent choices and the ones we recommend for you depend on your individual needs and circumstances....

This conversation will get you nowhere. The broker is dodging your question, most likely because *he* doesn't do his own research. So he won't recommend specific stocks until he talks to the firm's research analysts.

You are getting somewhere, however, in a conversation like this:

YOU: What do you recommend for conservative investors?

BROKER: We like solid, well-run blue chip companies for our conservative clients.

YOU: Which ones, specifically?

BROKER: My firm maintains a large list of recommendations, but I recommend just a handful from that list. I think oil stocks are an excellent investment now and that *Texaco, Chevron,* and *Exxon* are the best from the sector. All three are members of the Dow Jones Industrial Average, have huge market capitalizations, and have safe, high dividend yields. I like *American Express,* another Dow stock, because I think their new chairman will turn the company around by selling off divisions and returning it to their core business of credit cards and travel services. I think *British Gas* is an excellent buy with its yield at 9.2 percent, and I like three of the regional Baby Bells: *U.S. West, NYNEX,* and *Ameritech.*

YOU: What would you recommend for more aggressive accounts?

BROKER: First I would need to find out your risk tolerance and establish a time frame for reaching your investment goals.

YOU: Assume I want maximum capital gains, can take a lot of risk, and will invest for the long term.

BROKER: O.K., in that case some aggressive growth stocks I like from our recommended list are *Three-COM,* a computer network file server developer with outstanding earnings gains and terrific prospects, *QVC Network,* a home shopping television outfit whose new owners, I think, will make earnings soar, and *Tandycrafts,* a hobby and handicraft business with excellent earnings and huge potential given the aging population. I think that *COMPAQ Computer's* lower price strategy will allow them to compete with clone computer makers more effectively and really boost earnings. To round out the list, I also like *XTRA Corp.,* a transportation company with excellent earnings and a member of the Dow Jones Transportation Average, *Oracle Systems* and *Software Publishing,* two computer-oriented companies with outstanding earnings potential, and *Countrywide Credit,* a lender whose earnings are exploding because of the rush to refinance mortgages at today's lower rates.

This broker has given you a highly specific list of investment ideas for both conservative and aggressive accounts. While he may not base his reasons for recommending these stocks on factor analysis, you can still use the list to determine if the broker's recommendations will be any good.

Doing a Factor Analysis of the Broker's Suggestions

Just as we've done with mutual funds and money managers, enter the stocks in Value/Screen and follow the factor analysis process from Chap. 3. Analyzing the conservative recommendations first, we find the factor profile featured in Tables 10-1, 10-2, and 10-3, with the key and secondary factors listed in Tables 10-4 and 10-5.

The factors in our fictional broker's portfolio look exactly the same as those of the best value managers covered in Chaps. 7 and 8. When examining the broker's picks, you see that the key factors are the same as our five-factor value model used in Chap. 7 (which appears again in Table 10-6), but the minimums are substantially higher:

- The *minimum* market value is 313 percent higher than the database average.

Table 10-1. Factor Analysis of Conservative Picks Using Data from January 1, 1993

Variable	High	Low	Mean	Value Line mean	Difference (%)
Timeliness rank	4	3	3.25	3	8.33
Safety rank	3	1	1.38	3	−54
Financial strength	A++	B	A+	B+	Higher
Industry rank	81	20	60	46	26
Price stability rank	100	50	87	52	67
Beta	1.5	0.6	0.88	1.02	−14
Current EPS	6.51	2.11	4.20	1.71	146
Current dividend	4.64	1.00	3.12	0.7	346
Technical rank	3	2	2.63	3	−13
Recent price	84	24.75	56.42	29.28	93
52-week high	88.50	25.38	60.64	33.84	79
52-week low	69.13	20	48.55	22.05	120
Current P/E	16.3	9.70	13.4	17.8	−25
Current yield	9.20	4.0	5.58	2.2	153
Price-to-book	2.31	1.29	1.81	2.62	−31
13-week % price change	13.1	−7.40	0.16	9.1	−98
26-week % price change	10.2	−7.7	2.39	10	−76
Market value ($ mill)	76,538.3	11,686.1	24,761.54	2828.5	775

Table 10-2. Broker's Conservative Recommendations Factors from January 1, 1993

Variable	High	Low	Mean	Value Line mean	Difference (%)
Sales ($ mill)	102,847	10,577	32,071	3415	839
% ret net worth	16	5.8	12.65	12.6	0.40
% retained to common	11.1	1.0	5.5	9.1	−40
Book value per share	44.77	14.43	31.27	14.97	109
Debt as % of capital	58	20	36.4	32	14
Last qtr EPS % chg	23.3	−3.60	8.54	26	−67
12-month EPS % chg	10.8	−49.0	−21.0	17.2	−220
5-yr EPS growth	11.0	1.0	4.19	8.2	−49
5-yr divd growth	8.0	0.5	5.86	9.6	−39
5-yr bk val growth	12.5	−11.0	2.31	9.3	−75
Est. % chg EPS qt. 1	9.40	−6.40	2.04	34.7	−94.12
Est. % chg EPS qt. 2	41.8	1.3	11.29	41.9	−73.07
Est. % chg EPS fis yr	113.5	−24.2	12.9	29.9	−57
Prj 3-5 yr apprec %	51	14	31	74	−58
Prj EPS growth	10.0	3.0	6.38	15.3	−58
Prj div growth	11.5	4.0	6.0	6.6	−9
Prj book val growth	8.5	3.0	4.94	9.3	−47
Prj 3-5 yr av ret	14.0	8.0	11.75	16.0	−27

Table 10-3. Broker's Conservative Recommendations Factors from January 1, 1993

Variable	High	Low	Mean	Value Line mean	Difference (%)
Cash flow per share	17.42	3.78	9.53	3.02	215
% institutional	62.1	1.1	38.46	43.2	−11
Shares outstanding	1242	204.0	454.0	79.0	473
Price-to-cash-flow ratio	7.4	4.8	6.13	10.4	−41
Earnings yield	10.3	6.1	7.65	5.38	42
Margins	11.7	3.3	6.7	9.6	−31
Price-to-sales ratio	1.73	0.41	0.97	1.4	−31

Table 10-4. Broker's Conservative Recommendations
Key Factors

Key Factors

1. Annual sales are 839% higher than the database average.
2. Average market capitalization is 775% higher than the database average.
3. Average number of shares outstanding is 473% higher than the database average.
4. Average cash flow per share is 215% higher than the database average.
5. Average yield is 153% higher than the database average.

Table 10-5. Broker's Conservative Recommendations
Secondary Factors

Secondary Factors

1. 12-month earnings per share percentage changes are negative and 220% lower than the database average.
2. Last quarter earnings per share percentage changes are 67% lower than the database average.
3. Relative strength is negative.
4. All growth projections are substantially lower than the database average.
5. All "value" measurements are low. Price-to-sales ratios are 31% below the database average, price-to-earnings ratios are 25% lower, price-to-cash flow ratios are 41% lower, and price-to-book ratios are 31% below the database average.
6. Price stability of the stocks is 67% higher than the database average.

- The *minimum* annual sales figure is 209 percent higher than the database average.

- The minimum number of shares outstanding is 156 percent higher than the database average.

- The minimum cash flow per share is 25 percent above the database average.

Table 10-6. 5-Factor Value Model from Chap. 7

Variable	<=>	Value
Sales	≥	865
Market value	≥	908
Shares outstanding	≥	30
Cash flow per share	≥	Mean
Current yield	≥	7

So let's use the same model, but set the minimum cut-offs using these new figures. Thus, if the average market value for the database is $2.83 billion, we'll add 313 percent (or $8.85 billion) to arrive at a minimum acceptable market value of $11.68 billion. For sales, add 209 percent, and so on with each of the four factors before yield. Finally, as in Chap. 7, use yield as the relative factor, setting its minimum at a level that leaves you with ten stocks. Table 10-7 shows how the screen looks using data from January 1, 1993. Table 10-8 lists the 12 stocks resulting from the screen. (When two stocks tie on yield, include all those with equal yield; thus this portfolio has 12, not ten stocks.)

The stocks are giants: They have an average market capitalization of almost $23 billion, as well as strong cash flows and high yields. Since this list is substantially different from our model in Chap. 7, let's test its performance.

Table 10-7. Value/Screen Database Screen after Running the 5-Factor Model with Broker Recommendation Modifications

Variable	<=>	Value	Number of stocks
Market value	≥	11,680	83
Sales	≥	10,555	52
Shares outstanding	≥	203	50
Cash flow per share	≥	3.79	39
Current yield	≥	5.3	12

Table 10-8. 12 Stocks Making the List as of January 1, 1993

Ticker	Stock	Market capitalization ($ mill)	Yield (%)
BRG	British Gas	18,539.0	9.2
BCE	BCE Inc.	12,761.0	6.4
SC	Shell Trans. & Trading	28,242.0	5.9
RD	Royal Dutch Pet.	43,690.0	5.8
BP	British Pet.	20,225.0	5.6
USW	U S West	15,834.0	5.6
NYN	NYNEX	17,113.0	5.5
ELF	Societe Nationale Elf	16,476.0	5.5
TX	Texaco	15,348.0	5.4
AIT	Ameritech	18,698.0	5.3
BTY	British Tel.	37,421.0	5.3
GTE	GTE	30,556.0	5.3
Average		22,909.0	5.9

As you go through the years for the test, you'll find that the ten to 12 stocks meeting all the model's criteria tend to be the same year after year. They are huge stocks with high dividends, dominated by the telephone, oil, and auto industries. Bell Atlantic was on the list in June of 1987 *and* June of 1992, as were many of the other baby bell companies. Thus the turnover in this portfolio will be much lower than even the other conservative models we have developed.

Table 10-9 shows the seven-year performance. Wow! Too bad this wasn't a *real* broker instead of a factor-derived model! This model has a very low spread due to its low standard deviation, yet it also boasts an excellent total return. The risk-adjusted return is one of the best we've seen: 1.24. Over the seven years, you would have had a gain of 314.47 percent, or 22.53 percent compounded annually, while taking very low risk.

If you are a conservative investor and find a broker whose advice models this well, retain him—he'll be worth every cent!

The Aggressive Recommendations

Next, do a factor analysis of the broker's aggressive recommendations. Here we would find the factor profile featured in Tables

Table 10-9. Performance Results of the Big-Cap Income
Model December 31, 1985 through December 31, 1992

Time period	Portfolio performance (%)
December 31, 1985–June 30, 1986	17.40
June 30, 1986–December 31, 1986	14.80
1986, full year	**34.77**
December 31, 1986–June 30, 1987	29.30
June 30, 1987–December 31, 1987	−5.70
1987, full year	**21.93**
December 31, 1987–June 30, 1988	14.60
June 30, 1988–December 31, 1988	7.30
1988, full year	**22.97**
December 31, 1988–June 30, 1989	16.20
June 30, 1989–December 31, 1989	18.30
1989, full year	**37.47**
December 31, 1989–June 30, 1990	5.0
June 30, 1990–December 31, 1990	−5.10
1990, full year	**−0.36**
December 31, 1990–June 30, 1991	13.80
June 30, 1991–December 31, 1991	13.90
1991, full year	**29.62**
December 31, 1991–June 30, 1992	9.40
June 30, 1992–December 31, 1992	5.60
1992, full year	**15.53**
Average return	**11.06**
Standard deviation	**8.94**
Projected maximum 6-month return	**28.94**
Projected minimum 6-month return	**−6.83**
Spread	**35.77**
Risk-adjusted return	**1.24**

10-10, 10-11, and 10-12, with the key and secondary factors listed in Tables 10-13 and 10-14.

The factor profile and key and secondary factor differences of our fictional broker's aggressive recommendations look *exactly* the same as that of the best growth managers, with very little deviation from any of the other top growth managers studied so far.

The top five key characteristics are identical to CGM. So in this instance you don't need to build a separate emulation. If

Table 10-10. Broker's Aggressive Picks Factor Profile on
January 1993

Variable	High	Low	Mean	Value Line mean	Difference (%)
Timeliness rank	4	1	1.6	3	−44.44
Safety rank	4	3	3.56	3	19
Financial strength	A++	C	B+	B+	Same
Industry rank	52	5	30	46	−38
Price stability rank	65	5	23	52	−55
Beta	1.6	.55	1.23	1.02	21
Current EPS	4.12	.85	1.84	1.71	7
Current dividend	0.80	0.0	0.18	0.7	−75
Technical rank	5	1	1.9	3	−37
Recent price	63.25	8.0	33.9	29.28	16
52-week high	62.5	26.25	37.13	33.84	10
52-week low	28.5	6.75	14.4	14.40	−35
Current PE	34.4	8.6	21	17.8	20
Current yield	2.1	0	0.47	2.2	−79
Price-to-book	9.08	1.40	3.54	2.62	35
13-week % price change	110.7	−15.80	45.52	9.1	411
26-week % price change	171.4	−8.60	77.21	10	672.11
Market value ($ mill)	4083.8	96	1345	2828.5	−52

this broker sticks to his method of analysis, you'll get outstanding growth selections as well.

No Broker Is Ideal

This was a fictional broker. Rarely could you find a full-service broker who's mastered both aggressive and conservative investing and who's offered stock selections with such a highly defined factor profile. Yet comparing our ideal factor profiles to a broker's selections is easy. Most importantly, avoid using a broker whose stock picks come out with strange factor combinations—such as very high yields with very low Price Stability or Safety ranks. Just as ideal factor profiles are a recipe for success, *really odd* combinations are a recipe for disaster. Don't, however, dismiss a slightly unusual profile because the broker may be on to something. Go ahead and test a model based on the portfolio's key factors, and let the numbers tell you if he's on to something.

Table 10-11. Broker's Aggressive Recommendation's Factors from January 1993

Variable	High	Low	Mean	Value Line mean	Difference (%)
Sales ($ mill)	3271.4	130.9	773.28	3415	−77.36
% ret net worth	14.1	2.1	8.62	12.6	−32
% retained to common	14.1	2.1	7.99	9.1	−12
Book value per share	22.93	3.11	11.25	14.97	−25
Debt as % of capital	69	0	27.11	32	−15
Last qtr EPS % chg	567	85	173	26	566
12-month EPS % chg	224	−32	92	17.2	435.85
5-yr EPS growth	53	−21	15.3	8.2	87
5-yr divd growth	13.5	2	7.83	9.6	−18.4
5-yr bk val growth	52	−5	22	9.3	132
Est. % chg EPS qtr 1	64	−33	31	34.7	−12
Est. % chg EPS qtr 2	58	−28	26.26	41.9	−37
Est. % chg EPS fis yr	513.3	−7	111	29.9	272.61
Prj 3-5 yr apprec %	194	−12	55	74	−26
Prj EPS growth	43	7.5	27	15.3	74
Prj div growth	31.5	0	7.5	6.6	14
Prj book val growth	22	7.5	14	9.3	50
Prj 3-5 yr av ret	31	−3	10.11	16.0	−37

Table 10-12. Broker's Aggressive Recommendations Factors from January 1993

Variable	High	Low	Mean	Value Line mean	Difference (%)
Cash flow per share	12.37	0.91	3	3.02	−0.55
% institutional	78	13	45	43.2	3
Shares outstanding	140	5	40	79.0	−49
Price-to-cash-flow ratio	31.45	5	18	10.4	72
Earnings yield	11.6	3	6	5.38	10
Margins	18.3	1	6	9.6	−40
Price-to-sales ratio	3.69	0.67	1.79	1.4	28

Table 10-13. Broker's Aggressive Recommendations
Key Factors

Key Factors

1. Extremely high relative strength for both 13- and 26-week period. 26-week gains are 672% higher than the database average.
2. Last quarter earnings per share gains are 566% higher than the database average.
3. 12-month earnings per share percentage gains are 436% higher than the database average.
4. Estimated percentage change for earnings per share for the coming fiscal year are 273% higher than the database average.
5. All stocks except one have Timeliness ranks of 1 or 2.

Table 10-14. Broker's Aggressive Recommendations
Secondary Factors

Secondary Factors

1. Market value is 52% lower than the database average, with a high of $4.08 billion.
2. Average annual sales is 77% lower than the database average.
3. Yield is 79% lower than the database average.
4. Average shares outstanding is 49% lower than the database average.
5. Average price stability is 55% lower than the database average.
6. Safety ranks are confined to 3 and 4.

You should take the time to develop a model for *any* prospective broker who selects stocks with a factor profile that differs markedly from the best models used by the top stock pickers. For example, suppose you had this conversation on January 1, 1993:

YOU: Are you comfortable with both aggressive and conservative investing?

BROKER: No, I must admit I'm not. I think investing for yield doesn't make any sense, and the only way to beat the market in the long run is to invest in outstanding growth issues.

YOU: Which stocks do you like right now?

BROKER: I recommend four issues very highly. They are *Ann Taylor, Holly Corp., Univar,* and *Seagate Technology.* Their earnings gains last quarter were outstanding, and the consensus on Wall Street is that their earnings gains next year will top everything in the market.

You don't have to do a full factor profile to see how different this broker's recommendations are from the ideal growth profiles previously studied. As Table 10-15 shows, these stocks have *enormous* forecasted earnings gains for the next quarter and fiscal year. The *minimum* forecasted earnings gain for the coming fiscal year is 173 percent! That's extraordinarily high. More, these stocks also have an average earnings *loss* over the last 12 months of 19.23 percent and negative relative 26-week price strength. This is highly idiosyncratic and doesn't look promising. But let's test the factors in 1991, one of the best years for growth stocks in the last decade.

The model we'll develop to test the broker's recommendations is very simple. A test portfolio will need to contain stocks that have great earnings gains over the last quarter and very high forecasted gains for the next quarter, yet it must show earnings declines over the last 12 months and negative relative strength. The following four-factor model captures those characteristics nicely:

Table 10-15. Aggressive Growth Broker's Recommendations Key Factors

Key Factors
1. Estimated change in earnings per share for the coming fiscal year are 2139.30% higher than the market, with a minimum of 173.40%.
2. Last quarter earnings per share percentage gains are 934% higher than the market average.
3. Estimated gain for earnings per share for the next quarter are 620% higher than the market.
Yet...
1. 12-month earnings per share percentage change are *negative* and 212% below the database average.
2. 26-week price changes are 20% *lower* than the market, indicating negative relative strength.

1. Earnings per share last quarter ≥ Mean

2. 12-month earnings per share percentage gain ≤ Mean

3. 26-week price percentage change ≤ 0

4. Estimated change in earnings per share for the next quarter ≥ Number to leave 10 stocks (111% on January 1, 1991)

We set the 26-week price percentage change at zero or under because the figure for the database as a whole on January 1, 1991 was a loss of 16.1 percent. Using zero lets us have a figure of −20.3 percent, which is 26 percent lower than the database average, much like the figure we found when analyzing the broker's recommendations. Table 10-16 lists the stocks that made the cut on January 1, 1991.

Let's look at 1991 performance. For the first half of the year, the ten stocks gained just 8.4 percent, well below our Momentum Growth Model's gain of 50.50 percent for the same period. For the second half of 1991, this model turned in a gain of 7.4 percent, making the full return for 1991 16.43 percent, well below the S&P 500 and 130 percent lower than our Momentum Growth Model's return for the same year.

This poor performance is predictable when using factor analysis, since the strategy relies on an unnatural combination of fac-

Table 10-16. 10 Stocks Meeting the Model's Criteria as of January 1, 1991

Ticker	Stock	Industry
CLRK	CLARCOR	Packaging/container
OXY	Occidental Petroleum	Petroleum
SPW	SPX Corp.	Auto Parts
STX	Sterling Chemical	Chemical
OCAS	Ohio Gas Corp.	Insurance
MANT	Manitowoc, Inc.	Machinery
SQA	Sequa Corp.	Diversified
LMS	Lamson & Sessions Co.	Machinery
FRM	First Mississippi	Chemical
WOL	Wainoco Oil	Petroleum

tors. Strong earnings gains over the last quarter go hand-in-hand with strong earnings gains over the last 12 months and positive relative strength. For example, if we screened just on:

1. Last quarter earnings per share ≥ 100

2. Estimated change for earnings per share for quarter one ≥ 100

3. Estimated gain for earnings per share for the next fiscal year ≥ Number to get 10 stocks

We would find that the resulting ten stocks *also* had 12-month earnings per share gains that were 2233 percent higher than the market *and* positive relative strength, with a 26-week price gain some 300 percent ahead of the market. That's normal. Combining great gains over the last quarter, lousy gains in the last year, and negative relative strength is not normal. Rather, it's a recipe for disaster.

Avoiding Misfortune

The word *broker* is very old. According to Sereno Pratt's *The Work of Wall Street*, many believe that the word is derived from the Saxon word *broc*, which means misfortune, since the first brokers appear to have been men who failed in business as principals and had to earn an uncertain living as agents.

By asking specific questions of brokers and forcing them to give you a detailed list of recommendations, and then doing a factor profile of their recommendations, you can avoid misfortune and be on your way to something many investors would envy: a profitable and satisfying relationship with a full-service broker.

11
Newsletters, Books, and Individuals— Separating the Good Few from the Mediocre Many

Thousands of books and newsletters offering stock market advice manage to state the simple in the terms of the incomprehensible. If you think a broker is difficult to pin down, try plucking a few good recommendations from books or newsletters. They are so legendary in hedging their bets and obfuscating their advice that E. B. White uses them as an example when explaining that writers owe it to their readers to be clear: "Even to writers of market letters, telling us (but not telling us) which securities are promising, we can say, 'Be cagey plainly! Be elliptical in a straightforward fashion!' "

Yet all is not lost. Of the thousands of books and newsletters, a few emerge giving clear, concise, and worthwhile advice.

First the Sifting

When evaluating newsletters, knowing what to avoid saves much time. If the trial newsletters you get don't have direct stock recommendations with a review of previous performance, either from a model or an actual group of stocks, forget them. If the newsletter is quantitative, expect it to list how the stock selection method has performed historically; if it's written by a conventional stock picker, expect to see all the stocks recommended and how they did from buy to sell. If the newsletter contains lots of extraneous information, ranging from what the writer did over the holidays to his views on the most recent political crisis, you're usually wise to throw it in the trash. Such people publish newsletters as vanity items with the quality of their advice taking a distinct backseat to their rambling, know-it-all pronouncements.

Finally, look for specific current recommendations. It's easy to do a factor analysis on them to see if the newsletter is worth following at all. Do a factor profile on these stocks just as you would with a mutual fund or broker. Few newsletters are worth the investment. Those that are tend to be highly quantitative, like the *Value Line Investment Survey* and *The MPT Review.*

Judge a Book by Its Factors, Not by Its Cover

Books are more difficult. Newsletters eventually *have* to get around to recommending stocks. Not so with books. They can go from start to finish with only the writers' reminiscences on their fabulous careers, why they bought certain stocks a few years back, or how they were among the *only* managers to avoid the crash of 1987 completely! Unless the author is a highly interesting or entertaining person, you're best off not bothering with these books at all.

Books really can't offer specific stock picks, unless they are updated on a consistent basis, since all the information will have changed considerably when the book is published. Therefore, when trying to learn things from books, look for those that outline a particular *strategy* or *method* for picking stocks. Make sure it's highly specific and can be tested. Narrow down the field by going through the book looking for specific advice on stock selection. If you can't find any that is concrete and sensible, skip the book. Fortunately, several books meet this test, and a few of them are excellent.

William O'Neil's
C-A-N S-L-I-M[*] Method

Bill O'Neil's *How to Make Money in Stocks* is one such book. O'Neil certainly has a good track record. He bought a seat on the New York Stock Exchange at age 30 using profits generated from an initial investment of just $3,000, and he was one of the first people to build a daily computer database of the United States stock market. He currently publishes *Investor's Business Daily.*

His book is unusual because it offers specific, direct advice on how to pick stocks. O'Neil calls his method C-A-N S-L-I-M, with each letter standing for one of his criteria. An abridged version of his criteria is:

1. Current quarterly earnings per share gains must show a major increase.

2. Five-year earnings per share percentage gains must be high.

3. The company should have new products, new management, and new highs. (For factor analysis, we'll focus on the new highs.)

4. The number of shares outstanding should be low, with less than 25 million being ideal. The stock should have *some* institutional backing, but not be overwhelmingly owned by them.

5. The stock should have strong relative strength.

O'Neil lists many other considerations, but these are the specific ones we'll use to build a model to test his advice. We can skip any factor analysis since we are testing his advice, not looking at stocks.

Building a Model

O'Neil's advice is specific and easy to model. His first criterion, an excellent quarterly gain in earnings per share, sounds like our Momentum Growth Model. So we'll use the minimum from that model of 20 or greater. Thus our first factor is:

Last quarter earnings per share percentage gains ≥ 20

*C-A-N S-L-I-M is a registered trademark of William O'Neil & Co.

Next he wants high five-year earnings per share growth rates. Between 1987 and 1992, the average stock in the Value Line database had an average five-year earnings per share growth rate of approximately 7.6 percent. If we roughly double that figure to 15 we'd be assured of very high five-year earnings per share growth rates. Thus, our second factor is:

Five-year earnings per share growth rates ≥ 15

O'Neil next says that the company should have new products, have new management, and be trading close to a high. We can't measure the new products or management, but we can use the *User Defined* section of the database to find out how close to its high a stock is trading. Go to the *Define User Variable* section. Create a variable that equals current price divided by its 52-week high price, and set it as a percentage. Name the variable *Percentage of high price*. Thus, if a stock's price was $70 and its 52-week high price was also $70, the Percentage of High Price would be 100 percent.

After entering this new variable, go to the Tabular Reports section and see what the average is for the database. On January 1, 1993, the average for the database was 85.7 percent, so we'll use that number as a minimum for our next factor:

Percentage of high price $\geq$ Mean

O'Neil's next suggestion is that the stock have a low number of shares outstanding, preferably under 25 million. Thus our fourth factor is:

Shares outstanding ≤ 25 million

He also says that the stock should have some institutional backing, but not be dominated by institutional investors. Stocks that are more than 60 percent institutionally owned are often heavily controlled by them. So we'll make that our fifth factor:

Percentage institutional $\leq 60\%$

Finally, O'Neil mentions the importance of relative strength several times in his book. So we'll make it the sixth and final factor, setting it at the number that leaves ten stocks. On January 1, 1993, setting the 26-week price percentage gain to 32 percent or better left ten stocks. Tables 11-1 and 11-2 show the full model as run on January 1, 1993 and the ten stocks that met all of the model's criteria.

Tables 11-3 and 11-4 list the key and secondary factors that emerge from looking at a factor analysis of the ten stocks. O'Neil's advice produces a factor profile that shares four of the five key factor differences with our Momentum Growth Model; high estimated earnings per share gain for the coming fiscal year is the only one missing. Interestingly, O'Neil's model uses only *historical data,* with no reliance on any forecasts or projections. Many think that's a better way to select stocks since forecasts are so often wrong. So we'll just make a note of it and look

Table 11-1. Value/Screen Database Screen after Running Our Model Using C-A-N S-L-I-M Criteria on December 31, 1992

Variable	<=>	Value	Number of stocks
5-year EPS growth	>	15	357
Last qtr EPS % chg	≥	20	106
Shares outstanding	≤	25	29
Percentage of high	≥	85.7	22
% Institutional	≤	60	13
26-wk % price chg	≥	32	10

Table 11-2. 10 Stocks Recommended by 6-Factor C-A-N S-L-I-M Model for the First Half of 1993

Ticker	Stock	Industry
CNC	Conseco	Insurance
J	Jackpot Enterprises	Hotel/gaming
JBM	Jan Bell Marketing	Retail
LUK	Leucadia National	Financial services
MSCA	M.S. Carriers	Truck/transportation
OLS	Olsten Corp.	Industrial services
PHSYA	Pacificare Health	Medical services
PHM	PHM Corp.	Home-building
SFE	Safeguard Science	Electronics
WERN	Werner Enterprises	Truck/transportation

Table 11-3. C-A-N S-L-I-M Model's Key Factors

Key Positive Factors

1. 12-month earnings per share percentage gains are 634% higher than the database.
2. 26-week price percentage gain is 397% higher than the database.
3. Last quarter earnings per share percentage gains are 283% higher than the database.
4. Five-year book value growth rates are 239% higher than the database.
5. Five-year earnings per share percentage gains are 199% higher than the database.

Key Negative Factors

1. Average annual sales are 83% lower than the database, with a maximum of $1.24 billion.
2. Average market capitalization is 79% lower than the database, with a maximum of $1.14 billion.
3. Average shares outstanding are 79% lower than the database, with a maximum of 25.

Table 11-4. C-A-N S-L-I-M Model's Secondary Factors

1. Return on net worth is 77% higher than the database.
2. Average yield is 76% below the database.
3. Average price-to-sales ratio is 17% lower than the database.
4. Average PE ratio is 2% lower than the database.

at the other differences. In addition to the four key factors it shares with our Momentum Growth Model, O'Neil's adds very high five-year earnings per share and book value growth rates, more historical evidence of the companies success at expanding earnings.

The companies are small. The low shares outstanding factor served as a proxy for small market capitalization, with the average of the ten just $586 million, 79 percent below the average stock in the database. Finally, two additional deviations are the classic value factors, price-to-earnings ratio and price-to-sales ratio. With most growth stock portfolios, these measures are significantly higher than the database. Yet we find that both are marginally *lower*, giving this portfolio a margin of safety that most growth portfolios don't have. All together, an interesting and consistent profile that we can expect to perform well.

The Model's Historical Performance

In testing the model's performance, we find the excellent results listed in Table 11-5. Not only does this model beat every mutual fund in the Morningstar database, it does so using small-cap stocks that were generally out of favor during this period. The strategy offers a good spread and an excellent risk-adjusted return of 0.84, similar to many of the best growth models we've tested.

Our results show that O'Neil knows what he's talking about with growth stocks, and that his book would be a worthwhile addition to any market enthusiast's library.

Use This Method to Evaluate All Market Advice

Books, brokers, and newsletters are just a few sources of market tips or information, but most can be evaluated using this method. Perhaps you have a friend who's done very well in the market over the past year. You can use factor analysis to find out exactly what method he or she is using to select stocks, and discern whether the success is due to true skill or just a lucky streak. Even ridiculous strategies can have a few good quarters before their ignorance and foolishness bring them crashing down! Your friend may not like to hear that the strategy provided a negative return over the last seven years, but you, and anyone who might seek advice from him or her, will most certainly want this information.

Conversely, you might use factor analysis to improve on a great natural investing talent. You might have a friend who does very well but could do much, much better with an additional factor or two. People are creatures of habit, and if there is anything harder than breaking an old habit, it's starting a new one. Investors may ignore highly relevant information either because

Table 11-5. Performance Results of 6-Factor Model
Based on O'Neil's C-A-N S-L-I-M System
December 31, 1985 through December 31, 1992

Time period	Portfolio performance (%)
December 31, 1985–June 30, 1986	36.19
June 30, 1986–December 31, 1986	−4.0
1986, full year	**30.74**
December 31, 1986–June 30, 1987	24.91
June 30, 1987–December 31, 1987	−12.30
1987, full year	**9.55**
December 31, 1987–June 30, 1988	15.20
June 30, 1988–December 31, 1988	1.30
1988, full year	**16.69**
December 31, 1988–June 30, 1989	23.20
June 30, 1989–December 31, 1989	10.44
1989, full year	**36.06**
December 31, 1989–June 30, 1990	18.20
June 30, 1990–December 31, 1990	−9.86
1990, full year	**6.55**
December 31, 1990–June 30, 1991	48.2
June 30, 1991–December 31, 1991	43.6
1991, full year	**112.82**
December 31, 1991–June 30, 1992	0.3
June 30, 1992–December 31, 1992	21.7
1992, full year	**22.07**
Cumulative return	**529.42**
Average annual return	**30.06**
Average 6-month return	**15.51**
Standard deviation of return	**18.39**
Projected maximum 6-month return	**52.29**
Projected minimum 6-month return	**−21.28**
Spread	**73.56**
Risk-adjusted return	**0.84**

they are habitually used to looking at stocks a certain way or simply because they want to avoid information overload. Factor analysis can help them understand that adding new, relevant information may really boost their gains.

Suppose you have a friend who has been getting great results using a growth strategy. When asked what she likes in a stock, she replies that she only buys stocks with outstanding five-year earnings per share growth rates, low debt levels, consistent earnings growth from year to year, and very high profit margins. Building a model that uses these criteria and testing it for

1991 shows a gain of 69.4 percent. This is very good. Yet you know from doing other factor profiles that a growth strategy can be greatly improved by including high estimated earnings for the next year and by limiting the number of stocks to ten. By convincing your friend to consider only the top ten stocks ranked by five-year growth rates, she could increase her return by over 14 percent. And if you also convinced her to buy only stocks that had forecasted earnings growth rates for the next fiscal year higher than the average, you could bump her return up another 13 percent for a gain of 96.6 percent in 1991.

Factor Analysis of Individual Stocks

You can also look at individual stocks in terms of factor profiles. Let's say you're an aggressive investor who wants to buy stocks whose earnings are expected to soar in the next year. On January 1, 1993, your broker recommends two stocks: *Tandycrafts* and *Times Mirror*. Both have excellent prospects for earnings increases. Yet if you used forecasted earnings gains as your only criterion, you'd buy Times Mirror, since Value Line is estimating that it will increase earnings by 103.1 percent next fiscal year, whereas Tandycraft is expected to increase earnings by only 40.8 percent.

Looking at the overall factor profile of the two stocks gives you a much different picture, however. Times Mirror is a newspaper company with high price stability, a Timeliness rank of 4, *negative* 12-month earnings per share change, and a 26-week price change of −9.7 percent, putting it in the *bottom* quarter of stocks ranked by relative strength. This is hardly the ideal growth stock, and something you wouldn't know if you didn't look at the stock's overall factor profile.

Tandycrafts is a different story. This seller of hobby items has a very small number of shares outstanding, Timeliness and Technical ranks of 1, a high price stability, a *huge* 12-month earnings per share gain of 137.8 percent, and a 26-week price change of 171.4 percent, giving it one of the best relative strength ratings in the entire database. This stock's profile is far more similar to an ideal growth stock's profile, so it's the more promising growth stock to buy.

A Cohesive Framework

You'll never again be without moorings when evaluating *any-one's* advice on stocks. You now have a cohesive framework with which to review any suggestion, whether it is from a book recommending a specific strategy or from an individual recommending particular stocks. Factor analysis lets you test what you previously took on faith, and gives you the ability to separate the hundreds of mediocre approaches from the few that shine.

12
Getting the Best from All Styles

So far, we've created portfolios from single models that reflect a strong style, such as the Momentum Growth Model using CGM's key factors and the Big-Cap Income model from Chap. 10. Many of you, however, may enjoy the more involved process of using several different models to create a single portfolio.

Multimodel Stock Selection

Many of the portfolios I develop use as many as eight independent multifactor models, allowing me to "cherry-pick" the best stocks these models have to offer. As you develop your own models, you'll no doubt find several with superior performance. Testing them more deeply than we have here (an analysis that's outside the scope of this book) reveals that in many instances you can narrow down the number of stocks a model recommends to even fewer than ten by insisting that they meet even more stringent criteria than the original model. The resulting stocks possess a more highly defined factor profile that, when joined with stocks from other models, lets you utilize your strategy in a more thorough and profitable fashion.

Selecting Stocks Meeting the Criteria of Several Models

While developing multiple models that cherry-pick stocks can get complicated, a simple way to increase your certainty about a stock is to require that it be recommended by *several* models before putting it on your buy list. This also lets you find stocks that are closer to your ideal. For example, you may think that the Momentum Growth Model uncovers great opportunities in growth stocks, but you also find merit in the small-capitalization and low price-to-earnings style used by the model developed with Delaware Trend's key factors in Chap. 5. The simple solution is to add a stock to your list only if it's found in *both models*. Thus, on January 1, 1993, only Kysor Industrial would have made it onto your list. Kysor is essentially a small-cap, rapidly growing company with tremendous relative strength and great expectations for continued rapid growth that also sells at modest price-to-sales and price-to-earnings ratios. This approach is most useful when you are adding to an existing portfolio or only want to focus on a handful of prospective stocks.

Uniting Models

Uniting two models from a similar style and buying *all* the stocks on each model's recommended list is an excellent way to diversify your portfolio for any given style. Our Momentum Growth Model and the C-A-N S-L-I-M model developed in Chap. 11 are good examples. Each model has excellent earnings growth and high relative strength. But the C-A-N S-L-I-M model focuses on small-cap stocks, which also have outstanding five-year earnings per share growth rates, whereas the Momentum Growth Model gives far greater weight to stocks that have high *forecasted* earnings growth rates for the coming fiscal year.

These two styles are often slightly out of sync with each other, with one rising while the other rests. For example, in the second half of 1990, the C-A-N S-L-I-M model got hurt because of its small-cap exposure, losing almost 10 percent for the period. The Momentum Growth Model was unaffected, showing a gain of 2.60 percent. The opposite occurred, on the other hand, during the first half of 1992. Portfolios with huge estimated earnings were hit hard—the Momentum Growth Model lost 15.5 percent—while small-cap offerings avoided the blood bath: The C-A-N S-L-I-M portfolio showed a slight gain of 0.3 percent.

You can reduce overall risk (as measured by standard deviation) and enhance risk-adjusted return by uniting these two portfolios. Tables 12-1 and 12-2 review the performance of each model individually. Table 12-3 shows the results of investing half your money in the Momentum Growth Model and half in the C-A-N S-L-I-M model, always splitting your funds between the two when rebalancing in December and June. Uniting these models gives you broader style coverage and lowers your standard deviation of return. As we've seen, lowering a strategy's standard deviation may not sound so great historically, but the merged model's loss of 7.6 percent in the first half of 1992

Table 12-1. Performance Results of the Momentum Growth Model December 31, 1985 through December 31, 1992

Time period	Portfolio performance (%)
December 31, 1985–June 30, 1986	+47.1
June 30, 1986–December 31, 1986	−7.26
1986, full year	**36.42**
December 31, 1986–June 30, 1987	33.65
June 30, 1987–December 31, 1987	−9.90
1987, full year	**20.42**
December 31, 1987–June 30, 1988	6.0
June 30, 1988–December 31, 1988	21.99
1988, full year	**29.31**
December 31, 1988–June 30, 1989	21.8
June 30, 1989–December 31, 1989	9.47
1989, full year	**33.33**
December 31, 1989–June 30, 1990	14.8
June 30, 1990–December 31, 1990	2.60
1990, full year	**17.78**
December 31, 1990–June 30, 1991	50.50
June 30, 1991–December 31, 1991	63.80
1991, full year	**146.52**
December 31, 1991–June 30, 1992	−15.50
June 30, 1992–December 31, 1992	18.20
1992, full year	**−0.12**

Table 12-2. Performance Results of the Low Price-to-Earnings Ratio Model December 31, 1985 through December 31, 1992

Time period	Portfolio performance (%)
December 31, 1985–June 30, 1986	36.19
June 30, 1986–December 31, 1986	−4.0
1986, full year	**30.74**
December 31, 1986–June 30, 1987	24.91
June 30, 1987–December 31, 1987	−12.30
1987, full year	**9.55**
December 31, 1987–June 30, 1988	15.20
June 30, 1988–December 31, 1988	1.30
1988, full year	**16.69**
December 31, 1988–June 30, 1989	23.20
June 30, 1989–December 31, 1989	10.44
1989, full year	**36.06**
December 31, 1989–June 30, 1990	18.20
June 30, 1990–December 31, 1990	−9.86
1990, full year	**6.55**
December 31, 1990–June 30, 1991	48.2
June 30, 1991–December 31, 1991	43.6
1991, full year	**112.82**
December 31, 1991–June 30, 1992	−0.3
June 30, 1992–December 31, 1992	21.7
1992, full year	**22.07**

would surely have been easier to take than the Momentum Growth Model's 15.50-percent loss. Also remember that styles move into and out of fashion. Small-cap stocks may really shine for a string of quarters, while the Momentum Model's portfolio languishes. So this united model lets you benefit from both strategies.

Momentum Growth and C-A-N S-L-I-M are models with a great deal in common. However, when uniting models you'll frequently want to chose those whose factor profiles and return patterns are highly *dissimilar*. Doing so dramatically lowers risk while preserving overall returns; often one strategy will be taking a breather while the other soars, and vice versa.

Table 12-3. Performance Results Uniting the Momentum Growth Model and the C-A-N S-L-I-M Model December 31, 1985 through December 31, 1992

Time period	Two models joint performance (%)
December 31, 1985–June 30, 1986	41.65
June 30, 1986–December 31, 1986	−5.63
1986, full year	**33.67**
December 31, 1986–June 30, 1987	29.28
June 30, 1987–December 31, 1987	−11.10
1987, full year	**14.93**
December 31, 1987–June 30, 1988	10.6
June 30, 1988–December 31, 1988	11.65
1988, full year	**23.48**
December 31, 1988–June 30, 1989	22.50
June 30, 1989–December 31, 1989	9.96
1989, full year	**34.69**
December 31, 1989–June 30, 1990	16.50
June 30, 1990–December 31, 1990	−3.63
1990, full year	**12.27**
December 31, 1990–June 30, 1991	49.35
June 30, 1991–December 31, 1991	53.70
1991, full year	**129.55**
December 31, 1991–June 30, 1992	−7.60
June 30, 1992–December 31, 1992	19.95
1992, full year	**10.83**
Average return	**16.94**
Standard deviation of return	**20.08**
Maximum	**57.09**
Minimum	**−23.21**
Spread	**80.30**
Risk-adjusted return	**0.84**

Uniting Styles from Different Schools of Investing

An even more effective way to diversify a portfolio is to unite models from the growth and value schools. Doing so follows a philosophy not unlike the one John Donne expounds in his poem *The Good Morrow*, "Where can we find two better hemispheres without sharp North, without declining West. Whatever

Table 12-4. Portfolio Containing Stocks from Momentum Growth Model and Big-Cap Model Income on January 1, 1993 (listed by industry)

Ticker	Stock	Industry
LPX	Louisiana-Pacific	Paper
BGEN	Biogen	Drug
RD	Royal Dutch	Petroleum
SC	Shell Transport	Petroleum
BP	British Petroleum	Petroleum
TX	Texaco, Inc.	Petroleum
ELF	Elf Aquitaine	Petroleum
JSTN	Justin Industries	Building material
ARV	Arvin	Auto parts
LUV	Southwest Air	Air transport
BCE	BCE	Telecommunications
GTE	GTE	Telecommunications
NYN	NYNEX	Telecommunications
USW	US West	Telecommunications
AIT	Ameritech	Telecommunications
BTY	British Telecom	Foreign telecom
QVCN	QVC Network	Special retail
BK	Bank of New York	Bank
PGR	Progressive	Insurance
VRLN	Varlen	Diversified
KZ	Kysor Industrial	Diversified
BRG	British Gas	European diversified

dies was not mixed equally..." Mixing growth and value strategies equally gives you the best of both hemispheres, substantially reducing the volatility of strategies based on growth alone and increasing the capital appreciation potential of strategies centered on value. Consider the portfolio in Table 12-4, the result of joining the Momentum Growth Model with the Big-Cap Income model from Chap. 10.

This blended portfolio's factor profile is fascinating. Look at the list of some of the portfolio's factors in Table 12-5! You have

Table 12-5. Cross Section of the Portfolio's Factor Differences with the Database on January 1, 1993

Factor	Portfolio	Value Line database	Difference
Price stability rank	66	52	27% higher
Financial strength rank	B++	B+	Higher
Beta	0.94	1.02	8% lower
Price-to-earnings ratio	16.8	17.8	6% lower
Price-to-book ratio	2.41	2.62	8% lower
Current yield	3.7%	2.1%	76% higher
Market capitalization	$13.2 billion	$2.8 billion	371% higher
Last quarter earnings per share	98.5%	26%	279% higher
Percentage gain 12-month earnings per share	71.1%	17.2%	313.37% higher
Percentage gain 26-week price gains	22.1	10.0%	121% higher
Estimated change in earnings per share for coming fiscal year	119.5%	29.9%	300% higher

a big-cap portfolio with high price stability, a low beta, a low price-to-earnings ratio, and a yield 76 percent higher than the market—all the best of value. Yet you also have a portfolio with positive relative 26-week price strength, huge recent earnings gains, and earnings forecasts for more of the same—or for the best of the growth style. From a factor standpoint, you've got all the bases covered.

The portfolio's performance is outstanding, gaining over 515.90 percent between December 31, 1985 and December 31, 1992. That's 29.65 percent compounded annually! Over the last five years the strategy had an average annual return of 29.93 percent, beating all but two nonspecialty funds in Morningstar's database on an absolute basis.

Making Risk Tolerable

Yet this strategy really shines on a risk-adjusted basis, since it achieved these stellar returns with a standard deviation of

Table 12-6. Performance Results of the Combined
Model December 31, 1985 through December 31, 1992

Time period	Portfolio performance (%)
December 31, 1985–June 30, 1986	32.25
June 30, 1986–December 31, 1986	3.77
1986, full year	**37.24**
December 31, 1986–June 30, 1987	31.48
June 30, 1987–December 31, 1987	−7.80
1987, full year	**21.22**
December 31, 1987–June 30, 1988	10.3
June 30, 1988–December 31, 1988	14.65
1988, full year	**26.45**
December 31, 1988–June 30, 1989	19.0
June 30, 1989–December 31, 1989	13.89
1989, full year	**35.52**
December 31, 1989–June 30, 1990	9.90
June 30, 1990–December 31, 1990	−1.25
1990, full year	**8.53**
December 31, 1990–June 30, 1991	32.15
June 30, 1991–December 31, 1991	38.85
1991, full year	**83.49**
December 31, 1991–June 30, 1992	−3.05
June 30, 1992–December 31, 1992	11.90
1992, full year	**8.49**
Cumulative return	**515.90**
Average annual return	**29.65**
Average 6-month return	**14.72**
Standard deviation of return	**13.99**
Projected maximum 6-month return	**42.70**
Projected minimum 6-month return	**−13.27**
Spread	**55.98**
Risk-adjusted return	**1.05**

return of 13.99 percent, just a few points above the S&P 500's
and well below the two top Morningstar funds. *On a risk-adjusted basis, this strategy beat all the funds in Morningstar's database.*
Table 12-6 shows the returns of the combined portfolio, along
with other risk-adjusted figures.

In Chap. 6 we saw that it's best for an aggressive investor to
choose the strategy with the largest spread and highest risk-
adjusted return. Our merged model has a very high risk-adjust-

ed return of 1.05 but a low spread of 55.98 percent, which should make aggressive investors steer clear. Even here, that holds true. But that advice was for models based on single schools of investing. And even then, how many investors are truly that aggressive? In reality, where emotions and other considerations are always weighing on investment decisions, reducing a strategy's overall risk makes up for the lost return. Using the Momentum Growth Model alone, your maximum expected loss from for any six-month period is 27.22 percent, a high number. Adding the Big-Cap Income Model's stocks cuts the figure in half, changing the maximum expected six-month loss to 13.27 percent. The Big-Cap stocks act as ballast to the Momentum Growth's sails, dragging down performance a bit but ensuring that the portfolio will not sink.

Intellectually, it's easy to exude great bravado and claim all you care about is your portfolio's total return. Yet examples of the overwhelming influence emotions have on investment decisions abound. Nine out of ten investors using the Momentum Growth Model or investing in an aggressive growth strategy might buckle when the strategy or fund approaches maximum loss, letting an emotional decision destroy all the good the strategy did in the past. Selling at the bottom of *any* strategy's cycle destroys the reason for following it in the first place. Yet it happens time and again.

Uniting the two strategies makes risk tolerable by significantly reducing the maximum potential loss. It allows those who would not even consider an aggressive strategy to give it a second look, and lets truly aggressive investors get a better night's sleep. You give up some *potential* reward, but you also dramatically increase the likelihood that you'll *actually receive* that reward.

The Best Mix

Rare is the investor that's all fish or all fowl. Most seek growth for their capital, but would also like a good income and a risk level that lets them sleep well at night. Uniting models and the investment strategies from the growth and value school allows you to achieve just that, smoothing out variability, at the same time preserving the best of both investment strategies.

13

Avoiding Pitfalls:
Four Rules for
Investment Success

According to Peter Hay's *The Book of Business Anecdotes*, Bernard Baruch, a legendary investor and presidential adviser, once said that he had ten rules for investing. But pressed, he once honed them down to two commandments: First, never pay any attention to what a company president says about his stock. Second, sell when good news about the market hits the front page of *The New York Times*.

Pressed, we'll give four rules that you must follow if you are to be successful at multifactor model building:

1. Never use a single factor on a broad universe like the Value Line.

2. Never use "strange" factor combinations.

3. Always do multiyear evaluations of any model.

4. Always look at the risk-adjusted return.

Let's see why these are so important.

Never Use a Single Factor on a Broad Universe

In 1991, over the Christmas holiday, you read a terrific article extolling the virtues of buying stocks with very low price-to-book ratios. It cites the historical research of Ben Graham and David Dodd, which showed that stocks with low price-to-book ratios consistently outperformed the market. The article also reports on the more recent findings of Roger Ibbotson, which showed that, between 1967 and 1984, the 10 percent of stocks on the New York Stock Exchange with the lowest price-to-book ratio returned 14.36 percent compounded annually, outperforming the 10 percent with the highest by 8.5 percent per year. The article went on to say that Marc Reinganum, a finance professor at the University of Iowa, did an extensive study of 222 stocks that tripled in price in any given calendar year between 1970 and 1983, finding that one of the things most winners had in common was price-to-book value ratio below 1.

As you read the article, you get more and more excited, since such a contrarian stock-picking method really appeals to you! You resolve to follow up on this great investment idea and march off to the library, get the Value Line Investment Survey, and locate the ten stocks with the lowest price-to-book ratios. You take the list home (see Table 13-1) and call your broker, instructing him to buy all ten stocks. He says that a few of them

Table 13-1. 10 Stocks with Lowest Price-to-Book Ratios in the Value Line Database on December 31, 1991

Ticker	Stock	Price-to-book ratio
CAL	CAL Fed	0.05
WPPGY	WPP Group	0.06
SAA	Saatcchi & Saatchi Plc.	0.08
TFC	Transcapital Financial	0.10
MIDL	Midlantic Corp.	0.14
NSD	National Std.	0.14
NTK	Nortek, Inc.	0.14
DME	Dime Savings Bank	0.16
GLN	Glenfed	0.18
ADP	Allied Products	0.21

Table 13-2. Percentage Change in Share Prices
December 31, 1991 to June 30, 1992

Ticker	Stock	6-month return (%)
CAL	CAL Fed	72.2
WPPGY	WPP Group	−6.7
SAA	Saatcchi & Saatchi Plc.	N/A
TFC	Transcapital Financial	−63.7
MIDL	Midlantic Corp.	225
NSD	National Std.	92.3
NTK	Nortek, Inc.	193.3
DME	Dime Savings Bank	85.1
GLN	Glenfed	−10.9
ADP	Allied Products	−24.0
Average gain		56.26

are quite interesting turnaround candidates, but implores you not to buy several of the stocks, like WPP Group, which he says is teetering at the edge of bankruptcy. You thank him but remain firm, telling him to buy all ten stocks.

On June 30, 1992, you're stunned when you review your portfolio. Your ten stocks—listed with the gains shown in Table 13-2—are up over 56 percent in just six months! The S&P 500 *lost* 2.2 percent for the same period. Midlantic Corp. did the best, gaining over 225 percent in just six months! You run back to the library, find the current ten stocks with the lowest price-to-book ratios, go home and bark out buy orders to your broker like a pro. This time he doesn't argue with you; if you *were* a pro, you'd have the best six-month investment record in the entire country. You think you've discovered the perfect investment strategy. You're wrong.

Anything Can Work for a Few Quarters

In options trading, the worst thing you can do is make money on your first trade, since your success is usually based on a naive model or just dumb luck. The same is true here. During the second half of 1991, your ten stocks would have *lost* 14.8 percent, compared to a gain of 10 percent for the S&P 500. Still, you say, you made almost 33 percent for the year compared to a tiny gain for the S&P 500. You might continue to be intoxicated by that 56 percent run-up, convinced that, if you stick with the program, you'll continue to do very well.

Willingness to stick to the program is exemplary. But reliance on a single-factor screen when using a broad universe like the 1600 stocks in the Value Line is one of the most dangerous, foolish things you can do—especially if you are narrowing down the selection to just a handful of stocks. And it doesn't matter *which* single factor you use, you'll always end up with a highly unstable, volatile portfolio.

Testing Single-Factor Portfolios in Down Years

One of the best ways to see the devastating results from a single-factor portfolio is to look at its performance in a bad year. In 1990, the S&P 500 lost 3.17 percent. Let's look at how a variety of single-factor portfolios did in that year. Tables 13-3 and 13-4 list the ten stocks with the lowest price-to-book ratios as of December 31, 1989 and June 30, 1990, along with their subsequent six-month performances. In the second half of 1990, the low price-to-book portfolio would have lost an astounding 56 percent of its value. The return for all of 1990 was a stunning loss of 60.53 percent! To match such horrible performance you'd had to have bought the S&P 500 in 1929 and held on until the market bottomed in 1932! Meritor Savings, Fairfield Commu-

Table 13-3. 10 Stocks with Lowest Price-to-Book Ratios as of December 31, 1989

Ticker	Stock	Price-to-book ratio
IRE	Integrated Resources	0.01
ICA	Imperial Corp.	0.05
CRL	Crossland Savings	0.10
MDC	M D C Holding	0.11
FSB	Financial Corp. Santa Bar.	0.19
TFC	Transcapital Financial	0.23
MTOR	Meritor Savings	0.28
WKR	Whittaker Corp.	0.28
MLIS	Micropolis	0.31
DME	Dime Savings Bank	0.32
Total return, December 31, 1989–June 30, 1990	−10.30%	

Table 13-4. 10 Stocks with Lowest Price-to-Book Ratios as of June 30, 1990

Ticker	Stock	Price-to-book ratio
TFC	Transcapital Financial	0.14
FWF	Far West Financial	0.16
ABCP	Ambase	0.20
MGA	Magna International	0.20
NTK	Nortek	0.22
FCI	Fairfield Communities, Inc.	0.23
UMM	United Merchants	0.23
DME	Dime Savings Bank	0.24
MTOR	Meritor Savings	0.25
UH	U.S. Home Corp.	0.27
Total return, June 30, 1990–December 31, 1990	−56.0%	

nities, and Ambase all lost more than three-quarters of their value. The *best* performing stock was Nortek, *losing* 13.1 percent. For the three years between December 31, 1989 and December 31, 1992, buying the ten stocks with the lowest price-to-book ratios, rebalancing the portfolio every six months, would have netted you a loss of over 48 percent of your capital!

The same is true of other single-factor portfolios. Tables 13-5 and 13-6 list portfolios based on the ten stocks with the lowest price-to-earnings ratios. Those stocks did even *worse*, losing almost 65 percent during the year. A yield strategy fared only slightly better, as Tables 13-7 and 13-8 show.

It's not just value strategies that did so poorly. While 1990 was much kinder to growth strategies, portfolios based on *single* growth factors also suffered. Tables 13-9 through 13-14 show the results of using several popular growth factors as single screens on the Value Line 1600. In each case, the single-factor portfolios did significantly worse than both the market and the multifactor models that included the single factor as one of their variables. As we've seen time and again, using a single factor to narrow 1600 stocks down to ten leads to a huge factor instability in a portfolio.

Let's use yield as an example. Not all high-yield stocks are created equal. Stocks with high yields *may* be good investments, *depending on their other factors*. It's one thing if a stock has a yield

Table 13-5. 10 Stocks with Lowest Price-to-Earnings Ratios
as of December 31, 1989

Ticker	Stock	Price-to-earnings ratio
WHX	Wheeling Pittsburgh Steel	0.5
LTV	LTV Corp.	0.6
RAY	Raytech Corp.	2.8
BKNE	Bank of New England	3.1
EPI	Eagle Picher Ind.	3.7
NVR	Nvryan, L.P.	3.9
SPF	Standard Pac Corp.	4.0
MNCO	Michigan National	4.1
F	Ford Motor	4.4
N	INCO Ltd.	4.6
Total return, December 31, 1989–June 30, 1990	−24.32%	

Table 13-6. 10 Stocks with Lowest Price-to-Earnings Ratios
as of June 30, 1990

Ticker	Stock	Price-to-earnings ratio
LTV	LTV Corp.	0.9
EPI	Eagle Picher Ind.	1.1
FEXC	First Executive	2.3
GLN	Glenfed	3.1
HFD	Homefed	3.3
GGC	Georgia Gulf Corp.	3.4
NVR	Nvryan, L.P.	3.4
SPF	Standard Pac Corp.	3.4
ENST	Enstar Group	4.0
DME	Dime Savings Bank	4.0
Total return, June 30, 1990–December 31, 1990	−53.68%	
Total return, 1990	−64.95%	

of 9 percent *and* a market capitalization above $20 billion with sales above $20 billion, a financial strength rating of A++ and a projected dividend growth rate of 7.0 percent. It's quite another if a stock is yielding 9.0 percent, *and* it is losing money, has a tiny market capitalization, carries a financial strength rank of C, and

Table 13-7. 10 Stocks with Highest Yields as of December 31, 1989

Ticker	Stock	Yield (%)
NVR	Nvryan, L.P.	19.2
BKNE	Bank of New England	16.2
SPF	Standard Pac Corp.	16.1
KOG	Koger Properties	11.8
MHC	Manufacturers Hanover	9.9
SLP	Sun Energy Partners L.P.	9.9
FG	USF&G Corp.	9.9
PE	Philadelphia Electric	9.7
BPL	Buckeye Partners L.P.	9.4
UXP	Union Expl. Partners	9.4
Total return, December 31, 1989–June 30, 1990	−17.38%	

Table 13-8. 10 Stocks with Highest Yields as of June 30, 1990

Ticker	Stock	Yield (%)
NVR	Nvryan, L.P.	24.4
SPF	Standard Pac Corp.	18.6
LYO	Lyondell Petrochemical	13.5
TT	Transtechnology	13.2
KOG	Koger Properties	12.7
MIDL	Midlantic Corp.	11.9
SLP	Sun Energy Partners L.P.	11.7
FG	USF&G Corp.	10.7
FUN	Cedar Fair L.P.	10.6
CHL	Chemical Banking	10.6
Total return, June 30, 1990–December 31, 1990	−21.82%	
Total return, 1990	−35.41%	

is expected to cut its dividend. Yet both stocks might make it into a high-yield portfolio where high yield is the only criterion.

Looking at the second half of 1990, when the S&P 500 de-clined by 7.80 percent and the broader market, as measured by the Value Line Index, plummeted by 20.40 percent, you can see how adding

Table 13-9. 10 Stocks with Highest 12-Month Earnings per Share Percentage Gains as of December 31, 1989

Ticker	Stock	12-month EPS % gain
AZ	Atlas Corp.	998.8
SGAT	Seagate Technology	722.2
FCA	Fabri Centers America	693.3
LUK	Leucadia National	682.6
AHC	Amerada Hess Corp.	668.2
BNS	Brown & Sharpe	642.9
USR	U.S. Shoe	600.0
WN	Wynns International	600.0
OH	Oakwood Homes Corp.	575.0
EME	Emerson Radio	566.7
Total return, December 31, 1989–June 30, 1990	10.10%	

Table 13-10. 10 Stocks with Highest 12-Month Earnings per Share Percentage Gains as of June 30, 1990

Ticker	Stock	12-month EPS % gain
COHR	Coherent Inc.	900.0
JBBB	JBS Restaurants	628.6
CUC	Culbro	585.7
USHC	U.S. Healthcare	572.7
DTX	Dominion Textile	561.5
OXM	Oxford Industries	537.5
DYA	Dynamics Corp	475.0
PWJ	Paine Webber	442.9
CE	California Energy	387.5
VLSI	VLSI Technology	387.5
Total return, June 30, 1990–December 31, 1990	−21.2%	
Total return, 1990	−13.21%	

additional factors can affect performance tremendously. Table 13-15 shows the ten stocks with the highest 12-month earnings per share percentage gains as of June 30, 1990, while also showing how those stocks scored on several other factors. Had you just bought the ten stocks with the best 12-month earnings gains, you

Table 13-11. 10 Stocks with Highest 5-Year Earnings
per Share Growth Rate as of December 31, 1989

Ticker	Stock	5-year EPS growth rate(%)
GNE	Genetech	97.5
ORCL	Oracle Systems	91.5
AR	Asarco	82.5
SMC	A.O. Smith	80.5
SUP	Superior Industries	71.0
LK	Lockheed	70.0
NSH	Nashua Corp.	70.0
TATE	Ashton Tate	64.5
CLE	Claire's Stores	64.0
BMET	Biomet	63.5
MX	Measurex	63.5
Total return, December 31, 1989–June 30, 1990	12.1%	

Table 13-12. 10 Stocks with Highest 5-Year Earnings
per Share Growth Rate as of June 30, 1990

Ticker	Stock	5-year EPS growth rate (%)
CCN	Chris Craft	92.5
BEN	Franklin Resources	84.5
GNE	Genetech	80.0
GR	Goodrich, B.F.	77.0
AMAT	Applied Materials	75.0
RES	Renaissance Energy	73.0
MNCO	Michigan National	72.5
LPX	Louisiana Pac	67.0
CCTV	Carlton Communications	65.5
APWR	Applied Power	63.5
BMET	Biomet	63.5
Total return, June 30, 1990–December 31, 1990	−21.70%	
Total return, 1990	−12.23%	

Table 13-13. 10 Stocks with Highest Estimated Fiscal
Year Earnings per Share Percentage Gains as of
December 31, 1989

Ticker	Stock	Estimated EPS % gain coming fiscal year
AZE	American Maize	945.5
DTX	Dominion Textile	685.7
CUC	Culbro	600.0
NMG	Neiman Marcus	566.7
NBL	Noble Affiliates	483.3
BPC	BP Cda, Inc.	472.7
IHS	IPCO	400.0
KSU	Kansas City Southern	391.8
BVI	Bow Valley Industries	375.0
PCR	Perini	371.8
Total return, December 31, 1989–June 30, 1990	−7.41%	

Table 13-14. 10 Stocks with Highest Estimated Fiscal Year
Earnings per Share Percentage Gains as of June 30, 1990

Ticker	Stock	Estimated EPS % gain coming fiscal year
BGEN	Biogen	900.0
NMG	Neiman Marcus	866.7
HDYN	Healthdyne	777.2
KNO	Knogo Corp.	733.3
MOSI	Mosinee Paper	672.7
RELL	Richardson Electronics	650.0
CAO	Carolina Freight	537.5
CHF	Chock Full O'Nuts	480.0
GH	General Host	480.0
HSC	Harsco	479.1
Total return, June 30, 1990–December 31, 1990	−12.40%	
Total return, 1990	−18.89%	

Table 13-15. 10 Stocks with Highest 12-Month Earnings per Share Percentage Gains as of June 30, 1990 with Additional Factors

Ticker	Stock	12-month EPS % gain	26-week price change (%)	Estimated EPS gain for coming fiscal year (%)
COHR	Coherent, Inc.	900.0	−11.1	−32.1
JBBB	JBS Restaurants	628.6	16.7	17.6
CUC	Culbro	585.7	−24.7	18.6
USHC	U.S. Healthcare	572.7	42.1	75.0
DTX	Dominion Textile	561.5	−32.8	221.4
OXM	Oxford Industries	537.5	−28.9	17.6
DYA	Dynamics Corp.	475.0	−13.5	−3.8
PWJ	Paine Webber	442.9	19.8	4.8
CE	California Energy	387.5	−29.5	87.5
VLSI	VLSI Technology	387.5	47.4	N/A

would have lost 21.2 percent between June 30 and December 31 of 1990, worse than the Value Line Index's decline.

If, on the other hand, you looked at the list and applied additional criteria that we know are important to growth investing, performance soars. If you added only one other factor, relative strength in its simplest form, requiring that all stocks have positive 26-week price changes, only four of the ten stocks would qualify: JB's Restaurants, Paine Webber Group, U.S. Healthcare, and VLSI Technology. As a group, these four stocks lost just 10.23 percent, cutting in half the loss of our first ten. If you added *another* growth factor in its simplest form, requiring that each stock have a positive estimated change in earnings per share for the coming year, you'd be left with just JB's Restaurant, Paine Webber, and U.S. Healthcare. Those three *gained 4.90 percent.* Finally, if you used more rigorous requirements for the two additional factors and required each to be above 20 percent, you'd be left with just U.S. Healthcare, which gained 59.6 percent over the same period! This big difference is brought about simply by linking good factors.

Smaller Databases Are Different

Taking the single-factor approach with a smaller, predefined database like the Dow Jones Industrial Average isn't as risky, however. That's because the Dow is made up of some of the biggest, best-known blue chip companies in America, and in essence *already reflects* a multitude of factor differences from the broader market. The Dow's underlying factor profile would be similar to a group of stocks arrived at by screening the database for large, well-known blue chips with strong financial positions and high market visibility.

Let's compare the highest-yielding stock in the Dow Jones Industrial Average on December 31, 1989, General Motors, to the highest-yielding stock from broad Value Line database, Nvryan, LP. Nvryan's 16.2 percent yield appears more attractive than GM's 7 percent, but when we look at the other factors these stocks possess, a different picture emerges. GM had a market capitalization over $26 billion, a Safety rank of 1, a Financial Strength rank of A+, more than 600 million shares outstanding, and a price stability of 90. Nvryan L. P., on the other hand, had a market capitalization of only $125 million, a Safety rank of 4, a Financial Strength rank of B, 25 million shares outstanding, and a price stability index of 5, the lowest rank. Which stock is going to appeal to a conservative income-oriented investor more?

Table 13-16 lists the top ten yielding stocks in the Dow as of December 31, 1989. These are very well known companies. And because they're among the biggest and best-known stocks in the market, you see radically different performances: While the ten

Table 13-16. 10 Dow Stocks with Highest Yields as of December 31, 1989

Ticker	Stock	Yield (%)
GM	General Motors	7.0
S	Sears	5.90
TX	Texaco	5.40
ALD	Allied Signal	5.10
IBM	IBM	5.10
EK	Eastman Kodak	4.90
XON	Exxon	4.80
UK	Union Carbide	4.30
CHV	Chevron	4.20
GT	Goodyear Tire	4.10
Total return, 1990	−8.64%	

Table 13-17. 10 Dow Stocks with Highest Estimated Earnings Gains for the Coming Fiscal Year as of December 31, 1989

Ticker	Stock	Estimated earnings gain (%)
NAV	Navistar International	117.4
BA	Boeing	47.40
X	USX	35.40
MO	Philip Morris	35.10
PG	Procter & Gamble	25.30
DD	DuPont	25.10
MRK	Merck	24.60
T	AT&T	20.90
IP	International Paper	18.0
KO	Coca Cola	17.50
Total return, 1990	4.61%	

highest-yielding stocks in the Value Line database lost over 35 percent in 1990, these lost just 8.64 percent.

The same is true when looking at other factors. Look at Table 13-17. Compare the ten Dow stocks with the highest estimated earnings gains for the coming fiscal year with the ten Value Line stocks with the highest estimated earnings gains. You see again that the Dow stocks are a much better investment, gaining 4.61 percent, compared to the 10 Value Line stock's loss of nearly 19 percent.

Thus, unless you are using a preselected database like the Dow Jones Industrial Average, which already has strong factor differences from the market as a whole, never use just one factor to make stock selections.

Never Use "Strange" Factor Combinations

What's "strange"? A strange combination uses factors together that are neither intuitively nor logically connected: high yield linked to very low financial ranking, high earnings per share estimates linked with negative 12-month earnings per share percentage gains, huge earnings gains linked with negative forecasted changes for the coming year. All these go together about as well as pancakes and vinegar.

Use care, because some strange combinations might *sound* like good contrarian models. For example, on December 31, 1992, you read an article that says a great way to make money is to be a contrarian, buying what others are selling. One way to do this, opines the article, is to buy stocks that have had awful earnings changes over the last quarter and year (causing investors to sell the shares) and that also have very high expected earnings gains for the coming fiscal year. The author states that these shares will soar in price as their earnings recover and cites the previous year's gain of almost 28 percent versus a gain of little over 7 percent for the S&P 500 as proof of the method's effectiveness. The fictional article lists ten stocks (featured in Table 13-18)— that currently meet the criteria.

A quick factor profile—a cross section of which appears in Table 13-19—confirms that the portfolio conforms to the article's strategy. Yet this portfolio is the result of combining factors that *just don't go together.* High estimated earnings gains are a growth stock's turf, and, as our study of the best growth managers has shown, growth stocks have great earnings gains and great relative strength *as well as high forecasted gains.* This portfolio has no stocks with Timeliness ratings above 3; most growth stock portfolios never own stocks with Timeliness rankings *below 3!* The factors just don't make sense together and should warn you to

Table 13-18. 10 Stocks with Negative 12-Month Earnings per Share Gains and High Forecasted Earnings Gains for Coming Fiscal Year as of December 31, 1992

Ticker	Stock
HEM	Hemlo Gold Mines
CIC	Continental Corp.
BEP	BET Publications
UCL	Unocal
ITX	International Tech Corp.
BHI	Baker Hughes
TKOS	Tokos Medical
MTSC	MTS Systems
WBB	Webb Del
ASH	Ashland Oil

Table 13-19. Cross Section of Factor Differences Between 10-Stock Portfolio and Database Mean on December 31, 1992

Factor	10-stock portfolio	Value Line mean	Difference
Timeliness rank	4, no 1 or 2 ranks	3	33% worse
Safety rank	4, no 1 or 2 ranks	3	33% worse
Price-to-sales ratio	1.1	1.4	21% lower
PE	19.1	18.6	2.7% higher
12-month EPS change	−48.5%	17.2%	382% lower
Last quarter EPS change	−40.1%	26%	254% lower
Estimated EPS change coming fiscal year	106.3%	29.9%	256% higher
26-week price percentage change	−16.2%	10%	262% lower
Yield	2.8%	2.2%	27% higher

stay away. Yet the model gained more than 28 percent last year and it's hard to argue with success.

Always Do Multiyear Evaluations

This leads us to our next rule: Always do a multiyear evaluation of any strategy. *Any* strategy can have a good year, even a *few* good years, no matter how silly its methods. Yet foolish strategies rarely do well for long. When you look beyond a few years, they almost always break down.

In this example, a simple four-factor model defines the strategy:

1. 12-months, earnings per share must be equal to or less than zero.

2. Last quarter earnings per share must be equal to or less than zero.

3. Six-month price percentage change must be equal to or less than the mean for the above selections (e.g., the mean of the resultant stocks after running the two preceding factors).

4. Estimated earnings gains for the coming fiscal year must be equal to a number that leaves ten stocks.

Table 13-20. Performance Results of 4-Factor Model
December 31, 1985 through December 31, 1992

Time period	Portfolio performance (%)
December 31, 1985–June 30, 1986	23
June 30, 1986–December 31, 1986	−9.1
1986, full year	**11.81**
December 31, 1986–June 30, 1987	22.2
June 30, 1987–December 31, 1987	−27.60
1987, full year	**−11.53**
December 31, 1987–June 30, 1988	22.60
June 30, 1988–December 31, 1988	2.20
1988, full year	**25.29**
December 31, 1988–June 30, 1989	13.80
June 30, 1989–December 31, 1989	−4.30
1989, full year	**8.90**
December 31, 1989–June 30, 1990	10.10
June 30, 1990–December 31, 1990	−24.2
1990, full year	**−16.54**
December 31, 1990–June 30, 1991	26.60
June 30, 1991–December 31, 1991	4.90
1991, full year	**32.80**
December 31, 1991–June 30, 1992	18.50
June 30, 1992–December 31, 1992	7.90
1992, full year	**27.86**
Cumulative return	**91.28**
Average return	**6.19**
Standard deviation	**16.65**
Projected maximum 6-month return	**39.48**
Projected minimum 6-month return	**−27.11**
Spread	**66.59**
Risk-adjusted return	**0.37**

The strategy's performance in 1992 was outstanding, but how about before then? Table 13-20 shows the results of a seven-year test of the model. For the five years ending on December 31, 1990, the strategy showed a gain of just 12.65 percent! The S&P 500 did seven times as well, gaining 94.85 percent. Even the average *bond* fund did four times better! You'd have almost been better off keeping your money under your mattress. For the full seven years, the strategy gained just 91.28 percent compared to 173.62 percent for the S&P 500. This strategy's double-digit losses in 1987, the year of the crash, and in 1990, a mild bear market year, show that it's poison when the markets are bad. The other years show that it's simply mediocre when the market is bullish. 1991 was the best year for growth stocks in a decade, but you wouldn't know it looking at this strategy's return, as it gained just 2 percent more than the S&P 500.

The seven-year test gives you a context for reviewing the strategy's effectiveness and shows you what might have been apparent from a factor review: The strategy's performance in 1992 was a fluke. That's something *only those who do multiyear reviews will know.*

Always Look at Risk-Adjusted Returns

Not only was the strategy's return in 1992 a fluke; it was also dangerous. This leads to our final rule: Always look at risk-adjusted return. This strategy's low absolute return makes it fairly obvious that you shouldn't use it, but its risk-adjusted return makes the point even more clearly. Over the seven years of the test, the strategy's risk-adjusted return of 0.37 was one of the lowest we've seen. The strategy did horribly on an absolute basis *and* took tremendous risk. It's as if you lost a race by coming in last, and then found out your car also had a blind driver—putting you at the greatest risk for an accident.

Now this strategy was obviously bad. Risk-adjusted returns can guide you to the proper conclusion even with strategies that ostensibly make sense. The mediocre manager from Chap. 6 that masqueraded as a star is an even better example of the usefulness of risk-adjusted return since the absolute return was so good. That strategy's gain of 279 percent over the seven years beat all but a handful of the mutual funds in Morningstar's database. Yet its risk-adjusted return of 0.50 shows that the strategy was taking a great deal of risk to deliver the return. You *never* have to accept a low risk-adjusted return, and always reviewing it allows you to avoid all the hidden disasters others will never see until it's too late.

More Rules

Obviously, our list of commandments could go on to include many of the other points we've made on factor analysis. Yet if you follow these rules and use the factors that we've seen define almost all the top performing funds, you'll be on your way to trouncing the majority of investors.

14
The Final Factor

Remember the parable of the silver pieces? It's Matthew's account of a story Jesus told about a man embarking on a long journey. The man called in three servants, giving each a portion of his funds to manage during his absence. He gave each an amount that reflected his ability: To the first he gave 5000 silver pieces, to the second 2000, and to the third 1000. Immediately, the servant who'd been given 5000 invested the money and made another 5000. So too did the man with 2000, investing it for a gain of an additional 2000. But the man who received 1000 silver pieces feared his master and, rather than risk investing the money, dug a hole and buried it.

After a long absence, the master returned and called for his servants. The first came forward, showing his master that he had doubled the money entrusted to him. Pleased, the master told his servant that since he'd proved dependable in small matters, he'd now put him in charge of larger affairs. The same thing happened to the servant who had doubled the 2000. Finally, the man entrusted with 1000 silver pieces came forward and said that, because the master was a hard man, who reaped where he did not sow and gathered where he did not scatter, he feared losing his money so much that he buried it in order to return the amount intact.

The outraged master called this servant a lazy, worthless lout. He should at least have deposited the money with bankers so that he could offer his master interest on the silver pieces.

The master then gave the 1000 silver pieces to the man with 10,000. Those who have will get more, he told his servants, while those who have not will lose even the little that they have.

He then threw the unprofitable servant out into the night to wail and grind his teeth.

The Market Is the Master

The market is the master. Which servant are you? Too many investors empathize with the third man. Bombarded with innumerable, seemingly complicated options, they let their confusion paralyze them and bury their heads—and money—in the sand. The results are often the same as in the parable. Timid, aimless investors forfeit what little they have to the superior investors who have the courage to act. But action alone is not enough. Action without knowledge is foolish, and knowledge without action is futile. The key is informed action.

Reviewing Your Knowledge

You now have the tools to simplify and understand the unknown. You can tune out the cacophony of competing advice and look at the underlying structure of today's best managers' portfolios. You *know* that the best money managers employ superior strategies—strategies that are easy to uncover and define with factor analysis—consistently and rigorously. You *know* that you can uncover *any portfolio's* key factor differences from the market—the differences that are responsible for the portfolio's performance—by doing a factor analysis of the portfolio. You *know* that, while the top managers of a style may *say* they're different from one another and buy different stocks, their factor profiles show that they emphasize the *same key factors.* This is truly amazing, but shouldn't come as a big surprise. After all, what *is* a growth manager going to focus on if not growth in earnings and assets? What *is* a value manager going to focus on if not stocks selling at a bargain? While there are many factor differences among managers, with their many variations, those are secondary to the most important ones that are almost universally applied.

You *know* that the only way a portfolio can do significantly *better* than the market is to have a factor profile that is significantly *different* from the market. You know that the best managers keep their portfolio's factors highly skewed from the market and do so consistently. You know that portfolio factor profiles of mediocre managers are more similar to the market's profile. Finally, you know that poor managers use strange factor combinations, like extraordinarily large earnings forecasts linked to negative 12-month earnings gains.

You *know* that you can improve on these styles by using key factors efficiently and by religiously rebalancing your portfolio so that it consistently reflects those highly defined factors.

You *know* that what works for the pros can work for you.

The Final Factor

Knowing isn't enough, though. You must also act. And that leads to our final factor: *the will to act and stick with an intelligent investment program.* As Goethe said, "In the realm of ideas, everything depends on enthusiasm, in the real world, all rests on perseverance." Many get enthusiastic about good investment ideas but few succeed since they fail to persevere. None of the factors and models described in this book will do you any good if you fail to consistently act and use what you know.

Successful investors understand that simple, highly effective methods will not do them any good if they continually second-guess them. Successful investing is an act of will. To be a successful investor you must understand that you'll never be right all the time, that you'll almost never buy at the low or sell at the high, and that there are no sure things, only probabilities.

Obstacles to Investment Success

In many ways, successful investing runs contrary to human nature. For instance, it's natural to follow the crowd, to let your emotions dictate decisions, to buy stocks based on tips and hunches, and to approach investing with no underlying cohesiveness or consistency. It's also easy and natural to see things as you'd like them to be rather than how they are, and to see all investment strategies as hopelessly complex and unknowable, forcing you to take on faith that which you can easily test. And it's natural to fall into a habit of investing the same way you fall into a habit of brushing your teeth in the morning—never questioning if there is a better way.

Successful investors do not comply with nature; they defy it. There's nothing *natural* about successful investing. It's not natural to watch others get caught up in the spirals of greed and fear, causing booms and panics, and remain unmoved. It's not natural to be unemotional when your money is at stake. It's not natural to avoid fads and group fancies. It's not natural to persevere in a rigorous, consistent manner—no matter what the market is doing.

What about those investors, amateur and professional alike, who do break away from the herd, *use* superior strategies, and *still* get mediocre results? In this case, the missing element is most often consistency. They use a great strategy, but do so inconsistently or in a haphazard manner. One time they remove a stock because it no longer meets their criteria, but keep it another time because they have a "feeling" the stock will come back. Sometimes this works, but often it doesn't. The problem is that *you never know ahead of time which is which.*

These investors let their portfolios fill up with stocks that used to be good ideas. They ensure mediocrity by failing to consistently respond to changing conditions or by doing so intermittently. Often, they are tripped up by emotional factors.

Avoiding Emotional Traps

When making decisions, we tend to view everything in the present tense, and we time-weight information, giving the most recent the greatest weight. Think about the last time you really goofed. A year or so later you think: *What was I thinking! It's so obvious that I was on the wrong path, why didn't I see it?* The mistake is obvious in hindsight because you see the situation historically, drained of emotion and feeling. Stripped of the immediacy and vividness, you can look at the facts in a logical, unemotional manner. When you made the mistake, logic had to contend with emotion. Emotion often wins, since your ability to reason decreases as emotions increase.

Think of the present—right now. Does an investment strategy look irresistible to you? Chances are that it's just had a great quarter and a fabulous few years. Remember the mediocre manager from Chap. 6 who was able to masquerade as a star? If you'd looked at that manager on December 31, 1991, you would have wanted to hire him: Over the previous two years his portfolio more than doubled, gaining over 50 percent in the prior six months alone. If the manager's recent history received the bulk of weight in your decision making, you'd naturally want to hire him. Only an unemotional historical review, one that takes more time and other factors into consideration (such as risk) would have helped you avoid the manager.

Great opportunities can be missed through emotional decision making as well. If you started using the Momentum Growth Model in December of 1991, by June of 1992 you'd have lost 15 percent of your investment and be *absolutely convinced* that, while the model *used* to work, it no longer did. You'd be overwhelmed by your present experience and the information at hand. The 15 percent loss would carry the most weight in your calculations because it's the freshest. The emotional sting is real and hurts deeply. It would be *natural* for you to bitterly abandon the strategy at this point, blaming it for unreliability and failure. It happens often: A strategy gains popularity until finally it has a great quarter and a large group of investors embrace it. These marginal investors—those last in—will be the first out of the strategy when it cools, suffering the greatest disappointment and becoming increasingly convinced that the market makes no sense.

This isn't a phenomenon reserved for the unsophisticated. Pension sponsors have access to the best research and talent that money can buy. Yet they are notorious for investing heavily in stocks just as bear markets begin, and for firing managers at the absolute bottom of their cycle, just as they are about to rebound. Institutional investors *say* they make decisions objectively and unemotionally, but they don't. The authors of the book *Fortune & Folly* found that, while institutional investors' desks are cluttered with in-depth, analytical reports, the majority of pension executives select outside managers using "gut feelings" and will keep managers with consistently poor performance just because they have good personal relationships with them.

Thinking Historically

Successful investors look at history. They unglue themselves from the present and make decisions using historical information. They understand and react to the present in terms of its antecedents and what can reasonably be expected in the future.

Yesterday and tomorrow, as well as today, make up their *now*. Something as simple as a study of a strategy's spread is a good example. Knowing the potential parameters of a strategy gives the investor who thinks historically a tremendous advantage over the uninformed. If the maximum expected loss is 20 percent and the strategy is down 15 percent, instead of panicking, an informed investor can feel happy that things aren't as bad as they could be. This knowledge tempers expectations and emotions, giving informed investors a *perspective* that acts as an emotional pressure valve. Thinking historically, they let what they *know* transcend what they presently *feel*. This is the only way to do consistently well in investing.

Using Emotions Profitably

Emotions and intuition *do* have their place, however. Intuition is extremely important when *developing* market-beating strategies. You need all your creative juices flowing when designing models, and you should let them run wild. Try crazy combinations; you may stumble on to something others have overlooked. It costs you nothing and gives you invaluable insights into the factors that successful models contain. Designing models is inexorably linked to intuition and creativity. Only when *implementing* a strategy should you remove emotion and trial and error, for that is when they cease to be your allies.

Strong emotions can be excellent contrary indicators. If you are enormously happy about your investment results and bursting with pride about how smart you've been in the market, batten down the hatches because it's likely a storm is coming. Too much success is itself an ominous sign. Conversely, if you're certain that you'll never break even and that your stock selections are doomed to consistent failure, be happy, because a bottom is probably at hand.

It's Up to You

All the computer models developed in this book aren't substitutes for judgment; they're simply tools. Like any tool, the results you get are contingent on how you use it: If you use a hammer when you need a screwdriver, your results will be poor. Likewise, if you use these models in a haphazard or inconsistent manner, or if you try to find the *one stock* that will be the *absolute best performer,* you will certainly fail.

Used properly, however, the tools in this book can start you on the road to great market success. They can put the normally cruel laws of probability on your side. But first, *you* must decide on your goals and have the will to achieve them. Simply changing from a passive, randomly based investment strategy to one built on active, systematic goals will put you ahead of 90 percent of investors.

Finally, remember that the results you achieve are often contingent on what you expect. If you expect never to understand the market, to do poorly, to never do better than average, that's often what you'll get. If, on the other hand, you expect to translate your understanding into action, to do well, to move beyond those from whom you have learned, that's often where time will find you. Faith and expectation determine what you'll do and create.

Remember the story of the bricklayers? Three people were laying bricks, and each was asked what they were doing. The first replied, "I'm breaking my back and working my fingers to the bone for an ungrateful boss." The second said, "I'm earning a wage to care for my family." The third replied, "I'm helping to build a great cathedral."

Which person are you?

Bibliography

Barach, Roland. *Mindtraps: Mastering the Inner World of Investing.* Dow Jones-Irwin: Homewood, Ill., 1988.

Bell, David E., Raiffa, Howard, and Tversky, Amos. *Decision Making: Descriptive, Normative, and Prescriptive Interactions.* Cambridge University Press: Cambridge, England, 1988.

Brown, Stephen J. and Kritzman, Mark P., CFA. *Quantitative Methods for Financial Analysis.* DowJones-Irwin: Homewood, Ill., 1987.

Cottle, Sidney, Murray, Roger F., and Block, Frank E. *Graham and Dodd's Security Analysis,* 5th ed. McGraw-Hill: New York, 1988.

Coulson, Robert D. *The Intelligent Investor's Guide to Profiting from Stock Market Inefficiencies.* Probus Publishing Company: Chicago, 1987.

Dreman, David N. *Psychology and the Stock Market.* Warner Books: New York, 1977.

Dreman, David. *The New Contrarian Investment Strategy.* Random House: New York, 1980.

Ellis, Charles D., and Vertin, James R. *Classics: An Investor's Anthology.* Dow Jones-Irwin: Homewood, Ill., 1989.

Ellis, Charles D., and Vertin, James R. *Classics II: Another Investor's Anthology.* Business One Irwin: Homewood, Ill., 1991.

Fabozzi, Frank J. and Zarb, Frank G. *Handbook of Financial Markets: Securities, Options and Futures.* Dow Jones-Irwin: Homewood, Ill., 1986.

Farrell, James L. *Guide to Portfolio Management.* McGraw-Hill: New York, 1983.

Faust, David. *The Limits of Scientific Reasoning.* University of Minnesota Press: Minneapolis, 1984.

Gleick, James. *Chaos: Making a New Science.* Viking Penguin: New York, 1987.

Guerard, John, and Vaught, H.T. *The Handbook of Financial Modeling.* Probus Publishing Co.: Chicago, 1989.

Ibbotson, Roger G., and Brinson, Gary P. *Gaining the Performance Advantage: Investment Markets.* McGraw-Hill: New York, 1987.

Ingersoll, Jonathan E. Jr. *Theory of Financial Decision Making.* Rowman & Littlefield: Totowa, N.J., 1987.

Knowles, Harvey C. III, and Petty, Damon H. *The Dividend Investor.* Probus Publishing Co.: Chicago, 1992.

Kuhn, Thomas S. *The Copernican Revolution: Planetary Astronomy in the Development of Western Thought.* Harvard University Press: Cambridge, Mass., 1957.

Kuhn, Thomas S. *The Structure of Scientific Revolutions.* University of Chicago Press: Chicago, 1970.

Lewin, Roger. *Complexity: Life at the Edge of Chaos.* Macmillan: New York, 1992.

Lorie, James H., Dodd, Peter, and Kimpton, Mary Hamilton. *The Stock Market: Theories and Evidence.* Dow Jones-Irwin, Homewood, Ill., 1985.

Lowenstein, Louis. *What's Wrong with Wall Street.* Addison-Wesley: New York, 1988.

Mackay, Charles, LL.D. *Extraordinary Popular Delusions and the Madness of Crowds.* Bonanza Books: New York, 1980.

Maital, Shloml. *Minds, Markets, & Money: Psychological Foundation of Economic Behavior.* Basic Books: New York, 1982.

Nisbett, Richard and Ross, Lee. *Human Inference: Strategies and Shortcomings of Social Judgement.* Prentice-Hall: Englewood Cliffs N.J., 1980.

O'Barr, William M., and Conley, John M. *Fortune & Folly: The Wealth & Power of Institutional Investing.* Business One Irwin: Homewood, Ill., 1992.

O'Higgins, Michael, and Downes, John. *Beating the Dow.* HarperCollins Publishers: New York, 1992.

O'Neil, William J. *How to Make Money in Stocks: A Winning System in Good Times or Bad.* McGraw-Hill: New York, 1991.

O'Shaughnessy, James P. *Quantitative Models as an Aid in Offsetting Systematic Errors in Decision Making.* O'Shaughnessy Capital Management (privately published): St. Paul, Minn., 1988.

Paulos, John Allen. *Innumeracy: Mathematical Illiteracy and Its Consequences.* Hill and Wang: New York, 1989.

Peters, Edgar E. *Chaos and Order in the Capital Markets: A New View of Cycles, Prices, and Market Volatility.* John Wiley & Sons, Inc.: New York, 1991.

Schwager, Jack D. *The New Market Wizards.* Harper-Collins Publishers: New York, 1992.

Schwager, Jack D. *Market Wizards: Interviews with Top Traders.* Simon & Schuster: New York, 1989.

Sharp, Robert M. *The Lore and Legends of Wall Street.* Dow Jones-Irwin: Homewood, Ill., 1989.

Siegel, Laurence B. *Stocks, Bonds, Bills and Inflation 1992 Yearbook.* Ibbotson Associates: Chicago, 1992.

Thomas, Dana L. *The Plungers and the Peacocks: An Update of the Classic History of the Stock Market.* William Morrow: New York, 1989.

Train, John. *The Money Masters.* Harper & Row, Publishers: New York, 1980.

Train, John. *Famous Financial Fiascos.* Clarkson N. Potter: New York, 1985.

Train, John. *The New Money Masters: Winning Investment Strategies of: Soros, Lynch, Steinhardt, Rogers, Neff, Wanger, Michaelis, Carret.* Harper & Row, Publishers: New York, 1989.

Trippi, Robert R. and Lee, Jae K. *State-of-the-Art Portfolio Selection: Using Knowledge-Based Systems to Enhance Investment Performance.* Probus Publishing Company: Chicago, 1992.

Valentine, Jerome L., CFA, and Mennis, Edmund A., CFA. *Quantitative Techniques for Financial Analysis.* Richard D. Irwin, Inc.: Homewood, Ill., 1980.

Vince, Ralph. *The Mathematics of Money Management.* John Wiley & Sons: New York, 1992.

Watzlawick, Paul. *How Real is Real? Confusion, Disinformation, Communication.* Vintage Books: New York, 1977.

Index

About the Author

James P. O'Shaughnessy is founder and president of O'Shaughnessy Capital Management, a Greenwich, Connecticut-based investment advisory firm which manages hedge funds using the same investment style techniques that are shared in *Invest Like the Best*. Mr. O'Shaughnessy has served as a quantitative consultant to one of the nation's largest pension plans as well as to active money managers and foundations.